The Gulf monarchies after the Arab Spring

Manchester University Press

Series editors: Simon Mabon, Edward Wastnidge, and May Darwich

After the Arab Uprisings and the ensuing fragmentation of regime–society relations across the Middle East, identities and geopolitics have become increasingly contested, with serious implications for the ordering of political life at domestic, regional, and international levels, best seen in conflicts in Syria and Yemen. The Middle East is the most militarised region in the world, where geopolitical factors remain predominant in shaping political dynamics. Another common feature of the regional landscape is the continued degeneration of communal relations, as societal actors retreat into sub-State identities, whilst difference becomes increasingly violent, spilling out beyond State borders. The power of religion – and the trans–state nature of religious views and linkages – thus provides the means for regional actors (such as Saudi Arabia and Iran) to exert influence over a number of groups across the region and beyond. This series provides space for engagement with these ideas and with broader political, legal, and theological factors to create space for an intellectual reimagining of sociopolitical life in the Middle East.

Originating from the SEPAD project (www.sepad.org.uk), this series facilitates the reimagining of political ideas, identities, and organisation across the Middle East, moving beyond the exclusionary and binary forms of identity to reveal the contingent factors that shape and order life across the region.

Previously published titles

Houses built on sand: Violence, sectarianism and revolution in the Middle East   Simon Mabon

The Gulf States and the Horn of Africa: Interests, influences and instability   Robert Mason and Simon Mabon (eds)

Transitional justice in process: Plans and politics in Tunisia   Mariam Salehi

The labour movement in Lebanon: Power on hold   Lea Bou Khater

Surviving repression: The Egyptian Muslim Brotherhood after the 2013 coup   Lucia Ardovini

Saudi Arabia and Iran: The struggle to shape the Middle East   Edward Wastnidge and Simon Mabon (eds)

Saudi Arabia and the United Arab Emirates: Foreign policy and strategic alliances in an uncertain world   Robert Mason

The Gulf monarchies after the Arab Spring

Threats and security

Cinzia Bianco

MANCHESTER UNIVERSITY PRESS

This book will be made open access within three years of publication thanks to Path to Open, a program developed in partnership between JSTOR, the American Council of Learned Societies (ACLS), University of Michigan Press, and The University of North Carolina Press to bring about equitable access and impact for the entire scholarly community, including authors, researchers, libraries, and university presses around the world. Learn more at https://about.jstor.org/path-to-open/

Published by Manchester University Press
Oxford Road, Manchester M13 9PL

www.manchesteruniversitypress.co.uk

British Library Cataloguing-in-Publication Data
A catalogue record for this book is available from the British Library

ISBN 978 1 5261 7084 2 hardback
ISBN 978 1 5261 9556 2 paperback

First published 2024
Paperback published 2026

The publisher has no responsibility for the persistence or accuracy of URLs for any external or third-party internet websites referred to in this book, and does not guarantee that any content on such websites is, or will remain, accurate or appropriate.

EU authorised representative for GPSR:
Easy Access System Europe – Mustamäe tee 50,
10621 Tallinn, Estonia
gpsr.requests@easproject.com

Typeset by Newgen Publishing UK

Contents

Introduction

The year 2011 signalled the beginning of a transformative decade for the geopolitics of the Middle East and North Africa (MENA), posing daunting challenges, simultaneously, to countries all around the region. Popular political turmoil, economic instability, major geopolitical shifts, and asymmetric military challenges rose in just a few years to create a perfect storm, putting at risk a status quo crafted over decades. The region found itself on the brink of a watershed transition of political and economic power to new actors and new regimes, at times representing an alternative to existing models. Political groups with charismatic ideological charge and grassroots capabilities, such as Sunni Islamist groups – including the Muslim Brotherhood – were well placed to challenge and obtain power. A fault line emerged between actors determined to prevent that scenario – such as the United Arab Emirates (UAE), Saudi Arabia, and Egypt – and actors that supported that scenario, such as Turkey and Qatar. As Arab Spring protests descended into full-fledged civil and proxy wars, for example in Syria or Yemen, regional players entered into a geopolitical competition to fill power vacuums that involved a perceived Iranian advancement and encirclement. Even the monarchies of the Gulf Cooperation Council (GCC), considered islands of stability, were heavily affected by such a combination of game-changing events, which substantially put into question their existing perceptions of security at home and in the region, and led to the emergence of multi-dimensional and multi-layered security issues.

Starting from January and February 2011, popular uprisings began in North Africa, triggering the most widespread revolutionary wave in the modern history of the MENA region, known as the Arab Spring.[1] In little over a month protesters toppled the regimes of Zine El Abidine Ben Ali in Tunisia and Muhammad Hosni Mubarak in Egypt, both in power since the 1980s. These events had substantial reverberations in the entire region, as they demonstrated that popular revolts might take down regimes historically considered bastions of stability. In the Arabian Peninsula they inspired significant opposition rallies in Oman; Kuwait; Saudi Arabia's eastern

province; and, above all, Bahrain, where in March 2011 the Sunni ruling family of al-Khalifa cracked down on major protests by groups within
the Shi'a-majority population.[2] In Libya, aided by a North Atlantic Treaty
Organization (NATO) mission, protests ousted the decades-old regime of
Mu'ammar Qaddafi. Further away, in Yemen, popular protests created the
conditions to oust, in February 2012, the regime of Ali Abdullah Saleh, in
power since 1990, as a rebel group known as Houthis, inimical to Saudi
Arabia and supported by Iran, engaged in a campaign leading them to take
the capital, Sana'a, in 2014.[3] Between 2011 and 2012, a full-fledged civil
war reached the shores of Syria, after the Alawi regime of Bashar al-Assad
took arms against predominantly Sunni protesters.[4] While the international
community chose not to intervene, the military intervention of Russia and
Iran, a staunch ally of the al-Assad regime, advanced non-Arab influence in
the Levant.[5] Between 2014 and 2015, the strategic chaos in Syria allowed
the rise of a new jihadist group, Daesh,[6] which managed to proclaim a new
Caliphate in large swathes of territory between the two countries over a few
months, publicly declaring the annulment of the borders between them, as
drawn in the 1916 Sykes–Picot Agreement.[7] In July 2015, the USA and the
P5+1 – the five permanent members of the United Nations Security Council
plus Germany – signed a watershed deal with Iran (known as the Joint
Comprehensive Plan of Action (JCPOA)), designed to curb Iran's nuclear
capabilities and prevent thei weaponisation – which would have paved the
way for the normalisation of Iran's role in the region, too.

The Bahraini, Egyptian, and Syrian cases had a long-term significance.
The decision of the American administration not to stand by the US-allied
Egyptian regime, to support the Bahraini regime half-heartedly, and not to
intervene in Syria, put into question in unprecedented ways the reliability of
the United States as a partner to its regional allies, including in the GCC.[8]
It became clear in the GCC that the Arab Spring transition was happening
without a strategic arbiter of global stature.[9] The USA had initiated a policy
of retrenchment, a legacy of the disastrous 2003 Iraq war. Europeans were
as confused by the protests' intensity and capacity to spread among their
southern neighbours as they were dismayed at the USA's retrenchment and
policy of 'leading from behind'.[10] Other global players – such as Russia and
China – hesitated to step into the USA's role.[11]

In this geopolitical vacuum, some of the GCC monarchies – especially
those that had been less crippled by the Arab Spring – stepped forward to
shape the political future of the region with an unprecedented assertiveness
and unilateralism.[12] In doing so, the GCC leaders attempted an unprecedented step: to transform from security consumers to security producers.[13] They increasingly leveraged their political networks and vast financial
resources, accumulated since the oil boom of the 2000s, as instruments of

riyalpolitik, to become shapers of the post-2011 MENA regional order.[14] Their growing proactivity and assertiveness even went as far as to engage militarily in Libya and in Yemen. Their intervention represented a game-changer, from North Africa to the Levant, from the Suez Canal to the Bab al-Mandab and the Strait of Hormuz.[15] In all of these theatres, the GCC monarchies split on both sides of the trenches. These fundamental intra-GCC disagreements, especially on the role of political Islam and of Iran in the political future of the region, escalated into the two gravest internal political crises in the GCC's history, in 2014 and 2017, featuring Saudi Arabia, the UAE, and Bahrain breaking relations with Qatar.[16] In 2018, the intense lobbying efforts of Riyadh and Abu Dhabi in Washington, DC, contributed to the decision of US president Donald Trump to pull out of the JCPOA. This paved the way for the escalation of an asymmetrical conflict in and around the Gulf, as Iran sponsored low-intensity attacks against US targets as well as Saudi Arabia and the UAE, including via its allies in Iraq and Yemen.[17] In 2019, these attacks hit several oil tankers off the UAE coast and critical infrastructures of the Saudi State-owned energy major ARAMCO. The USA refrained from responding kinetically to any of these 2019 events. It was a true turning point for the Gulf monarchies, as they interpreted this US hesitation as the final proof of retrenchment and MENA fatigue. In fact, the USA increasingly signalled the intention to divert politi-cal focus and resources away from the MENA region and towards the Asia-Pacific, to contain China. As a reaction, the GCC monarchies set out on a path to diversify their security relations, by deepening ties on defence, trade, and technology with China, Russia, the United Kingdom, and France, among others.[18] The UAE and Bahrain also expanded this pool to Israel, with whom they normalised relations in 2020.[19] Interested to reinforce its regional position since the 2015 intervention in Syria, and to attract invest-ments, Russia increasingly presented itself as a security provider willing to back up regional regimes without interfering in their internal affairs.[20] Becoming ever more dependent on oil and gas from the Gulf, China also embraced a new strategic posture vis-à-vis the region, by making it a cen-trepiece of its Belt and Road Initiative (BRI), which promotes infrastructure projects connecting the region's economies to China.[21] This diversification remained a key vector of the GCC countries' approach to the emerging competitive multi-polar order. However, this was meant to create a mosaic of security partners rather than new dependencies, as they doubled down to try and develop their own security capabilities and geopolitical credentials.

After 2019, the GCC monarchies thus reassessed their security agendas and opened a new phase in their regional policies, characterised by consoli-dation and diplomatic manoeuvre, embracing a strategic pause to escala-tion.[22] This included some limited outreach to Iran – encouraged especially by the UAE – and a *détente* with Qatar and Turkey – driven by Saudi Arabia – that resulted in the end of the 2017 crisis and the signing of the al-Ula communiqué in January 2021. Both Oman and Kuwait welcomed the de-escalation, as they faced pivotal leadership changes when, in 2020, Sultan Qaboos bin Sa'id al-Sa'id of Oman and Emir Sabah al-Ahmad al-Jaber al-Sabah of Kuwait passed away. Another element encouraging de-escalation was the outburst of the global coronavirus (or COVID-19) pandemic in early 2020, which acted as a multiplier of existing vulnerabilities in the six GCC countries.[23] As a result of the economic lockdowns implemented around the world to contain the pandemic, the energy market plunged into chaos, driving prices to historic lows. Saudi Arabia managed to push other oil producers within the Organization of the Petroleum Exporting Countries (OPEC) in the OPEC+ group – which includes non-OPEC oil producers such as Russia – to embrace production cuts, thus reversing a free-fall in prices.[24] However, the 2020 energy prices crisis, just like the 2014 crisis before it, highlighted the structural vulnerabilities in the GCC countries' political economic rentier model: i.e. the idea that the State reallocates the externally driven oil-and-gas-related rents it receives through government-granted privileges such as tax exemption and a very generous welfare and subsidy system, in exchange for unquestioned loyalty to the regimes.[25] On the contrary, a substantial new surge in energy prices in 2022 strengthened the GCC regimes, domestically, regionally, and internationally. As a response to the Russian invasion of Ukraine in February 2022, the USA and Europe led a coalition of governments imposing sanctions on Russia, resulting in the collapse of energy relations between Moscow and Europe, which hitherto had relied on its eastern neighbour for 40 per cent of its energy needs.[26] These dynamics interacted with pre-existing imbalances in the oil market, pushing oil prices to a whopping 130 USD per barrel in March 2022.[27] Gulf producers, holding the means to release additional energy and relieve pressure on the market, acquired new leverage internationally. In just a few months, GCC capitals received dozens of world leaders and officials, at an unprecedented pace. Regional leaders, persevering in their strategy for partnership diversification and driven by still-acute security perceptions, reacted by leveraging their newly found geopolitical relevance, and embracing strategic hedging.[28]

Ten years after the Arab Spring the established trend was the transfer of the region's geopolitical centre of gravity to the monarchies in the Arabian Peninsula. The unprecedented assertiveness shown by Saudi Arabia, the UAE, and Qatar, together with the growing weight of active neutrality embraced by Kuwait and the passive neutrality chosen by Oman, redefined regional equilibria. While more a rules-taker than a rules-maker, small

Bahrain became a microcosm and political laboratory for all the emerging fault lines, which came to define the post-Arab Spring decade.

Identikit of the book

The changing status of regional politics and the new course of the GCC states call upon studies on regional security to evolve and keep pace with the disruptive developments of the post-2011 decade. This book aims to unpack the core elements in the formation of threat perceptions and the strategic calculus of these regional actors, risen to a new and prominent geopolitical role, thus providing the fundamental reading keys to policy-making in the Gulf monarchies. To do so, given how the decision-making and policy-making processes in the Gulf monarchies are largely limited to a small number of individuals within leaderships, this book addresses the questions of how the GCC policy-makers' definition of threats has changed, what the factors are shaping their perceptions and prioritisation, and how to use this information in analysing the short- and medium-term impacts on the security agendas and policies of the regimes. While focusing on the ten years between 2011 and 2021, the book contextualises its findings in the academic literature of the past three decades, providing historical background and references, and it sketches possible long-term trends. In reflecting on how the Arab Spring transformed security perceptions and agendas in the GCC, the book challenges established pre-Arab Spring narratives that saw the GCC monarchies as having shared security concerns on external threats – primarily, from Iran – and internal threats of insurgencies, by showing how and why key divergences had long existed within the bloc. Rather than coordination within established alliance patterns, such as the GCC, intensifying threats resulted in extreme polarisation and fragmentation, both within the GCC and between individual regimes and societies. Such polarisation and fragmentation emerged especially during the 2014 and 2017 intra-GCC crises, and the two issues at their core – namely the Muslim Brotherhood and Iran-supported Shi'a groups – became catalysts of these perceptions. In this sense, these issues and circumstances are identified here as suitable case studies to investigate the weight of sectarianism and transnational ideologies, and to identity fault lines versus geopolitical calculations in the making of the monarchies' security agendas.

This book's main research question is: how has the interpretation of the notion of threat evolved since 2011 at the level of each of the GCC regimes? In the process of answering this question, other issues spontaneously arise. Is there still a shared understanding of the idea of Gulf security and a shared prioritisation of threats among the GCC regimes? Did new threats emerge in addition, substitution, or modification to traditional ones? How do endogenous and exogenous threats interact when they materialise simultaneously at the global, regional, and domestic levels? How can threats be categorised when so many emerge from different sources? What is the impact of these evolutions on the GCC countries' relations among themselves and with other regional actors?

In the attempt to find answers to these questions, this volume deploys an original theoretical framework that would serve as a fundamental instrument to interpret and systematise the security thinking in the Gulf region in the ten years following the Arab Spring. Rejecting the generalisations and hyper-securitisation that characterised the post-Arab Spring discourse, often as a by-product of state narratives, the book introduces new concepts (threat vs risk, intermesticism, vulnerabilities) and instruments (for categorisation) to seek an in-depth, nuanced, detailed understanding of how security perceptions are formed at the leadership level in each of the six GCC monarchies, at the intersection between identity and geopolitical questions.

This framework is applied to six case studies – the six GCC monarchies – in six chapters, through a combination of quantitative and qualitative research methods. Empirical data are extracted from a variety of sources, such as statistics; political and media discourse, subjected to speech analysis; where possible, official documents or diplomatic and political communications, such as the Riyadh Agreements; and over 100 interviews gathered in the course of more than six years of research in all of the monarchies. The interviewees, pseudonymised for security reasons, included local diplomats and officials, as well as local academics and analysts, who – beneath biases and political agendas, always acknowledged – provided an invaluable window onto the perception of threats at the level of the GCC regimes: the author wishes to acknowledge their contribution and pay tribute to them.

This volume responds to the growing interest in the Gulf and the recognition of the rising relevance of the monarchies as geopolitical actors. This interest has been growing in the circles of academia and policy, as well as among the general public. It has crossed the traditional latitudes of Europe and the USA towards Asia, as Asian countries – including China, Russia, Pakistan, India, Japan, South Korea, and Singapore – strengthened their political, security, economic, and energy relations with the Gulf monarchies. And yet, the literature still hasn't provided enough resources looking at the post-2011 geopolitical outlook comprehensively, or an analysis of the trends in all six GCC monarchies individually and in a single volume. This author intends to fill this gap by offering a text that covers the entirety of the GCC region and speaks to academia, policy, and the general public. The book serves students, researchers, and scholars interested in the security dynamics of the MENA region and the Gulf as well as their international relations, based upon security and threat deterrence, by providing theoretical Innovations within the framework of existing concepts and theories – in combination with findings from extensive fieldwork on a large set of case studies – and ideas to push the research agenda further. In addition to more theoretical sections, the volume also includes large descriptive and analytical sections, where readability is prioritised. Finally, the text is relevant for practitioners and policy-makers seeking to unpack the new gravitational centre for the geopolitics of the MENA region and the Horn of Africa, by bridging the gap between theory and operationalisation, offering a diachronic overview of the fundamental policy-drivers lying behind regime narratives in all six GCC monarchies, and an in-depth analysis based on dozens of interviews from a diverse range of perspectives in and around the monarchies' leaderships. The choice to focus on post-2011 affairs, cover several domains, and contextualise the findings in the new competitive multi-polar order has been made to support policy-makers who would look at the GCC from a holistic perspective.

The book opens with an introductory chapter providing an analytical and descriptive overview of the transformation, polarisation, and fragmentation of the politics of the MENA region and the GCC in the ten years after the Arab Spring, ending with the 2021 strategic pause and the 2022 Russian invasion of Ukraine. The second chapter is the core of the book's contribution to the academic and scholarly debate, as it provides an original theoretical framework enabling a more nuanced analysis of security perceptions in the GCC monarchies. The framework is subsequently applied to an analysis of threat perceptions in each of the six GCC states, in six empirical chapters. In each chapter, one per state, the first section is dedicated to measuring the impact of the Arab Spring on the leadership's security perceptions, as a central argument of this book is that the fragmentation of the security calculus across the GCC regimes has crystallised since 2011. The two following sections analyse security perceptions triggered by Iran and the Muslim Brotherhood. The last and most substantial section fleshes out the essential drivers and key elements of the country's security calculus, the overarching priorities in the ten years after 2011, and likely future evolutions. Finally, in the last chapter, the author draws conclusions on threat prioritisation in the region by comparing and contrasting the findings of the six chapters and contextualising the findings in regional and global dynamics, ending with considerations specifically geared to inform policy-making vis-à-vis the region, and suggestions for further research.

Existing literature and contributions to the field

The literature on Gulf security produced since the early 1980s is extensive and diverse, and can be systematised into categories, or waves, drawing similarities and patterns. The presented theories have in common that, while they remain valid and applicable to the present, no single one of them seems exhaustive enough to provide a comprehensive analysis of the phase of GCC security thinking that began in 2011. This book sets to fill this gap, while embracing a holistic approach that encompasses elements from the existing literature.

First-wave studies focus on state entities as unitary actors and their effort to protect their strategic interests, mainly with a realist or neo-realist approach. Actual and potential security challenges are usually defined as conventional military threats from external powers. First-wave studies are epitomised by Anthony Cordesman's comprehensive study on *The Gulf and the Search for Strategic Stability*.[29] The study is heavily based on realist assumptions regarding power metrics – size, population, resources, military capabilities – and geographic features, such as the proximity to a threatening big power, i.e. Iran.[30] A similar approach is embraced by Joseph Kostiner's analysis of the campaign to construct a GCC collective defence arrangement in the aftermath of the 1990–1991 war.[31] Kostiner also focuses on conventional threats and realist considerations, arguing that longstanding intra-GCC tensions over territorial boundaries pushed smaller states, such as Kuwait and Bahrain, to prefer bilateral defence agreements with the United States and Britain instead of looking towards closer cooperation within the GCC. Subsequently, David Priess offers a modification of first-wave arguments, arguing that states react to increases in the level of threat that they face rather than to changes in the power of external actors, shifting the policy-driver from balance of power to balance of threat.[32] He defines threats as determined by aggregate power, geographical proximity, offensive power, and aggressive intentions, thus broadening the traditional interpretation of threat, including subversion, terrorism, espionage, and even political propaganda in the semantic camp of offensive-power capabilities.[33] For this reason, Priess argues, in early 1981 the six smaller Arab monarchies of the Gulf put aside their rivalries with one another and set up the GCC in order to face Iran, which had begun to encourage or sponsor subversive movements throughout the region, and therefore posed a direct and proximate threat to their continued existence. While incorporating the balance-of-threat rationale of first-wave studies, this book recognises and unpacks the centrality increasingly attributed by GCC states in their security perceptions to non-state actors, such as Islamist groups, which were fully neglected in first-wave studies.[34]

In between the first and second waves, area studies have moved to explore the processes of internationalisation and their impacts on the security calculus of the GCC countries. A large part of them have focused on the role of the external powers in the regional security balance, including on the USA's security role as a powerful deterrent to the expansionist ambitions of neighbouring actors.[35] Likewise, scholars have pointed to the fact that this US–GCC security alliance triggers a significant security dilemma, in particular in Saudi Arabia: while representing an effective deterrent, the presence of US military on Saudi soil, where the Holy Cities of Mecca and Medina are located, has generated considerable domestic criticism of the regime.[36] Indeed, depending on the United States highlights the failure of local regimes to protect their citizens, and is particularly problematic because criticism of US policy in the Middle East has traditionally been strong in Arab public opinion.[37] Geoffrey Gresh has put forward a policy interpretation for such a dilemma, arguing that host nations' leaders facing significant external threats – i.e. the threat of invasion from an outside aggressor or rivalry over contested territory – are more likely to accept US bases, while host nations' leaders pressed by extensive internal security threats – i.e. social upheaval, violent opposition movements, or mounting economic grievances against the ruling regime – are more likely to reject them.[38] His research incorporates the principle of the conflation of regime security with national security as a feature of policy-making in the Gulf, overwhelmingly accepted by the area literature and in this volume.[39] As for global actors, while still crucial in the security equation of the region, they will not be the focus of this book, which joins a post-2015 academic trend to privilege regional perspectives on regional issues.[40]

Second-wave studies started to look at the long-term consequences of integrating the GCC into the globalised market and international community.[41] These studies broaden the notions of threat to incorporate a wide range of economic, social, environmental, and demographic challenges as threatening societal and therefore political stability. Themes include domestic political challenges, such as the demands for greater popular participation voiced in most GCC states in the 1990s;[42] the challenge of pushing liberalisation without democratisation;[43] the economic difficulties that accompanied the stagnation of oil prices after the first Gulf war;[44] the structural imbalances in the political economy of resource distribution and in the labour market;[45] demographic trends, in particular where nationals are a staggering minority of the total population;[46] the long-term impacts of climate change;[47] and the growing shortage of fresh water throughout the region.[48] Several scholars, interpreting the Arab Spring as driven primarily by socioeconomic grievances, highlight the events of 2011 as a demonstration of the fundamental argument presented by this wave of literature, that non-traditional challenges can become political.[49] *Insecure Gulf*, by Kristian Ulrichsen, embodies this literature well.[50] Adopting a constructivist approach, Ulrichsen argues that Gulf security is evolving as internal political and socioeconomic changes in the Gulf states interact with the processes of globalisation, and that stability in the GCC countries is threatened not only by the conventional hard security threats but also by so-called soft security challenges to human security. These, in fact, risk eroding the internal consensus and thus the ruling bargain that binds ruler and ruled in the region. In the context of the future depletion of energy resources, Ulrichsen reflects upon the fact that ruling elites won't be able to rely on oil rents as insulation from internal problems and demands caused by social inequalities. Finally, Ulrichsen effectively describes how internal and external security have become inextricably linked as domestic structural imbalances weaken the State's ability to react cohesively to external threats, a perspective that is also adopted here. This book also takes stock of the soft security challenges analysed by second-wave studies, but incorporates them into the idea of socioeconomic and sociopolitical vulnerabilities, addressing these as one of the elements forming the security perceptions and calculus of the GCC, rather than existential challenges per se. The same analytical framework will be applied to the impact of COVID-19 on the security agendas in the region, an issue that is yet to be properly addressed.

Third-wave studies instead postulate that competing ideologies of state organisation can come to constitute security threats. Such transborder threats flourish in the Arab world because sovereignty remains a contested concept and because, as Gregory Gause effectively described in his *The International Relations of the Persian Gulf*, the region includes a multitude of trans-border identities – ethnic, sectarian, tribal, ideological – that connect people from different countries and can be easily exploited to spread any given ideology.[51] In this sense the capacity of an external power to influence politics in other countries can be based not only upon material resources but also, as per constructivist theories, upon ideological power. One notable example is the work of Michael Barnett, who centred his arguments on ideologies and identity politics.[52] Barnett wrote that frequently the threat posed to Arab states was the successful portrayal of a rival model of state institutions and organising ideologies that potentially undermined the State's basis of existence. Ideologies such as pan-Arabism and pan-Islamism, especially when implying political unification as a way to safeguard the common Arab or Muslim interests, undermined the GCC states' sovereignty. For instance, Saudi Arabia was notoriously suspicious of Egyptian president Gamal 'Abd al-Nasser, who, brandishing pan-Arab rhetoric, had inspired the formation between the 1950s and the 1960s of a constellation of nationalist movements responsible for sustained instability in the Arabian Peninsula.[53] Ideological threats based on identity politics were discussed much in the post-Arab Spring context, as popular uprisings developed across ideological and identitarian fault lines: Shi'a vs Sunni, secularism vs Islamism. In this context, Matteo Legrenzi has argued that, bearing in mind the disequilibrium of societies in Middle Eastern states, the Arab Spring brought to the surface an identity split between states and their regime and an absolute divergence of interests between regime and society, with the latter becoming a threat to the former.[54] He further argues that while, after 2011, the traditional identity dichotomy between pan-Arabism and pan-Islamism dissolved, the politicisation of sectarian ties created a new dichotomy and a new security dilemma in the Arabian Peninsula. If Sunni GCC regimes counterbalance their Shi'a population, perceived as the fifth column of Iran, this in turn increases the societal fragmentation that feeds ideological and identitarian threats. This is the perspective adopted by several scholars dealing with the post-Arab Spring GCC, who additionally point at the cynical manipulation of identity politics by regimes as a tool to advance their domestic and foreign policy interests.[55] Gregory Gause explains sectarianism as a tool of power politics that Gulf regimes employ to counterbalance both domestic and foreign threats: part of a game played for regional influence that he calls the Middle East New Cold War, rather than a centuries-long inevitable religious dispute.[56] Anti-Shi'a mobilisation is thus viewed as an effective way of rallying the support of domestic populations around, respectively, an anti-Iranian or anti-Saudi foreign policy and anti-dissidents at the national level. This book relies substantially on third-wave studies, investigating the political and societal dimensions of ideological and identitarian challenges explored there. It also takes the questions further, by analysing the reasons why, within the GCC, some leaders perceived their countries as significantly more vulnerable than others did to the type of threats described by third-wave studies.

This volume will also introduce three specific innovations as contributions to this existing literature: differentiating between threats and risks, establishing how structural vulnerabilities interact with leadership cognition and other intangible factors in shaping security perceptions, and providing inputs on threat prioritisation.

The first innovation is to achieve a more nuanced and specific definition of the concepts of threats and security as perceived by GCC policy-makers in the ten years since the Arab Spring. It introduces new interpretations of concepts such as 'risk', 'vulnerabilities', and 'securitisation'. The author also departs from the uncritical and overly frequent use of the term 'threat', which has been predominant in the post-Arab Spring 'hyper-securitisation' literature.[57] While attributable to the polarised context that has characterised the past ten years, this lack of nuanced analysis has led to unfulfilled assumptions about policy trajectories, the clearest example – among others – being the assumption that Saudi Arabia and the UAE would behave coherently or identically towards Iran and the Muslim Brotherhood.[58]

The second innovation will be to unearth structural and ontological vulnerabilities – especially of a sociopolitical and socioeconomic nature – that are pre-existing in the context of the referent object (the GCC states), and to explore their role vis-à-vis decision-makers' perceptions when they operationalise the differentiation between threats and risks through securitisation.[59] Several authors engaged with unpacking the structural vulnerabilities in the GCC countries, some dating back to their foundation as sovereign states.[60] Many have evaluated the impact on these vulnerabilities of the Arab Spring.[61] However, very few scholars have provided an account of how those vulnerabilities are viewed from the perspective of the six GCC leaders individually, and how they interact with or impact upon their perceptions of their own security and that of fellow GCC states.[62] This book thus engages with these long-existing findings in an innovative and interdisciplinary way. It finds that vulnerabilities inform rather than determine the perceptions of policy-makers, which are equally impacted by a variety of other human factors.[63]

The third innovation is the provision of inputs into the prioritisation of threats, which has a major impact on policy choices. Few scholars have worked on proposing clear and testable hypotheses about how states prioritise among different kinds of threats. This author joins Gregory Gause in his assumption that a domestic threat that originated abroad, such as one abetted by foreign actors, would be prioritised over all others.[64]

A fourth innovation proposes an analytical framework to categorise perceived threats in their dimensions and types. While the relevant literature has provided us with clear descriptive categories, there has been little attention to the increasing multi-dimensionality of threats and their intersections, particularly those emerging after 2011. Most authors have refrained from accounting simultaneously for the economic, military, political, and societal dimensions of threats and investigating the links between those. This is what this book wants to do, by adapting the categorisation framework from Barry Buzan's *People, States and Fear*.[65] Furthermore, rather than arguing that threats can be categorised only as external or internal, this volume speaks of three types of threat: external threats, originating from external sources that affect the international interests of the country; internal threats, having endogenous roots and affect the internal stability of the country; and intermestic threats, having a mixed external and internal nature, such as those dervied from exogenous motives but having domestic implications, or vice versa. Kristian Ulrichsen used the term 'intermestic' in 2017 with specific reference to Middle East and Gulf security, arguing that the 'outbreak of the Arab Spring in 2011 and regional responses to the broader political upheaval across the Middle East and North Africa gave urgency to the porous relationship between internal and external security'.[66] This author follows in Ulrichsen's footsteps, by developing further the concept of the overlap between the regional and domestic dimensions of security that became more evident after 2011.

Notes

1 Simon Mabon, *Houses Built on Sand: Violence, Sectarianism and Revolution in the Middle East* (Manchester: Manchester University Press, 2021); Fawaz Gerges (ed.), *The New Middle East: Protest and Revolution in the Arab World* (Cambridge: Cambridge University Press, 2013).
2 Sean Yom and Gregory Gause, 'Resilient Royals: How Arab Monarchies Hang On', *Journal of Democracy* 23:4 (2012), 74–88.
3 Emile Hokayem and David Roberts, 'The War in Yemen', *Survival* 58:6 (2016), 157–186.
4 Christopher Phillips, *The Battle for Syria: International Rivalry in the New Middle East* (New Haven: Yale University Press, 2016).
5 *Ibid.*, 147–170.
6 Daesh is the Arab acronym for ISIS, Islamic State of Iraq and Syria. On its rise, see Fawaz Gerges, *Isis: A History* (Princeton: Princeton University Press, 2017).
7 Michael Berdine, *Redrawing the Middle East: Sir Mark Sykes, Imperialism and the Sykes–Picot Agreement* (London: Bloomsbury, 2018).
8 Tim Niblock and Steve Hook (eds), *The United States and the Gulf: Shifting Pressures, Strategies and Alignments* (Berlin: Gerlach Press, 2015).
9 Fawaz Gerges, 'The Obama Approach to the Middle East: The End of America's Moment?', *International Affairs* 89:2 (2013), 299–323.
10 *Ibid.*
11 Kristina Kausch, 'Competitive Multipolarity in the Middle East', *International Spectator* 50:3 (2015), 1–15.
12 Rory Miller, *Desert Kingdoms to Global Powers: The Rise of the Arab Gulf* (New Haven: Yale University Press, 2016).
13 Jean-Marc Rickli, 'New Alliances Dynamics in the Gulf and Their Impact on the Small GCC States', *Third World Thematics* 1:1 (2016), 132–150.
14 The term *riyalpolitik* indicates the pragmatic use of financial resources to attain foreign policy objectives. It appears in Abdullah Baabood, 'Dynamics and Determinants of the GCC States' Foreign Policy, with Special Reference to the EU', in Gerd Nonneman (ed.), *Analyzing Middle East Foreign Policies and the Relationship with Europe* (London: Routledge, 2005), 145–173.
15 For a comprehensive overview of the Gulf monarchies' role in the Horn of Africa, see Simon Mabon and Robert Mason, *Gulf States and the Horn of Africa: Interests, Influences and Instability* (Manchester: Manchester University Press, 2022).

16 Cinzia Bianco and Gareth Stansfield, 'The Intra-GCC Crises: Mapping GCC Fragmentation after 2011', *International Affairs* 94:3 (2018), 613–635.

17 Ross Harrison, 'The GCC versus Iran: Low Intensity War, High Intensity Conflict', Arab Center for Research and Policy Studies (2021), www.dohain stitute.org/en/Lists/ACRPS-PDFDocumentLibrary/The-GCC-versus-Iran-Low-Intensity-War-High-Intensity-Conflict.pdf (accessed 23 July 2023).

18 Kristian Ulrichsen, 'Rebalancing Regional Security in the Persian Gulf', Center for the Middle East, Rice University's Baker Institute for Public Policy (2020), www.bakerinstitute.org/research/rebalancing-regional-security-persian-gulf (accessed 23 July 2023).

19 Fatiha Dazi-Héni, 'The Gulf States and Israel after the Abraham Accords', Arab Reform Initiative (2020), www.arab-reform.net/publication/the-gulf-states-and-israel-after-the-abraham-accords/ (accessed 19 July 2023).

20 Roland Dannreuther, 'Russia and the Gulf States: Between West and East', in Nikolay Kozhanov (ed.), *Russia's Relations with the GCC and Iran* (Singapore: Palgrave Macmillan, 2021).

21 Jonathan Fulton, 'China between Iran and the Gulf Monarchies', *Middle East Policy* 28:3 (2021), 203–216.

22 Sanam Vakil and Neil Quilliam, 'Steps to Enable a Middle East Regional Security Process', research paper, Chatham House (2021), www.chathamhouse.org/2021/04/steps-enable-middle-east-regional-security-process (23 July 2023).

23 Elham Fakhro, 'COVID and Gulf Foreign Policy', International Crisis Group, 20 April 2020, www.crisisgroup.org/middle-east-north-africa/gulf-and-arabian-peninsula/covid-and-gulf-foreign-policy (accessed 12 September 2022).

24 OPEC+ is the enlarged version, in a flexible format, of OPEC, comprising the top oil producers in the world.

25 The 'rentier state system' is a political-economic system whose theory was expressed first in Hazem Beblawi, 'The Rentier State in the Arab World', in Hazem Beblawi and Giacomo Luciani (eds), *The Rentier State: Nation, State and the Integration of the Arab World* (London: Croom Helm, 1987).

26 'Energy Imports Dependency', *Eurostat* (2021), https://ec.europa.eu/eurostat/databrowser/view/nrg_ind_id/default/table?lang=en (accessed 23 July 2023).

27 'Crude Oil: 2022 Data', *Trading Economics*, 6 March 2022, https://tradingeconomics.com/commodity/crude-oil (accessed 6 March 2022).

28 Mohammad Salman, Moritz Pieper, and Gustaaf Geeraerts, 'Hedging in the Middle East and China–US Competition 1', *Asian Politics & Policy* 7:4 (2015), 575–596.

29 Anthony Cordesman, *The Gulf and the Search for Strategic Stability* (Boulder, CO: Westview, 1984).

30 Anthony Cordesman and Khalid R. Al-Rodhan, *Gulf Military Forces in an Era of Asymmetric Wars* (London: Greenwood, 2007).

31 Joseph Kostiner, 'The Search for Gulf Security: The Politics of Collective Defense', *Middle East Contemporary Survey* 16 (1992), 237–244.

32 David Priess, 'Balance-of-Threat Theory and the Genesis of the Gulf Cooperation Council', *Security Studies* 5:4 (1996), 143–171.

33 Scott Cooper, 'State-Centric Balance-of-Threat Theory', *Security Studies* 13:2 (2003), 306–349.

34 Vincent Durac, 'The Role of Non-State Actors in Arab Countries after the Arab Uprisings', *IEMed Mediterranean Yearbook* (2015), 37–41.

35 There is a general consensus on this argument that hasn't changed much over time. See for example J. E. Peterson, *Defending Arabia* (London: Croom Helm, 1986); and Amin Saikal, 'The United States and Persian Gulf Security', *World Policy Journal* 9:3 (1992), 515–531.

36 Fred Lawson, 'Security Dilemmas in the Contemporary Persian Gulf', in Mehran Kamrava (ed.), *International Politics of the Persian Gulf* (New York: Syracuse University Press, 2011); Clive Jones, 'Saudi Arabia after the Gulf War: The Internal–External Security Dilemma', *International Relations* 12:6 (1995), 31–51.

37 Fawaz Gerges, *The Far Enemy: Why Jihad Went Global* (Cambridge: Cambridge University Press, 2009).

38 Geoffrey Gresh, *Gulf Security and the US Military: Regime Survival and the Politics of Basing* (Stanford: Stanford University Press, 2015).

39 Anoushiravan Ehteshami and Raymond Hinnebusch, 'Foreign Policymaking in the Middle East: Complex Realism', in Louise Fawcett (ed.), *International Relations of the Middle East* (Oxford: Oxford University Press, 2013).

40 Scholarly work seeking to update this type of literature with the new regional and global power balances has been published after 2011, including Jonathan Fulton and Li-Chen Sim (eds), *External Powers and the Gulf Monarchies* (London: Routledge, 2018).

41 Lawrence Potter and Gary Sick, *Security in the Persian Gulf: Origins, Obstacles, and the Search for Consensus* (New York: Macmillan, 2002); Jamal Al-Suweidi (ed.), *Arabian Gulf Security: Internal and External Challenges* (Abu Dhabi: ECSSR, 2008); Anoushiravan Ehteshami, *Dynamics of Change in the Persian Gulf: Political Economy, War and Revolution* (London: Routledge, 2013).

42 Neil Partrick and Francis Toase (eds), 'Gulf Security: Opportunities and Challenges for the New Generation', RUSI Whitehall Papers 51 (London: RUSI, 2000).

43 Anoushiravan Ehteshami and Steven M. Wright (eds), *Reform in the Middle East Oil Monarchies* (New York: Ithaca Press, 2008).

44 Gregory Gause, 'The Political Economy of National Security in the GCC States', in Gary Sick and Lawrence Potter (eds), *The Persian Gulf at the Millennium* (New York: St Martin's, 1997).

45 Martin Baldwin-Edwards, 'Labour Immigration and Labour Markets in the GCC Countries: National Patterns and Trends', Kuwait Programme on Development, Governance and Globalisation in the Gulf States, London School of Economics and Political Science, Research Paper 15 (2011), http://eprints.lse.ac.uk/55239/1/Baldwin-Edwards_2011.pdf (accessed 23 July 2023).

46 Ingo Forstenlechner and Emilie Jane Rutledge, 'The GCC's "Demographic Imbalance": Perceptions, Realities and Policy Options', *Middle East Policy Journal* 18:4 (2011), 25–45.

47 James Russell, 'Environmental Security and Regional Stability in the Persian Gulf', *Middle East Policy* 16:4 (2009), 90–101.

48 Geoffrey Kemp and Janice Gross Stein, 'Enduring Sources of Conflict in the Persian Gulf Region', in Geoffrey Kemp and Janice Gross Stein (eds), *Powder Keg in the Middle East: The Struggle for Gulf Security* (Washington, DC: Rowman and Littlefield, 1995); Michael Bonine, 'Population Growth, the Labor Market and Gulf Security', in David Long and Christian Koch (eds), *Gulf Security in the Twenty-First Century* (London: IB Tauris, 1997).

49 Bahgat Korany, 'The Middle East since the Cold War', in Fawcett, *International Relations*, 90.

50 Kristian Ulrichsen, *Insecure Gulf: The End of Certainty and the Transition to the Post-Oil Era* (New York: Columbia University Press, 2011).

51 Gregory Gause, *The International Relations of the Persian Gulf* (Cambridge: Cambridge University Press, 2009).

52 Michael Barnett, 'Institutions, Roles and Disorder: The Case of the Arab States System', *International Studies Quarterly* 37:3 (1993), 271–296.

53 Fred Halliday, *Arabia without Sultans* (London: Saqi, 2013).

54 Matteo Legrenzi (ed.), *Security in the Gulf: Historical Legacies and Future Prospects* (London: Routledge, 2013).

55 *The Gulf's Escalating Sectarianism*, POMEPS Briefing 28 (Jaunary 2016), Project on Middle East Political Science, http://pomeps.org/wp-content/uploads/2016/01/POMEPS_BriefBooklet28_Sectarianism_Web.pdf (accessed 23 July 2023).

56 Gregory Gause, 'Beyond Sectarianism: The New Middle East Cold War', Brookings Institution, 22 July 2014, www.brookings.edu/research/beyond-sectarianism-the-new-middle-east-cold-war/ (accessed 9 May 2022).

57 The term 'threat' was employed with reference to several different dangers and often implied a GCC-wide perspective; for instance, Alexey Khlebnikov, 'The New Ideological Threat to the GCC: Implications for the Qatari–Saudi Rivalry', *Strategic Assessment* 17:4 (2015), 17–28. The concept of 'hyper-securitisation' is unpacked in, among others, Ferruccio Pastore, 'The Problematic Decentring of Migration Policy Studies', *Territory, Politics, Governance* 11 (2022), 1–6.

58 See for instance Rafeef Ziadah, 'The Importance of the Saudi–UAE Alliance: Notes on Military Intervention, Aid and Investment', *Conflict, Security & Development* 19:3 (2019), 295–300; and Matthew Hedges and Giorgio Cafiero, 'The GCC and the Muslim Brotherhood: What Does the Future Hold?', *Middle East Policy* 24:1 (2017), 129–153, available at https://mepc.org/journal/gcc-and-muslim-brotherhood-what-does-future-hold (accessed 7 August 2023).

59 Ole Wæver, *Securitization and Desecuritization* (Copenhagen: Centre for Peace and Conflict Research, 1993).

60 These include Mohammed Ayoob, *The Third World Security Predicament: State-Making, Regional Conflict and the International System* (Boulder, CO: Lynne Rienner, 1995); Forstenlechner and Rutledge, 'The GCC's "Demographic Imbalance"'; Steffen Hertog, 'The Sociology of the Gulf

Rentier Systems: Societies of Intermediaries', *Comparative Studies in Society and History* 52:2 (2010), 282–318; Ulrichsen, *Insecure Gulf*; Sick and Potter, *The Persian Gulf at the Millennium*; and Rosemarie Said Zahlan, *The Making of the Modern Gulf States: Kuwait, Bahrain, Qatar, the United Arab Emirates and Oman* (London: Routledge, 2016).

61 These include *The Gulf's Escalating Sectarianism*; Legrenzi, *Security in the Gulf*; and Ehteshami, *Dynamics of Change.*

62 David Roberts tackled this question partially in 'Qatar and the UAE: Exploring Divergent Responses to the Arab Spring', *Middle East Journal* 71:4 (2017), 544–562. Laurence Louër has also looked at the same question in an academic article looking only at Bahrain: 'Sectarianism and Coup-Proofing Strategies in Bahrain', *Journal of Strategic Studies* 36:2 (2013), 245–260. Neil Quilliam looked at Saudi security perceptions, but limited to the Qatar crisis: 'The Saudi Dimension: Understanding the Kingdom's Position in the Gulf Crisis', in Andreas Krieg (ed.), *Divided Gulf* (Singapore: Palgrave Macmillan, 2019).

63 Robert Jervis, *Perception and Misperception in International Politics* (Princeton: Princeton University Press, 2017).

64 Gregory Gause, 'Balancing What? Threat Perception and Alliance Choice in the Gulf', *Security Studies* 13:2 (2003), 273–305.

65 Barry Buzan, *People, States and Fear* (Boulder, CO: Lynne Rienner, 1991).

66 Kristian Ulrichsen, 'Links between Domestic and Regional Security', in Kristian Ulrichsen (ed.), *The Changing Security Dynamics of the Persian Gulf* (London: Hurst, 2017), 23.

1

The geopolitics of globalisation in the Gulf

Is the GCC a security community?

Threats and security perceptions are so central to the foreign policies of the GCC countries that the GCC itself was created for collective deterrence against common threats.[1] The emergence in 1979 of a revolutionary regime in Tehran with expansionist intent and the subsequent outbreak of the Iran–Iraq War in September 1980 were perceived as threatening the very survival of the monarchies: by coming together, the six countries wanted to present something of a common front to common security needs.[2] Over the years, scholars have acknowledged some of the limits that prevented the GCC from becoming an effective organism for collective defence and security.[3] However, many also often looked at the security of the bloc as almost a unitary good.[4] The existence of a common perception and prioritisation of threats among the six monarchies has rarely been questioned, and the GCC itself has often been described as a 'security community'.[5] The 2014 and 2017 crises instead suggest that GCC security is not a one-dimensional phenomenon but a complex matrix of domestic and regional factors each playing a distinctive role in formulating the definition, categorisation, perception, and prioritisation of threats.

The history of relations among the six GCC monarchies is abundant with instances of cooperation and unity, as well as controversies and divisions. This dichotomy can be found even in the circumstances of the very foundation of the modern states, after forces from the British empire, which had held established protectorates in the littoral areas of the Arabian Peninsula since the late nineteenth century, announced their withdrawal from east of Suez in 1968. The leaders of the small littoral emirates of the Gulf – today's UAE, Bahrain, and Qatar – announced a 'Federation of Arab Emirates' to 'take effect from 30 March 1968'.[6] Ultimately, however, while the seven Trucial States formed the UAE, Qatar and Bahrain went their separate ways, unable to overcome centuries-old conflictual relations and territorial claims.[7] There were in fact border disputes among all of the GCC countries, with some still unresolved six decades later.[8] In fact, as Louise Fawcett has noted, because the GCC see themselves as young nation-states, 'sovereignty was a prize to be nurtured, not one to be sacrificed on the altar of a pan-Arab movement, or one that extolled the virtues of integration'.[9]

In particular, while the GCC was primarily formed as a common defence mechanism, security and defence cooperation remained chronically under-developed.[10] The process to establish a collective military force – named Peninsula Shield – in 1984 highlighted a divergence of purposes, with Saudi Arabia and Oman hoping that it would emerge as a competent force able to contribute to regional self-defence, and the smaller GCC monarchies preferring to rely on the more effective assistance of the USA.[11] In fact, hesitations to commit to a GCC-wide large military standing force have been linked to the concerns that such a force would probably be led and dominated by Saudi Arabia and could possibly be used at some stage even to intimidate and influence the other monarchies.[12] This fear, in turn, pushed individual GCC member states to reach security arrangements or defence pacts with external actors, such as the United States or NATO, to balance against Saudi interference in what Gerd Nonneman calls 'omnibalancing'.[13] The Peninsula Shield case is exemplary of the difficulty in integrating security institutions, centralised commands, or defence systems.[14] This poor level of integration has long been one of the main arguments against defining the GCC countries as a security community, i.e. 'a group of states sharing values, identities – and agendas – tied together by supranational formal and informal links and collective security mechanisms, which are sufficiently strong and widespread to assure peaceful interaction among the group members'.[15]

And yet, when considering foreign policy choices, in the past the GCC could be considered a 'heterogeneous security community'.[16] In 2010, Christian Koch wrote that 'the monarchies have moved beyond the minimalist conception of an association – based on the lowest common denominator principle – towards a broader and more inclusive concept of the GCC as a regional organisation coordinating strategy and policy', especially on the Arab–Israeli conflict, alignment with the West, and mistrust vis-à-vis Iran.[17] However, the conflictual foreign policies pursued by the six GCC countries in the post-Arab Spring era definitively challenge the argument that there was foreign policy coordination.

In this context, rather than as a security community the Gulf monarchies can be seen as members of the Persian Gulf security sub-complex, within the larger complex of the MENA region.[18] A security complex is a system in which members have intense security interdependence and frequent, positive or negative, interactions.[19] All Gulf states, individually, can be described as members of the larger MENA system. The swiftness with which the 2011 uprisings were able to spread from Tunisia all the way to Bahrain and Yemen is a primary example of how interconnected the security of regional countries is. At the same time, looking at the dynamics in the Gulf exclusively as an extension of events taking place in the larger MENA system would disregard just how intertwined the security dynamics are within the Gulf itself, ranging from the impact of the Iranian revolution on the formation of the GCC to the reverberations of the 2003 Iraq war on Iran–GCC relations, to the weight of civil wars in Yemen on the domestic policies of Saudi Arabia and Oman.

Domestic specificities of individual countries are also structurally relevant, and strongly encourage a detailed analysis covering each of the six monarchies individually.[20] For example, while the six countries are all absolute monarchies slowly introducing measures for limited political representation, the political system in Kuwait guarantees a much higher degree of representation than that in any of the other countries.[21] The macroeconomic indicators in the region have grown even more different across the years: those of Saudi Arabia are not comparable to Bahrain's, while those of Qatar are not comparable to Oman's. From a historical point of view, Omani and Bahraini pre-eighteenth-century history has a much more international character than the history of the other countries. The ruling regime in Oman belongs to the Ibadi sect, a branch of Islam that cannot be characterised as Sunni or Shi'a, and upholds very different principles than, for example, Saudi Wahhabism. These specificities have a role to play in the security perceptions – and, therefore, policies – of the GCC monarchies, and therefore need to be duly taken into account.

From a potential union to the fragmentation of the GCC

The popular uprisings of 2011 greatly impacted the security perceptions of the GCC monarchies and triggered a series of transformative events for the overall security calculus in the Gulf.[22] These events, in their national chapters, brought to the surface the different sociopolitical and socioeconomic vulnerabilities of the individual countries, which, interpreted by their leaders' perceptions, accelerated the fragmentation of a collective security calculus, setting the monarchies on a collision course that is extraordinary in the context of GCC history.

Each GCC country perceived the 2011 protest wave differently, as their own experiences of them were, per se, profoundly different.[23] The Arab Spring had a negligible domestic impact in Qatar and brought only small-scale and short-lived dissent in the UAE. On the contrary, there were sustained and large-scale street protests in the other monarchies, with Saudi

Arabia and Bahrain confronting organised groups with a clear, anti-regime, political agenda. Initially, when protests reached their own backyard, the monarchies closed ranks to push back against change. In March 2011 troops from Saudi Arabia and the UAE, under the umbrella of the Peninsula Shield, entered Bahrain at the request of the King to quell the riots that were threatening the rule of the royal family.[24] This kick-started a decade of full Bahraini alignment with Saudi Arabia and the UAE, but produced no long-lasting security and defence coordination or integration either among all the GCC countries, or among these three. In 2011, Saudi Arabia's Foreign Minister Saud Al Faisal al-Sa'ud relaunched the idea, first discussed in the 1980s, of establishing a Gulf Union, arguing that 'threats of all kinds require … to shift from a current formula of cooperation to a union formula'.[25] The proposal was supported by Bahrain but met a half-hearted response from the other countries, and was formally rejected by Oman in 2013.[26] By that time, it was clear that the six monarchies had divergent threat perceptions, agendas, and priorities.

Whilst the USA and global actors took a backseat regarding events in the MENA region, the Arab Spring enabled alternative regional actors to gain influence. The Obama administration, taking office in 2008, had entered the scene seeking to address growing American domestic fatigue with 'forever wars', in the Middle East, driven in large part by the human, financial, and political costs of the 2003 war in Iraq, where thousands of US troops were still stationed in 2008.[27] As such, the Obama administration did not actively intervene in the 2011 Arab Spring protests that brought about the overthrow of USA's Egyptian ally Hosni Mubarak and threatened the regime in Bahrain. This sparked fears of a US withdrawal from the region among the Gulf monarchies, which were confirmed when President Obama did not honour his 'red line' pledge to protect Syrian civilians from Bashar al-Assad's chemical weapons attacks in Syria in 2013.[28] This US reticence had created geopolitical vacuums in the region, and space for alternative regional players, including the Gulf monarchies themselves. And yet, the Gulf monarchies were sitting on opposite sides of the fault lines over the geopolitical future in the MENA region, and the confrontation was characterised by intense polarisation.

A constellation of Islamist actors, loosely linked to the Muslim Brotherhood, contested power in postrevolutionary Libya, Tunisia, Egypt, Syria, and beyond.[29] In most of these regional theatres, Islamists were actively supported by both Turkey and Qatar, and actively opposed by the UAE and Saudi Arabia. These two camps were on opposite sides during the 2013/2014 Libya civil war – with Saudi–Emirati support for General Khalifa Haftar's militias and Turkish-Qatari support for the UN-recognised Tripoli Government. They were again in opposite camps as Saudi Arabia, the UAE, and Kuwait sponsored a coup d'état by the Egyptian army against the Muslim Brotherhood Government of Mohammad Morsi in 2013.

Simultaneously, when protests descended into civil conflicts and wars in Yemen, Iraq, and Syria, Iran intervened – including militarily – to support its allies and proxies, severely heightening the threat perceptions of Saudi Arabia and the UAE, which already perceived an Iranian role in stoking the 2011 protests in Bahrain and eastern Saudi Arabia.[30] Iran supported directly and indirectly – via Lebanese militia Hezbollah – the regime of Assad in Syria, as it opened a civil war against protesters and militias who were funded, trained, and politically endorsed by Qatar and Saudi Arabia. Simultaneously, Oman was actively mediating talks between Iran and the P5+1 that led to the signing of the 2013 interim deal curbing Iran's nuclear programme, in exchange for relief for Tehran from international sanctions.[31] The deal was met with considerable concern in Saudi Arabia, the UAE, and Bahrain, which feared Iran could deploy the additional funds to finance its regional expansion.

These divergences in the security perceptions were revealed unequivocally to the public eye in the first intra-GCC crisis of 2014. In March 2014, just a few months after the idea of the Gulf Union was finally rejected, Saudi Arabia, Bahrain, and the UAE collectively withdrew their ambassadors from Qatar.[32] The action was taken in response to an alleged breach on the part of Qatar of a comprehensive security agreement dated November 2013, signed by the King of Saudi Arabia and the Emir of Qatar, and witnessed by the Emir of Kuwait.[33] The document, known as the Riyadh Agreement is quintessentially a demand that Qatar refrain from any controversial policy perceived as negatively impacting the regional status quo. It was signed only three months after Hamad bin Khalifa al-Thani – who had ruled Qatar since 1995 and had been the main architect of Qatari foreign policy autonomy from Saudi Arabia – abdicated in favour of his thirty-three-year-old son, Tamim bin Hamad al-Thani.[34] The missing GCC ambassadors returned to Doha in November 2014, after Emir Tamim signed a second security agreement, known as the Supplementary Riyadh Agreement, reiterating and reinforcing the points agreed upon the year before.

As part of the deal, in 2014 Qatar tried to establish some dialogue with the anti-Islamist military regime of al-Sisi in Egypt and ejected a number of individuals belonging to the Muslim Brotherhood, including acting leader Mahmoud Hussein and foreign relations officer Amr Darrag, to Turkey.[35] Qatar also agreed to soften the tone of Al Jazeera in all reports that could damage the GCC regimes' interests, and completely shut down Al Jazeera's affiliate in Egypt, Mubasher Misr. Crucially, Qatar did not join Saudi Arabia and the UAE when they designated the Brotherhood as a terrorist organisation in 2014.[36]

This Qatari commitment to alignment further emboldened the UAE and Saudi Arabia, especially after 2015. In January of that year, King Abdallah of Saudi Arabia died and his brother Salman bin Abdulaziz al-Sa'ud became king. In April, King Salman appointed his favourite son, Mohammad bin Salman, to the position of deputy crown prince.[37] Mohammad bin Salman forged an alliance with the Crown Prince of Abu Dhabi, Mohammad bin Zayed al-Nahyan, for an assertive regional project to support favoured factions and push back against geopolitical adversaries. In March 2015, Mohammad bin Salman announced that Saudi Arabia would conduct a military operation in alliance with the UAE against Iran-supported Yemeni rebels known as Houthi, who had taken over the country's capital, Sana'a, off the back of the Yemeni Arab Spring.[38] The following year the Saudi Government executed Shi'a cleric Nimr al-Nimr, who was the most high-profile leader in the 2011 protests in Saudi Arabia: when this triggered attacks by Iranian mobs on Saudi diplomatic missions in Iran, Riyadh cut diplomatic ties with Tehran, and the other GCC countries recalled their ambassadors from the country.[39] On the other front, anonymous Turkish officials accused the UAE of being the major supporter of a group from within the Turkish army that attempted and failed a coup d'état against the Turkish Government in July 2016.[40]

The election of Donald Trump as US president in November 2016 opened even more opportunities for the Saudi–Emirati duo.[41] Donald Trump's rhetoric and policies persuaded the Saudi and Emirati leaders that the USA would move away from retrenchment and would begin once again to become more involved in regional affairs, albeit by leaning further on its traditional partners, including Saudi Arabia and the UAE. Trump arranged to meet Mohammad bin Salman for a private lunch in the Oval Office as early March 2017, when Mohammad was only deputy crown prince, and took his first trip abroad to Saudi Arabia two months later, vowing full support to US partners in a large multi-lateral summit. This included support on countering Iran, Islamists, and their sponsors in Qatar and Turkey, as well as personal endorsement for the leaders of Trump's two closest partners, Saudi Arabia and the UAE.

Riding this momentum, in June 2017 Mohammad bin Salman ousted his cousin Mohammad bin Nayef and became the crown prince of Saudi Arabia.[42] A few months later, the Saudi authorities executed a sweeping operation against hundreds of Saudi officials, royals, and business tycoons – many of whom were linked to Mohammad bin Nayef. Accused of corruption charges, they were held in the Ritz-Carlton hotel in Riyadh and negotiated plea deals with the authorities.[43] An emboldened Saudi leadership continued to move against prominent Saudi dissidents and figures unsupportive of Mohammad bin Salman domestically and abroad. In October 2018, a team of individuals linked to Saudi institutions flew to Istanbul in pursuit of Jamal Khasoggi, a prominent Saudi journalist and former advisor to policy-makers, who had been living in self-exile in the United States.[44] Khashoggi was killed inside the Saudi consulate in Istanbul and his body was dismembered. The news was leaked to the press, triggering a years-long global outcry and investigations into the crime by the United Nations; several national security services, including the CIA; and the Turkish authorities, who confidentially provided evidence to foreign partners. These investigations raised suspicions that Crown Prince Mohammad bin Salman himself had greenlighted the killing.[45] What followed was a profound political falling-out between Ankara and Riyadh, as Saudi officials became convinced that the Turkish Government was trying to delegitimise Mohammad bin Salman to the extent of justifying his removal.[46] While the Saudi Crown Prince managed to consolidate his position domestically with the support of King Salman, the collapse of his reputation severely affected his standing within international politics and relations with global leaders, except President Donald Trump.

Break-up point

Soon after Trump's trip to Saudi Arabia in 2017, the GCC plunged into the most serious internal political crisis in its thirty-six years of existence.[47] On 24 May 2017, the Qatar News Agency (QNA) attributed controversial statements about Iran, Israel, and Hamas to Qatar's Emir Tamim.[48] Qatari officials quickly argued that QNA had been hacked, but these statements sparked a string of strong responses from Saudi and Emirati media, with editorials and articles accusing Qatar of funding terrorist groups – among which they included the Muslim Brotherhood and affiliates – and colluding with Iran and Iranian-backed militias to undermine the stability of the GCC. This latter accusation referred to a $700 million ransom paid by Qatar to free twenty-six members of a Qatari falconry party kidnapped in southern Iraq by an Iranian-backed Iraqi Shi'a militia known as Kata'eb Hezbollah in April 2017.[49] After weeks of such an intense media offensive, on 5 June 2017, Saudi Arabia, Bahrain, the UAE, and Egypt (i.e. the quartet) announced that they had cut all relations with Qatar and closed their land, air, and sea borders with the country. The quartet ejected Qatari diplomats; ordered Qatari citizens to leave their states within fourteen days; and halted all land, air, and sea traffic with Qatar. In the weeks after this initial move, the crisis underwent a significant escalation when the quartet issued a list of thirteen demands for Qatar to meet with them within ten days in order to resolve the dispute.[50] The demands included: curbing all ties except economic ones with Iran; severing all ties with individuals, groups, or organisations designated as terrorists by the quartet (i.e. the Muslim Brotherhood); shutting down Al Jazeera and news outlets that received Qatar funds; terminating any joint military cooperation with Turkey; disclosing and halting all contacts with political opposition figures in Saudi Arabia, the UAE, Egypt, and Bahrain, handing them over to their countries of origin; paying compensation for losses caused by Qatar's policies; consenting to audits for compliance; and aligning with the other Gulf and Arab countries militarily, politically, socially, and economically.

In July 2017, the quartet released a statement saying that these demands were in fact linked to the Riyadh Agreements, already signed by Qatar, which were leaked to the press that same month. These documents are, in fact, an unmatched written window onto the GCC's divergent security perceptions, and thus deserve closer scrutiny. The documents' gravity is quickly evident in their language: the words most often reiterated in the few pages are 'security' and 'stability'.[51] The 2013 Agreement, signed by the Saudi King and the Qatari Emir and witnessed by Kuwait's leader, laid out three commitments. The first is to avoid 'interference in the internal affairs of the GCC states, whether directly or indirectly, [including] not to give asylum/refuge or give nationality to any citizen of the Council states that has an activity opposing his country's regimes, and no support for antagonistic media'.[52] The emphasis is on political security, i.e. regime stability, that can, supposedly, be endangered by outside actors (in this case, Qatar) supporting dissidents. The second and third points specifically mention avoiding support of the Muslim Brotherhood as well as opposition groups in Yemen 'that could pose a threat to neighbouring countries', i.e. Saudi Arabia, the proponent of such agreement.[53] The following document, the 2014 Supplementary Agreement, is even more specific.[54] The list of signatories is expanded, as it includes King Abdullah bin Abdulaziz al-Sa'ud of Saudi Arabia; King Hamad bin Issa al-Khalifa of Bahrain; Sheikh Mohammed bin Rashed al-Maktoum, Prime Minister of the UAE and Ruler of Dubai; Mohammed bin Zayed al-Nahyan, Crown Prince of Abu Dhabi; and Emir Tamim bin Hamad al-Thani of Qatar. Tellingly, no Omani official signed the agreement, and similarly to what happened in 2017 Oman steered clear of the 2014 dispute altogether. The Emir of Kuwait did sign it, but was later identified as a neutral witness in the dispute, rather than an active signatory.[55] The document is explicitly divided into matters of domestic and foreign policy, and its underlying idea is that in vulnerable times, Qatar has provided financial, logistic, and political support (or simply airtime) to individuals or organisations opposing the security and stability of the GCC. The fact that this point appears both in the domestic and foreign affairs sections and that there is a specific call to '[prevent] external groups, parties and organisations that target the GCC from finding a place inside GCC countries' is a clear reference to intermestic threats.[56] A key reference is made to avoiding the provision of financial, media, or political backing to the Muslim Brotherhood – especially in Egypt – as well as to groups in Syria and Yemen.

To complement the Riyadh Agreements, in 2017 the quartet also published three blacklists of more actors considered hostile. While the threatening capacity of the blacklisted entities or individuals was in many cases inflated for an aggressive, rather than defensive, political hidden agenda, they do provide a window onto security perceptions and thinking. Moreover, the three categories of individuals and organisations included in the three lists released in 2017 fit into the frameworks of the Riyadh Agreements.

The first, large, category is that of political Islamists, namely the Muslim Brotherhood and organisations gravitating around its ideology. Alongside the international central organisation, the quartet singled out affiliated entities such as the Qatar-based International Union of Muslim Scholars and the International Islamic Council for Da'wah and Relief, and smaller associated entities such as the Al Karama Organization, the Foundation Sheikh Thani Ibn Abdullah for Humanitarian Services, the Cordoba Foundation in the United Kingdom, and the Al Islah Association. Additionally, the list featured dozens of prominent Brotherhood leaders from Egypt, the birthplace of the organisation, including the spiritual leader Yusuf al-Qaradawi, to whom Qatar gave refuge and a prominent platform; the organisation's acting general leader Alsayed Mahmoud Ezzat Ibrahim Eissa; and Mohammed Jamal Ahmed Hishmat Abdul Hamid, the key founder of Egypt's Freedom and Justice Party – the political wing of the Brotherhood. Many Egyptian nationals on the lists were accused of anti-regime activities in Egypt during the 2011 revolution and against the al-Sisi regime. Similarly, the Libyan entities on the lists included Islamist figures and militias who had been key opponents of the anti-Islamist Government of General Khalifa Haftar, supported by Riyadh and Abu Dhabi, such as the Benghazi Defence Brigades; Ismail Mohammed Sallabi of the Benghazi Revolutionaries Shura Council; Abdul Hakim Belhadj, former leader of al-Qa'ida's Libyan Islamic Fighting Group, the Tripoli Military Council, and the al-Watan Party; and Ali Mohammed Salabi, Ismail's brother – a Qatar-based preacher close to the Brotherhood. Several Libyan media – such as al Saraya Media Center; Boshra News Agency; Nabaa TV; and the Tanasuh Foundation for Dawa, Culture, and Media in Libya – were also added to the lists, accused of receiving funds from Qatar to spread Islamist propaganda.

Another category on the blacklists was that of individuals and organisations supportive of or related to jihadist groups such as Syria's Jabhat al-Nusra, Yemen's al-Qa'ida in the Arabian Peninsula (AQAP) and Egypt's al Gama'a al Islamiyya. In this category, most of the individuals were of Qatari nationality, including members of the royal family, and there were many Qatari-funded charities, such as Qatar Charity.

The final category of blacklist is that of Shi'a Islamists, i.e. militias or individuals allegedly backed by Iran, most prominently represented by Hezbollah and its leaders, designated as a terrorist organisation by the GCC in March 2016.[57] Individuals and militias associated with the 2011 uprisings in Bahrain feature most prominently in this category, among them Bahraini national Hassan Ali Mohammed Juma Sultan, a Shi'a cleric who undertook his religious studies in Iran and has been a leader of the Islamic Dawa Party as well as of Bahrain's al-Wefaq, and was allegedly affiliated to several activities with the Lebanese Hezbollah.[58] Sultan was featured in an audio recording of a phone conversation with Hamad bin Khalifa al-Attiyah, special advisor to Qatar's Emir, seemingly aimed at coordinating Qatar's Bahrain policy with the opposition's stances.[59] Also on the list was Mohammed Suleiman Haidar Mohammed al-Haidar, a Qatari businessman accused of financing armed groups active in the Bahraini opposition to the ruling family. Many of the Shi'a groups involved in armed struggle against the Bahraini royals, such as the Saraya Al Ashtar, the February 14 Youth Coalition, the Saraya Al Muqawama (or Resistance Brigades), Hezbollah al-Bahraini, Saraya Al Mukhtar, and Harakat Ahrar Bahrain, were also blacklisted. These radical demands gave Doha the sense that the quartet was looking for full capitulation. While calling for dialogue with their GCC neighbours, Qatari leaders expressed their firm rejection of the demands, arguing that they equated to ceding Qatar's sovereignty, and the crisis plunged into a diplomatic limbo.[60]

The unprecedented media and information offensive of May 2017, which went as far as attacking the legitimacy of Qatar's Emir, was an early signal of just how unique this crisis would be vis-à-vis previous ones.[61] Speculations transpired via the media, vehemently denied by Saudi Arabia and the UAE, that a military invasion of Qatar was also considered.[62] The crisis also transferred into the social domain, economic relations *tout court*, international politics, and regional geopolitics. Vitriolic campaigns on traditional and social media extended to the public opinions of the countries involved, in a way that was deeply wounding to the idea of a 'khaliji community', increasingly replaced by a top-down nationalism.[63] The expulsion of Qatari citizens and the introduction of restrictions on cross-border movements posed serious questions on the long-term impacts of the crisis on the GCC's social fabric.[64] The extension of a full-ranging economic closure against a single fellow GCC state was historically unprecedented, and the measures against Qatar were particularly dramatic given that the country depends heavily on the globalised liberal economic order to survive, importing over 80 per cent of its food and exporting energy, the proceeds of which cover approximately 70 per cent of the Government's revenue.[65] The substantial level of economic integration attained by the GCC thus became an enabling context for the offensive, magnifying the effects of the economic measures employed and showing Qatar's leadership that, in spite of the wealth and political weight acquired through it, the emirate remains a geographically small entity depending on its neighbours to thrive.

The crisis also expanded to regional and international politics. Qatar established air bridges from Turkey and Iran to obtain essential goods, and had to reroute its energy exports through Iranian and Omani waters in order to avoid crossing those of the quartet.[66] In fact, both Oman and Kuwait refused to join the anti-Qatar camp and strongly pledged their neutrality in the crisis, with Kuwait becoming the major mediator in resolution attempts.[67] Turkish president Recep Tayyip Erdoğan emerged as the strongest supporter of Qatar's Emir, even deploying Turkish troops on Qatari soil to deter any hypothetical military escalation of the crisis.[68] Doha experienced a pragmatic rapprochement with Iran because of Tehran's willingness to provide options for Doha to escape total isolation.[69] By the end of June, Iran's president Hassan Rouhani, was already taking a public political stance backing Qatar and declaring the 'siege' against it 'unacceptable'.[70] In turn, in August 2017, Qatar's Foreign Ministry restored full diplomatic relations with Iran.[71] In the wider region, the quartet received tepid support from several African and Middle Eastern countries, including, most convincingly, the Saudi protégé in Yemen, the Government of Abd Al Mansour al-Hadi, and the Emirati protégé in Libya, General Khalifa Haftar.[72] Most other regional actors, from Morocco to Jordan, claimed neutrality and supported the Kuwaiti efforts in favour of reconciliation.[73] This was the same position embraced by the Europeans – including the European Union, France, Germany, Italy, and the UK – and by many other global players such as China or India, simultaneously dependent on Saudi oil and Qatari gas.[74] The common objective of the international community was to guarantee the free flow of energy. The USA was in a more complicated position, given how President Trump had supported the Saudi and Emirati position publicly and privately even before the crisis was triggered, effectively enabling the hostilities against Qatar.[75] Despite that, the state and defence departments voiced support for de-escalation, albeit to no avail, with then Secretary of State Rex Tillerson and then Secretary of Defence Jim Mattis involved in mediation attempts and even appointing a special envoy for the crisis, General Anthony Zinni.[76]

A strategic pause

The Trump administration, featuring several anti-Iran hawks, also overturned US policy on Iran. Under Trump, the White House started an incremental 'maximum pressure' sanctions campaign against Iran and finally withdrew from the JCPOA in May 2018.[77] This escalation between the USA and Iran was received very differently across the GCC, even beyond the unique position of Qatar.

Riyadh and Abu Dhabi – like Tel Aviv – fully supported Trump's maximum pressure campaign and the withdrawal from the JCPOA. Abu Dhabi tightened the space for trade with Iran, reigning in Dubai-based banks and companies that had links to Iran and sending instructions via the UAE central bank for commercial banks to close the accounts of Iranian companies and nationals.[78] As mentioned, Saudi Arabia's posture vis-à-vis Iran had already become more hostile by 2017. In November that year, Saudi Crown Prince Mohammad bin Salman gave an interview to the *New York Times* calling the Supreme Leader of Iran 'the new Hitler of the Middle East'.[79] Oman was instead particularly concerned about a potential escalation between Iran on one side and the USA, Saudi Arabia, and the UAE on the other. Muscat also had concerns on the reliability of its key security partnership with the USA, as Trump officials shunned their Omani counterparts, vieweing them as too close to Iran and too far from the UAE, whose influence in south-east Yemen was considered the primary threat in Muscat.[80] Kuwait did not join the Saudi–Emirati line on Iran either: holding the chairmanship of the GCC in 2017, Kuwait's Emir Sabah al-Ahmad al-Jaber al-Sabah sent a letter to the Iranian Government offering to mediate a dialogue between Iran and its fellow GCC states.[81] The attempt was unsuccessful, but clearly showed divergences between the two more senior GCC leaders – Kuwait's Emir Sabah and Oman's Sultan Qaboos – and the two younger de facto leaders – Emirati Crown Prince Mohammad bin Zayed and Saudi Prince Mohammad bin Salman.

The outlook deteriorated in 2019, when Iran launched a 'maximum resistance' strategy with the aim of transferring the risks and costs of maximum pressure onto the regional and international community.[82] Tehran started substantially breaching the JCPOA, increasing its stockpiles of enriched uranium and installing new centrifuges. Within the region, Iran increased the frequency of missile and drone attacks both directly – such as with the 2019 downing of a US drone adjacent to Iranian airspace – and via proxy groups, against US interests in Iraq, oil tankers, and critical infrastructures in the wider Gulf. In 2019, UAE and international tankers were targeted in Emirati territorial waters, and Saudi oil facilities in Abqaiq and Khurais were hit with a coordinated attack by drones and cruise missiles. Despite the close ties among Riyadh, Abu Dhabi, and Washington, the Trump administration did not react to these attacks against its partners, dramatically weakening the confidence of local leaders in the solidity of US deterrence. Months later, when a US contractor was killed by Iranian-allied Iraqi militias, Trump authorised a response that resulted in the killing of Qassem Soleimani, commander of the Islamic Revolutionary Guard Corps's (IRGC) Quds Force. The Gulf monarchies, despite being on the frontline of a potential Iranian retaliation, were not consulted or alerted beforehand.[83]

The events of the end of 2019 dramatically changed the security calculus of the GCC monarchies, with even Saudi Arabia and the UAE no longer feeling able to rely on the USA as their security guarantor vis-à-vis the growing regional polarisation. Both actors then embraced a new geopolitical phase to dial down tensions and de-escalate rivalries with both Iran and Islamists while they worked to rebuild their deterrence credentials by diversifying away from an overreliance on the USA. Momentous shifts and a growing sense of vulnerability ushered in a strategic pause.

The outbreak of the COVID-19 pandemic in early 2020 and the subsequent collapse in the price of oil, which averaged at below 40 USD per barrel that year, reinforced this sense of vulnerability and the urgency of refocusing, away from resource-draining geopolitical rivalries and towards domestic stability.[84] The electoral defeat of Donald Trump in the 2020 presidential election, bringing into office a Democratic administration led by Joe Biden, also called for a rethink of the monarchies' relations with the USA and the US role in regional security.[85] Upon taking office in January 2021, the Biden administration launched negotiations with Iran – in the P5+ 1 format – to rejoin the JCPOA. In August 2021, Biden hastily withdrew all remaining US troops from Afghanistan, and the country was back under Taliban control in two weeks. During his campaign, Biden vowed to make Saudi Arabia 'a pariah' in retribution for the killing of Jamal Khashoggi and all other human rights violations.[86] These elements further highlighted the perceptions of a US retrenchment from its traditional geopolitical role in the MENA region and, therefore, the need for the Gulf monarchies to pursue a strategic pause.

By the end of 2020, Saudi Arabia had reached out to Qatar via the Kuwaiti channel to put an end to the intra-GCC crisis that had begun three years earlier.[87] Back-channel negotiations led by Kuwait resulted in a formal reconciliation at the al-Ula Summit in January 2021. Riyadh also led the UAE, Egypt, and – albeit more reluctantly – Bahrain to reconcile with Doha, which in turn vowed to cut ties with the Muslim Brotherhood and tone down media and political hostilities towards the the quartet regimes. The borders between Qatar and its neighbours were reopened, diplomatic relations were reinstated, and the parties explored opportunities for cooperation, including the 2022 World Cup, due to be hosted in Doha. Both Saudi Arabia and the UAE then also engaged in contact with Turkey, leading to meetings at leadership level in 2021 and 2022 and concrete steps to reset and improve political and economic ties.[88]

The UAE, which had initiated talks on maritime security with Iran as early as December 2019, sent COVID-19 aid both to Iran and to the Syrian regime of Bashar al-Assad, who officially visited Abu Dhabi and Dubai in 2022.[89] The UAE also started to allow once again the re-export business to Iran: in 2022, it became the world's biggest exporter to Iran, shipping $16.5 billion in goods.[90] Both the UAE and Kuwait sent their ambassadors back to Iran in 2022. Alongside these attempts at de-escalation, the UAE (and Bahrain) signed the Abraham Accords normalising relations with Israel in 2020. Given its advanced military and cyber-security capabilities, Israel represented an 'extra layer of deterrence vis-à-vis Iran' for the UAE.[91] In fact, technical cooperation on air defence with Tel Aviv enabled the interception of several of the missiles fired by Iranian proxies in Yemen in early 2022.[92] Having also reached out to Iran for a confidential first contact in 2019, Saudi officials held several more rounds of dialogue with their Iranian counterparts.[93] Riyadh agreed to reopen the Iranian delegation at the Organization of Islamic Cooperation in Jeddah, and joined a regional summit – the Baghdad Conference for Cooperation and Partnership – including Iran in August 2021. As in the case of the UAE, the aim of the dialogue for Riyadh was to give Iran stakes in the halting of asymmetric attacks against its territory or interests, especially from Yemen. In the spring of 2022, Iran in fact encouraged Yemen's Houthis to sign a UN-sponsored truce, which led to a significant decrease in the frequency of asymmetric attacks against Saudi territory.

Kuwait and Oman welcomed this turn towards a strategic pause. In addition to external challenges, Kuwait and Oman also had to confront in 2020 the deaths of their leaders, Sultan Qaboos and Emir Sabah.[94] Both had led their countries for decades, and both – especially the former – played a pivotal role in internal and external affairs. Resources were diverted to confront these leadership transitions amid the COVID-19 pandemic, low oil prices, economic instability, and reshuffles in regional and global geopolitics. The UAE also witnessed a major leadership transition in 2022 because, after the death of Khalifa bin Zayed al-Nahyan, Mohammad bin Zayed was officially appointed president of the Federation. Unlike Kuwait and Oman, the leadership transition for the UAE was not a moment of vulnerability but instead an opportunity for Abu Dhabi to consolidate and double down on its policy choices.

The sense of GCC vulnerability was assuaged with the end of the COVID-19 pandemic and a newly regained centrality after the Russian invasion of Ukraine in February 2022. The USA and Europe reacted to the invasion by introducing stringent sanctions against Russia that also targeted the export of oil and gas, on which Europe had previously depended. This significantly tightened the supply available on the energy market, pushing oil prices to above 100 USD per barrel, and left European countries looking for alternative energy suppliers.[95] Qatar, among the largest liquefied natural gas (LNG) producers in the world, became heavily involved in negotiations to provide LNG to Europe.[96] Officials from the USA and Europe also sought the support of Oman, Kuwait, Saudi Arabia, and the UAE, both to upgrade energy relations and to increase general supply levels at lower prices.[97] Despite his campaign promises and political reticence, US president Joe Biden had to travel to Saudi Arabia and publicly meet with Crown Prince Mohammad bin Salman as several other European officials had done before, ending the Crown Prince's isolation.[98]

However, no GCC monarchy chose to join the USA and Europe in sanctioning, ostracising, and alienating Russia. The UAE, holding one of the rotating non-permanent seats for 2022–2023 in the United Nations Security Council (UNSC), abstained in the vote for a US-sponsored UNSC resolution condemning the Russian invasion of Ukraine.[99] The UAE also became a destination for Russian capital and individuals escaping western sanctions.[100] Saudi Arabia, despite American insistence, refused to break cooperation with Russia at OPEC+ or to boost oil production to lower prices.[101] Leaders of the GCC met US president Joe Biden when he travelled to Saudi Arabia in July 2022 to hold the Jeddah Security and Development Summit with officials from the GCC countries Jordan, Iraq, and Egypt. Yet they had also held an official summit with Russian Foreign Minister Sergey Lavrov two months earlier, and another with Chinese president Xi Jinping in December 2022.

In fact, the Gulf monarchies' reticence to align with the USA against Russia was evidence that, perceiving the US retrenchment from its position as a security guarantor, the Gulf monarchies no longer felt bound to support Washington when going against their direct interests, including financial ones. This was a watershed moment, signalling a substantial change in their foreign policy tradition. The monarchies moved from decades of alignment with the USA and Europe to a gradual embrace of strategic hedging and manoeuvring, amid the emergence of an increasingly competitive multi-polar system vis-à-vis Russia but also China. Between 2018 and 2022, Saudi Arabia and the UAE signed strategic partnership agreements with both Moscow and Beijing, and the two countries (plus Oman) emerged as pillars of Beijing's critical infrastructures project, the Belt and Road Initiative.[102] In 2020, China replaced the EU as the GCC's largest trading partner, with bilateral trade valued at $161.4 billion, becoming a top investor into the region.[103] Saudi Arabia surged to be among the top two providers of oil to China, and China emerged as by far the most important client for Omani oil.[104] In their quest to strengthen their own defence capabilities, easing the reliance on the USA for their security, Saudi Arabia and the UAE also upgraded defence cooperation with Beijing and Moscow. Chinese arms sales to Saudi Arabia rose from $35 million to $170 million between 2015 and 2020, and to the UAE from $45 million to $121 million over the same period.[105] Russia signed military cooperation agreements with the UAE in 2018 and with Saudi Arabia in 2022, kick-starting joint investments in the military industrial sectors.[106] Once again, Qatar emerged as a unique case: Doha maintained a lower-level engagement with both Russia and China, and instead further strengthened ties with the USA, becoming a major non-NATO ally in March 2022.[107]

The Arab Spring in 2011 had highlighted the vulnerabilities of the GCC countries as well as their internal divergences and divisions. But these events had also lit the fuse for watershed changes in the geopolitics of the Gulf and the wider MENA region that affected the regional order as much as the role of global powers within it. Ten years after the Arab Spring had triggered new security perceptions in the GCC monarchies and therefore the rethinking of their security calculus, these perceptions and this calculus had directly impacted the geopolitics of the entire region and the interests and role of global powers there. In this sense, understanding those perceptions remains more than ever at the root of understanding the policies and positioning of the Gulf monarchies.

Notes

1 This argument is found in most of the relevant literature, and argued at length in Matteo Legrenzi, *The GCC and the International Relations of the Gulf: Diplomacy, Security and Economic Coordination in a Changing Middle East* (London: Bloomsbury, 2015).

2 *Ibid.*

3 Neil Partrick, 'The GCC: Gulf State Integration or Leadership Cooperation?', Kuwait Programme on Development, Governance and Globalisation in the Gulf States, London School of Economics (2011), Research Paper 19, http://eprints. lse.ac.uk/55660/1/__lse.ac.uk_storage_LIBRARY_Secondary_libfile_shared_ repository_Content_Kuwait%20Programme_Partrick%202011%20paper.pdf (accessed 20 July 2023); J. E. Peterson, 'Sovereignty and Boundaries in the Gulf States: Settling the Peripheries', in Kamrava, *International Politics of the Persian Gulf*, 21.

4 See for example Christian Koch, 'The GCC as a Regional Security Organization', *KAS [Konrad-Adenauer-Stiftung] International Reports* (2010), 24–35; and J. E. Peterson, 'The Historical Pattern of Gulf Security', in Potter and Sick, *Security in the Persian Gulf*.

5 A 'security community', as defined in Emanuel Adler and Michael Barnett (eds), *Security Communities* (Cambridge: Cambridge University Press, 1998), 12, is 'a group of states sharing values, identities – and agendas – tied together by supranational formal and informal links and collective security mechanisms, which are sufficiently strong and widespread to assure peaceful interaction among the group members'. This definition was used with reference to the GCC in Michael Barnett and Gregory Gause, 'Caravans in Opposite

Directions: Society, State and the Development of a Community in the Gulf Cooperation Council', *Cambridge Studies in International Relations* 62:1 (1998), 161–197, among others.

6 William Brewer, 'Yesterday and Tomorrow in the Persian Gulf', *Middle East Journal* 23:2 (1969), 149–158 (154).

7 Malcolm Peck, *The United Arab Emirates: A Venture in Unity* (Boulder, CO: Westview Press, 1986), 49–52.

8 Peterson, 'Sovereignty and Boundaries in the Gulf States'.

9 Louise Fawcett, 'Alliances, Cooperation and Regionalism in the Middle East', in Fawcett, *International Relations*, 196.

10 For the original charter, refer to the website of the GCC, www.gcc-sg.org/ (accessed 24 July 2023); and for a collection of statements from ruling elites, see J. E. Peterson, 'The GCC and Regional Security', in John Sandwick (ed.), *The Gulf Cooperation Council: Moderation and Stability in an Interdependent World* (Boulder, CO: Westview Press, 1986), 171–173.

11 Yoel Guzansky, 'Defence Cooperation in the Arabian Gulf: The Peninsula Shield Force Put to the Test', *Middle Eastern Studies* 50:4 (2014), 540–654 (642).

12 Joseph Kostiner, 'GCC Perceptions of Collective Security in the Post-Saddam Era', in Kamrava, *International Politics*, 102.

13 Gerd Nonneman, 'Determinants and Patterns of Saudi Foreign Policy: "Omnibalancing" and "Relative Autonomy" in Multiple Environments', in Paul Aarts and Gerd Nonneman (eds), *Saudi Arabia in the Balance: Political Economy, Society, Foreign Affairs* (New York: New York University Press, 2005).

14 Guzansky, 'Defence Cooperation in the Arabian Gulf', 646.

15 Adler and Barnett, *Security Communities*, 12.

16 Koch, 'The GCC as a Regional Security Organization'.

17 *Ibid.*, 33.

18 Barry Buzan refers to the Persian Gulf as a sub-complex in Ole Wæver and Barry Buzan, *Regions and Powers* (Cambridge: Cambridge University Press, 2003). Among the area scholars an example of this conceptualisation is in Cilja Harders and Matteo Legrenzi (eds), *Beyond Regionalism? Regional Cooperation, Regionalism and Regionalization in the Middle East.* (London: Ashgate, 2013).

19 The regional security complex theory first appears in Buzan, *People, States and Fear*, 24.

20 An approach that emphasises domestic factors in security policy-making is not too different from the theory of neoclassical realism, which has already been applied successfully to the GCC case, for example in Rickli, 'New Alliances Dynamics in the Gulf'.

21 All the political, economic, sociological, and historical differences among the GCC monarchies appear clearly in Christopher Davidson, *Power and Politics in the Persian Gulf Monarchies* (London: Hurst, 2011), where all of these aspects are treated in separate chapters, for each GCC state respectively.

22 Cinzia Bianco, 'Gulf Security after 2011: A Threat Analysis', *Middle East Policy* 25:2 (2018), 27–41.

23 *Ibid.*

24 Guzansky, 'Defence Cooperation in the Arabian Gulf'.

25 Prince Saud Al Faisal's speech was delivered on 28 April 2012 at the 'Conference of Gulf Youth, Arab Gulf States from Cooperation to Union' in Riyadh. It can be read at 'Toward a Union Formula – Prince Saud Al Faisal', website of the Saudi–US Relations Information Service, http://susris.com/2012/04/30/toward-a-union-formula-%E2%80%93-prince-saud-al-faisal/ (accessed 25 August 2022).

26 Abdullah Baabood, 'The Future of the GCC amid the Gulf Divide', in Krieg, *Divided Gulf*.

27 Marc Lynch, 'Obama and the Middle East', *Foreign Affairs*, September/October 2015, www.foreignaffairs.com/articles/middle-east/obama-and-middle-east (accessed 20 July 2023).

28 *Ibid.*

29 Beverley Milton-Edwards, *The Muslim Brotherhood: The Arab Spring and Its Future Face* (London: Routledge, 2015).

30 Dalia Dassa Kaye, Frederic Wehrey, and Michael Scott Doran, 'Arab Spring, Persian Winter: Will Iran Emerge the Winner from the Arab Revolt?', *Foreign Affairs*, 1 July 2011, 183–188, www.foreignaffairs.com/articles/middle-east/2011-07-01/arab-spring-persian-winter (accessed 23 July 2023).

31 P5+1 refers to the UN Security Council's five permanent members (the P5) – China, France, Russia, the United Kingdom, and the United States – plus Germany.

32 Jamal Abdullah, 'Motives and Consequences of Ambassador Withdrawals from Doha', *Al Jazeera Centre for Studies* 24 (2014), https://studies.aljazeera.net/en/reports/2014/04/201441061248251708.html (accessed 24 July 2023).

33 The two documents, the 2013 and 2014 Riyadh Agreements, were leaked to the press in July 2017. CNN, which originally obtained the documents, has provided both the original Arabic versions and English translations at http://i2.cdn.turner.com/cnn/2017/images/07/10/translation.of.agreementsupdated.pdf (accessed 25 August 2022).

34 Kristian Ulrichsen, *Qatar and the Gulf Crisis: A Study of Resilience* (Oxford: Oxford University Press, 2020).

35 *Ibid.*, 45.

36 *Ibid.*

37 Madawi Al-Rasheed, *The Son King: Reform and Repression in Saudi Arabia* (Oxford: Oxford University Press, 2021).

38 Hassan Ahmadian, 'Iran and Saudi Arabia in the Age of Trump', *Survival* 60:2 (2018), 133–150.

39 *Ibid.*

40 David Hearst, 'UAE "Funnelled Money to Turkish Coup Plotters"', *Middle East Eye*, 29 July 2016, www.middleeasteye.net/fr/news/exclusive-uae-funnelled-money-turkish-coup-plotters-21441671 (accessed 25 August 2022).

41 Kristian Ulrichsen, 'Fire and Fury in the Gulf', *IndraStra Global* 4:2 (2018), www.ssoar.info/ssoar/handle/document/55716 (accessed 24 July 2023).

42 Ben Hubbard, *MBS: The Rise to Power of Mohammed bin Salman* (New York: Tim Duggan Books, 2020).

43 *Ibid.*

44 Ben Hubbard covers in great detail the killing of Jamal Khashoggi and the events that followed, in *ibid*.

45 *Ibid.*

46 Interview by the author of a senior Saudi diplomat, Brussels, 13 June 2022.

47 Ulrichsen, *Qatar and the Gulf Crisis*.

48 Marc Owen Jones, 'Hacking, Bots and Information Wars in the Qatar Spat', in Lynch, *The Qatar Crisis*, 8–10.

49 Erika Solomon, 'The $1bn Hostage Deal that Enraged Qatar's Gulf Rivals', *Financial Times*, 5 June 2017, www.ft.com/content/dd033082–49e9–11e7-a3f4-c742b9791d43 (accessed 17 September 2022).

50 Ulrichsen, *Qatar and the Gulf Crisis*.

51 The Riyadh Agreements (original and English translation) can be found at http://i2.cdn.turner.com/cnn/2017/images/07/10/translation.of.agreements updated.pdf (accessed 25 August 2022).

52 *Ibid.*, 1.

53 *Ibid.*

54 *Ibid.*, 2.

55 Abdulhadi Alajmi, 'The Gulf Crisis: An Insight into Kuwait's Mediation Efforts', *International Relations* 6:10 (2018), 537–548.

56 The Riyadh Agreements, 3.

57 David Pollock, 'Hezbollah Labelled Terrorist by GCC States', *Fikra Forum*, Washington Institute for Near East Policy, 8 March 2016, https://www.washingtoninstitute.org/policy-analysis/hezbollah-labeled-terrorist-gcc-states-what-do-their-people-think (accessed 24 July 2023).

58 *Ibid.*

59 The original recording is available at ' "Emir" from Qatar Heard Conspiring against Bahrain', *Al Arabiya*, 17 June 2017, https://english.alarabiya.net/en/News/gulf/2017/06/17/Who-is-this-Emir-from-Qatar-heard-conspiring-against-Bahrain-.html (accessed 25 August 2022).

60 Ulrichsen, *Qatar and the Gulf Crisis*.

61 Jones, 'Hacking, Bots and Information Wars'.

62 'UAE Planned to Invade Qatar with Blackwater-Linked Mercenaries: Report', *Middle East Eye*, www.middleeasteye.net/fr/news/uae-planned-invade-qatar-blackwater-linked-mercenaries-report-1742295879 (accessed 17 September 2022); Jennifer Jacobs, 'Trump Warned Saudis off Military Move on Qatar', Bloomberg, 19 September 2017, www.bloomberg.com/news/articles/2017-09-19/trump-is-said-to-have-warned-saudis-off-military-move-on-qatar (accessed 17 September 2022); Abdulrahman al-Rashed, 'The Story of the Saudi–UAE "Invasion" of Qatar', *Al Arabiya*, https://english.alarabiya.net/views/news/middle-east/2017/09/21/The-story-of-the-Saudi-UAE-invasion-of-Qatar (accessed 17 September 2022).

63 Courtney Freer, 'Social Effects of the Qatar Crisis', *Indrastra Global* 10 (2017), 1–4 (4).

64 *Ibid.*

65 Steven Wright. 'The Political Economy of the Gulf Divide', in Krieg, *Divided Gulf.*

66 Ulrichsen, *Qatar and the Gulf Crisis.*

67 Giorgio Cafiero and Theodore Karasik, 'Kuwait, Oman, and the Qatar Crisis', Middle East Institute, 22 June 2017, www.mei.edu/publications/kuwait-oman-and-qatar-crisis (accessed 17 September 2022).

68 Bülent Aras and Pınar Akpınar, 'Turkish Foreign Policy and the Qatar Crisis', IPC Policy Brief (Istanbul: Istanbul Policy Center, 2017).

69 Sébastien Boussois, 'Iran and Qatar: A Forced Rapprochement', in Krieg, *Divided Gulf.*

70 'Iran's Rouhani Backs Qatar, Rejects "Siege"', Reuters, 25 June 2017, www. reuters.com/article/us-gulf-qatar-iran/irans-rouhani-backs-qatar-rejects-siege-idUSKBN19G0X2 (accessed 25 August 2022).

71 'Qatar Says Its Ambassador to Return to Iran: Foreign Ministry', Reuters, 23 August 2017, www.reuters.com/article/us-gulf-qatar-iran/qatar-says-its-ambassador-to-return-to-iran-foreign-ministry-idUSKCN1B32J6 (accessed 25 August 2022).

72 Lynch, *The Qatar Crisis.*

73 *Ibid.*

74 Máté Szalai, 'The Crisis of the GCC and the Role of the European Union', *MENARA Future Notes* 14 (2018), https://www.iai.it/sites/default/files/menar a_fn_14.pdf (accessed 24 July 2023); Mohammed Sinan Siyech, 'India–Qatar Relations: Navigating Turbulent Seas', Middle East Institute, 9 April 2019, www.mei.edu/publications/india-qatar-relations-navigating-turbulent-seas (accessed 25 August 2022); Jonathan Fulton, 'China's Approach to the Gulf Dispute', *Asia Dialogue*, 3 May 2018, https://theasiadialogue.com/2018/05/ 03/chinas-approach-to-the-gulf-dispute/ (accessed 25 August 2022); Elena Melkumyan, 'Emir of Qatar in Russia: Low Profile and Modest Outcome', Valdai Club, 30 March 2018, http://valdaiclub.com/a/highlights/emir-of-qatar-in-russia/ (accessed 25 August 2022).

75 Michael Stephens, 'Why Key Arab Countries Have Cut Ties with Qatar – and What Trump Had to Do with It', Lynch, *The Qatar Crisis*, 12–13.

76 Giorgio Cafiero, 'The "Trump Factor" in the Gulf Divide', in Krieg, *Divided Gulf*, 128.

77 Michael Doran, 'The Trump Doctrine in the Middle East', in Stanley A. Renshon and Peter Suedfeld (eds), *The Trump Doctrine and the Emerging International System* (Cham: Palgrave Macmillan, 2021).

78 'Fresh US–UAE Sanctions Will Hit Iran's Weakening Rial', Emerald Expert Briefings, Oxford Analytica (2018), https://www.emerald.com/insight/content/ doi/10.1108/OXAN-ES233702/full/html (accessed 25 July 2023).

79 Ben Hubbard, 'Saudi Crown Prince Likens Iran's Supreme Leader to Hitler', *New York Times*, 15 March 2018, www.nytimes.com/2018/03/ 15/world/middleeast/mohammed-bin-salman-iran-hitler.html (accessed 17 September 2022).

80 Cinzia Bianco, 'Intra-GCC Security Dynamics: The Case of Oman', Monograph Series 9, Gulf Studies Center, Qatar University (2020), http://www.qu.edu.qa/static_file/qu/research/Gulf%20Studies/documents/Monograph%20N9.pdf (accessed 25 July 2023).

81 Kristin Smith Diwan, 'Kuwait: Finding Balance in a Maximalist Gulf', Arab Gulf States Institute in Washington, 29 June 2018, https://agsiw.org/kuwait-finding-balance-maximalist-gulf/ (accessed 17 September 2022).

82 Kayhan Barzegar, 'The Hard Chess Puzzle: Trump's "Maximum Pressure" versus Iran's "Maximum Resistance"', Al Jazeera Centre for Studies, 15 June 2020, https://tinyurl.com/54wa2y35 (accessed 17 September 2022).

83 Interview by the author of a former official from the United States National Security Council, Rome, 6 October 2021.

84 Fakhro, 'COVID and Gulf Foreign Policy'.

85 Joshua Shifrinson and Stephen Wertheim, 'Biden the Realist', *Foreign Affairs*, 9 September 2021, https://www.foreignaffairs.com/articles/united-states/2021-09-09/biden-realist (accessed 23 July 2023).

86 *Ibid.*

87 Marwan Kabalan, 'The Al-Ula GCC Summit', *Insight Turkey* 23:1 (2021), 51–59.

88 Anchal Vohar, 'Erdoğan's War with Arab Monarchies Is Over', *Foreign Policy*, 22 March 2022, https://foreignpolicy.com/2022/03/22/erdogan-turkey-uae-saudi-arabia-monarchy-islamism/ (accessed 17 September 2022).

89 Julien Barnes-Dacey and Cinzia Bianco, 'Order of Engagement: Assad's Visit to Abu Dhabi', 24 March 2022, European Council on Foreign Relations, https://ecfr.eu/article/order-of-engagement-assads-visit-to-abu-dhabi/ (accessed 17 September 2022).

90 Benoit Faucon, 'UAE Trade Provides Iran with Western Goods, from Perfume to Laptops', *Wall Street Journal*, 5 July 2022, www.wsj.com/articles/u-a-e-trade-provides-iran-with-western-goods-from-perfume-to-laptops-11657048268 (accessed 11 August 2022).

91 Comments by an Emirati expert during the Royal United Services Institute Roundtable on the UAE within Iran in the Global Security Context project, 2 November 2021.

92 Interview by the author of a senior Emirati professor of political science, Dubai, 31 May 2022.

93 Simon Mabon, Samira Nasirzadeh, and Eyad Alrefai, 'De-Securitisation and Pragmatism in the Persian Gulf: The Future of Saudi–Iranian Relations', *International Spectator* 56:4 (2021), 66–83.

94 Cinzia Bianco, 'The Deaths of the Mediators-in-Chief: Oman, Kuwait, and De-Escalation in the Gulf', European Council on Foreign Relations, 9 October 2020, https://ecfr.eu/article/commentary_the_deaths_of_the_mediators_in_chief_oman_kuwait_and_de_escalati/ (accessed 17 September 2022).

95 Guntram Wolff, 'The EU without Russian Oil and Gas', *Intereconomics* 57:2 (2022), 66–67.

96 Ben Hubbard, 'The War in Ukraine Could Empower Qatar', *New York Times*, 16 May 2022, www.nytimes.com/2022/05/16/world/middleeast/russia-gas-ukraine-qatar.html (accessed 17 September 2022).

97 Interview by the author of a senior EU official, Brussels, 14 September 2022.

98 Hesham al-Ghannam and Mohammed Yaghi, 'Biden's Trip to Saudi Arabia: Successes and Failures', Carnegie Endowment for International Peace (2022), https://carnegieendowment.org/sada/87662 (accessed 17 September 2022).

99 Zainab Fattah, 'UAE Joined China, India in Abstaining on UN Ukraine Vote', Bloomberg, 26 February 2022, www.bloomberg.com/news/articles/2022-02-26/uae-abstained-in-un-vote-on-ukraine-to-put-emphasis-on-diplomacy (accessed 17 September 2022).

100 Ben Bartenstein, 'Wealthy Flock to the UAE as War Spurs Russian Capital Flight', Bloomberg, 16 June 2022, www.bloomberg.com/news/articles/2022-06-14/world-s-wealthy-flock-to-uae-as-war-spurs-russian-capital-flight (accessed 17 September 2022).

101 'Russia, Saudis Remain Committed to OPEC+, Oil Market Stability', Bloomberg, 29 July 2022, www.bloomberg.com/news/articles/2022-07-29/russia-saudis-remain-committed-to-opec-oil-market-stability (accessed 17 September 2022).

102 Nesibe Battaloglu, 'Saudi and Emirati Pivot to Russia and China: Shift of Axis or Extreme Hedging?', *Politics Today*, 5 July 2022, https://politicstoday.org/saudi-and-emirati-pivot-to-russia-and-china/ (accessed 17 September 2022).

103 *Ibid.*

104 *Ibid.*

105 *Ibid.*

106 *Ibid.*

107 Clarke Cooper, 'As Qatar Becomes a Non-NATO Ally, Greater Responsibility Conveys with the Status', Atlantic Council, 3 March 2022, www.atlanticcouncil.org/blogs/menasource/as-qatar-becomes-a-non-nato-ally-greater-responsibility-coveys-with-the-status/ (accessed 17 September 2022).

2

Theoretical framework

This chapter builds up the theoretical framework employed in the book for the empirical analysis of GCC regimes' security perceptions in the post-2011 context. The scope is to provide reading keys and instruments to systematise threat analysis, thus also allowing for generalisation. The chapter first engages with the literature on security studies and the key conceptual debates within it to define the lexicon that will be employed in the framework – such as security, threat, and risk – also introducing the original concept of differentiation between threats and risks.

Then the chapter unpacks the concept of security perceptions, and explores the academic debate on how these are formed, engaging with the question of the predominance of structural versus contingent factors and on the impact of human factors. Security perceptions are then treated as pivotal in the operationalisation of the differentiation between threats and risks, via securitisation. In policy-making, perceptions are also a major factor informing policy choices when they interact with structural sociopolitical and socioeconomic vulnerabilities, which are here explored. Moreover, the choice to securitise a risk into a threat may be driven by genuine security perceptions as well as by ulterior motives, such as promoting a specific narrative for a political agenda. Offering methods and tools to distinguish narratives from genuine perceptions, thus also challenging hyper-securitisation, is one of the major objectives of this study.

The chapter then presents a framework to categorise threats and risks into three types – internal, external, and intermestic – and four dimensions – political, military, economic, societal. While the relevant literature has provided sufficient descriptive categories to define the diverse types of threats that are most common to the GCC regimes and their diachronic evolution, there has been little attention paid to the increasing multi-dimensionality of threats, their intersections, and how to schematise them coherently but comprehensively. In this context, the chapter puts forward a hypothesis for threat prioritisation, arguing that the threats perceived as intermestic are routinely prioritised by GCC leaders.

Two preliminary considerations that have emerged via a recollection of the main developments in the scholarship on security studies seem helpful in the process of building up the necessary theoretical background. First, the field has been liberated from epistemological assumptions, thus allowing scholars to broaden their theoretical perspective and indulge in a form of eclecticism while elaborating original theories. Second, there is a growing appreciation of the cultural and historical specificities and the observation of temporally contingent empirical reality that serve the intention of the author well.

Defining the terms: security, threats, risks

The debate on security

Definitions of the notion of threat are, of course, inextricably linked to that of security. The conceptual debate on security has gone from an uncontested, unidimensional definition in the pre-Cold War period, when the field was known as strategic studies, to a dynamic phase of the debate on the fundamental characteristics of the notion. For realists, the only way for states to be free from threats is to show power: security becomes a derivative, sometimes almost a synonym, of power.[1] This interpretation was particularly strong until the end of the Cold War: if military force was relevant to an issue, it was considered one of security; otherwise, that issue was consigned to the category of politics. However, after the end of the Cold War, and from the 1990s onwards, the debate was reopened with contributions from – *inter alia* – constructivism, critical security studies, poststructuralism, feminism, and the Copenhagen School. For instance, from a social constructivist approach, security is achieved once the perception and fears of security threats are allayed and overcome.[2] Security is, as such, conceived as an outcome of a process of social and political interaction where social values and norms, collective identities, and cultural traditions are essential to form perceptions. While some scholars continued to speak primarily of national security, taking the State as the major referent object for security, many others started to speak more often of human security, with individuals or humankind as the referent.[3] Further on, the idea of security has been subjected to a reconceptualisation by the process of globalisation, becoming even more multi-faceted and complex. In the western debate, security has been increasingly related to the prevention of and protection against uncertainties, more similar to societal crises than to manifest or latent dangers.[4]

Acknowledging the diversity of the debate, Barry Buzan described security as 'an underdeveloped concept', ambiguous, 'essentially contested', elastic in its meaning.[5] Within this contested and elastic space, however, security has to be defined on a daily basis – at least implicitly – in the context of policy-making. In this sense, while objective factors are instrumental in a security calculus, they are not sufficient: subjective factors inevitably weigh in. In fact, as Alexander Wendt argued, 'security is what actors make of it'.[6] While settling the rather contentious and broad dispute on defining security in a general and abstract sense is outside the scope of this book, it will offer an interpretation that strives to relate conceptual analysis to operationalisation and is relevant to the context of post-2011 GCC monarchies.

The lexicon of security

The security lexicon employed here builds on Barry Buzan's ideas about the comprehensiveness of the concept of security and his loose mix of classical neorealism and constructivism. In his book *People, States and Fear*, Buzan points out that the concept of security was 'too narrowly founded' and that his goal, therefore, was to offer a 'broader framework'.[7] Buzan explicitly suggests that to attempt formulating a precise definition of security would be to disregard the set of 'contradictions latent within the concept itself', in particular as the State's pursuit of security for itself may conflict with the pursuit of individuals' or international security.[8] Despite the soundness of the claim, this remains one of the trickiest spots of Buzan's theory in terms of operationalisation. Indeed, in the context of the crafting of a security agenda, contradictions are daily occurrences that, rather than preventing the definition of security, call for an even more detailed definition – in terms of degrees – and a constant effort to establish prioritisation.

In almost all cases, GCC regimes resolve the latent contradictions of security in favour of a State- and regime-centric definition. The coronavirus (COVID-19) pandemic that swept the world in 2020 offered a very appropriate case study to test this argument. As will be detailed in the analytical chapters of this book, while all GCC governments experienced significant challenges related to the spread of COVID-19 among their populations, this did not significantly alter their security calculus. The pandemic only acted as a multiplier of existing security concerns, heightening the perceptions of risks and threats that, ultimately, remained of a political nature.

A direct consequence of this overcentralisation of the decision-making process in the GCC, as well as the unique role played by the ruling families in the GCC countries' foundational myths, has been the complete conflation of regime security with national security, a point that has been examined extensively and validated often in the area literature.[9] Even those scholars who state the necessity of prioritising human security in the region often do so by arguing that a lack of attention towards public grievances is most likely to generate regime instability, thus implicitly reinforcing the regime-centric perspective.[10] Keeping in mind these context-specific characteristics, security – as perceived by the GCC regimes – is here taken to be about the ability of regimes to maintain their independent identity; their functional integrity; and sovereignty against forces of change, which they see as hostile. Such a definition assumes the basic primacy of political variables in determining the degree of security that states and regimes enjoy. This approach is grounded in the literature on security in the developing states, especially that authored by scholars from developing states themselves. For instance, David Priess and Mohammed Ayoob strongly criticised the legitimacy of the State as a homogeneous unit of analysis, distancing themselves from the idea of the nation-state as a unitary actor and focusing instead on State–society relations, often in opposition to one another.[11] Accordingly, they found that GCC rulers, similarly to other rulers who have not come into office through a democratic process, perceive threats chiefly through the lens of regime survival.

The matter of degree is indeed a second critical issue in Buzan's work. Regardless of what provisions, responses, or policies are taken by regimes vis-à-vis dangers, there is always only a partial chance of success, and thus a partial assurance of security. Buzan recognises this, but treats it as a logical problem and argues that if security is conceived as a matter of degree then 'complicated and objectively unanswerable questions arise about how much security is enough'.[12] Nonetheless, by focusing on the imperatives of operationalisation, the idea of varying degrees of security can be explained as a function of perceptions, and rationalised by introducing a distinction between threats and risks. Both terms have similar attributes, such as a negative connotation as damaging phenomena, the capacity to defy control, and ambiguity. At the same time, they also have a fundamental difference: risk has much less certainty of expectation and, most importantly, the scope of the potential negative impact is unsure. The term 'threat' is therefore employed here to define risks that become acute enough to take on an overtly political dimension and hinder the identity and sovereignty of the regime, or the functional integrity of its institutions.

This is not to say, however, that only political threats exist. Barry Buzan distinguished among five types of threats: military threats, i.e. seizure of territory, invasion, occupation, that can be direct or against the external interests of the State; economic threats, i.e. export or import restrictions, default on debt, economic instability; societal threats, i.e. damages to domestic stability and cohesion; ecological threats, i.e. environmental deterioration; and political threats, such as penetration by a hostile party or ideological competition, which can be international and exogenous or structural and endogenous.[13] Threats can even combine all five dimensions indicated by Buzan.

It is impossible, for instance, to rationalise the perception of Iran's regional influence in the GCC exclusively as a political and military threat, overlooking the factor of Iran's potential as an economic competitor. However, the political dimension remains the one enabling the definition. By the same token, in the GCC environmental dangers such as the increasingly evident effects of climate change have not yet been part of the security calculus, and they probably won't, unless they threaten to have political outcomes that affect the ability of states, or of the governing elites within those states, to survive.

In these definitions, decision-makers are those who operationalise the distinction between threats and risks, by assigning or not assigning the political variable to a given issue, through so-called securitisation. The core idea of securitisation, formulated by Ole Wæver, is that security can be analysed as a speech act, which brings certain referent objects and threats into existence by being uttered as such by securitising actors.[14] In a less fundamentalist interpretation of Wæver's theory, securitisation theory remains a useful framework to understand how actors securitise risks into threats with their speech acts.

Decoding perceptions

In the act of securitisation, actors are often driven by their security perceptions. When actors are political leaders, these impact policies and states' behaviour. The role of perceptions in states' behaviour is only partially addressed in the literature on international relations and security studies as well as in area studies literature. Gregory Gause, one of the few scholars who focused on the topic in the context of the Gulf, wrote that 'each state's behaviour is rooted in perception of both the international situation and its own status as a state'.[15] This implies that the actual threat matters less than the perceived threat in terms of policy-making, as studying the perceptions held by key actors 'casts a light on how officials decide which issues become securitised and subsequently acted upon'.[16] Gause also noted that very little literature existed on the topic, as 'there seems to be an assumption that the source of greatest threat is obvious to observers or subjects'.[17] What little literature exists arguably emphasises the opposite point: that the question of how security perceptions are formed is frequently controversial and conIingent to a time-scape matrix. Perceptions are the outcomes of dynamic processes to apprehend and interpret an issue in its damaging potential, and depend heavily on point of view.

There is a rationalist approach to the study of threat perceptions, arguing that when decision-makers lack the full picture on a potentially damaging issue, they feel compelled to identify it as a threat and react irrationally.[18] The emphasis of the rationalists is thus largely on the ability of the sender of the threatening signals – the source of the perceived threat – in formulating credible messages. Yet, actors also have strong incentives to bluff or deceive, to conceal their weaknesses or to exaggerate their capabilities, especially when they are entangled in the classic 'security dilemma', i.e. they themselves fear attack from the target.[19] The problem in the rationalist approach is that it largely neglects the role oI interpretation of the signals by the targets themselves, which is, instead, what constructivists focus on.[20] For example, in 1976 Robert Jervis looked at why states reacted differently to the same objective external situation, and concluded that diverging interpretations were the driving factors behind divergent reactions.[21] Though influenced by structural, systemic realities, interpretation is not restrained by them, and remains subjective and even irrational.

In this sense, sociocultural factors contribute to the process of forming perceptions.[22] For example, their identity as Arab-Islamic monarchies entails a number of sociocultural factors in shaping perceptions in the GCC monarchies. Another factor worth considering is collective memory. Alexander Wendt discussed it in the debate surrounding the causes of the Bosnian civil war, highlighting the role that collective Serb historical perception played in the conflict.[23] Collective memory is also relevant in the Gulf, for example when a more benign perception of Iran's regional role in Oman is put in correlation with the military assistance given by Iran's Shah to the Omani Sultan during the Dhofar war in the 1960s and 1970s, an assistance that was instrumental to the Sultan in quelling the insurgency and consolidating his reign. [24]

Specific events and actors also shape security perceptions.[25] While an event cannot be the exclusive source of threat, it is often the mechanism that brings the underlying threat to the attention of the target. Actors are of course key, as both senders and receivers of the threatening signals. The senders of the signals often represent the embodiment and personification of threats. The receivers – or threatened actors – are those who offer the signals' interpretation, influenced by 'human factors', such as individual cognition and even emotions. [26]

In political science, these 'human factors', including personality, political cognition, and socialisation into cultural environments, become all the more important as the role of individuals becomes more pivotal in polities.[27] The importance of keeping track of these features is keenly reflected in the nature of GCC politics, where states are highly autocratic and leaders are the final representatives of the national interest, able to act with very few constraints, especially in foreign and security policies.[28] Gregory Gause even went as far as writing: 'In the Gulf, the personal is the political, particularly in foreign policy'.[29] Policy-making isn't subject to bureaucratic scrutiny, nor to the critical review of the press, which addresses a scarcely engaged public opinion. Citizens do elect representatives in Parliament or local assemblies, but the constraints that those elected institutions can place on foreign policy or security decisions are non-existent.[30] It is therefore hard to dispute the notion that monarchs of the Gulf enjoy a formidable impact on the making of security policies. In this context, leaders can securitise any issue, operationalising the distinction between risks and threats and determining their prioritisation, even based on their individual cognition.

A particularly interesting and relevant case is that of perceptions of the Muslim Brotherhood in Qatar versus the UAE after 2011, when the Arab Spring erupted and Brotherhood-affiliated groups began to emerge, challenge, and obtain power. The then Emir of Qatar, Hamad bin Khalifa al-Thani, a longstanding practitioner of the art of international politics, saw the Brotherhood as an opportunity to strengthen Qatar's regional reach, while the then Crown Prince of Abu Dhabi and Deputy Commander of the Armed Forces, Mohammed bin Zayed al-Nahyan, a man of military culture, routinely described the group as a 'mortal enemy'.[31] Several scholars have analysed the roots of such different perceptions in countries that are very similar from a political, geopolitical, social, and economic perspective and, in many cases, a determining role has been attributed to the personal cognition and socialisation of the leaders.[32]

Such unrestrained ability to craft security narratives and policies also opened opportunities for GCC rulers to exploit securitisation for their political agendas. Scholars have clearly shown how, when oil prices plummeted in 2014, GCC rulers used securitisation to accrue political support by hyper-securitising risks.[33] Energy export revenues are instrumental in the GCC countries, as in all rentier economies, in distributing the economic benefits that the population expects to receive from the State. Having fewer energy revenues to distribute, GCC regimes chose to emphasise their ability to guarantee security by highlighting threats, thus reinforcing domestic backing and guaranteeing political quiescence. Moreover, authors focusing on sectarianism have argued that, by amplifying the dangers posed by Iran's interference in their countries, GCC rulers have been able to label the local Shi'a communities as Iran's 'fifth column' and therefore ignore and delegitimise their dissent.[34] Heightening security concerns, magnifying threats, and rallying the population against a common enemy are longstanding, effective political techniques to guarantee quiescence, and are largely in use in the region. The choice to securitise a risk into a threat may be driven by genuine security perceptions as well as by ulterior motives, and, therefore, distinguishing the narrative from genuine security perceptions is critical to an effective threat analysis.

Addressing vulnerabilities

In spite of the vast power that GCC rulers enjoy, they rarely operate against their own countries' structural features, especially when they represent vulnerabilities. Borrowing the definition from Fabien Nathan's environmental studies work, vulnerabilities are here defined as conditions that determine the incapacity of the State to contain, cope with, adapt to, and recover from a damaging phenomenon.[35] These are structural, objective, and systemic factors, which interact with intangible factors, such as perceptions. In line with the work on developing states' security, this book will especially focus on sociopolitical and socioeconomic vulnerabilities.

Edward Azar and Chung-in Moon operationalised the concept of 'security software' by disaggregating it into three primary components: legitimacy, integration, and policy capacity.[36] These scholars argue that not enough time has been available to state-makers in MENA countries to develop the intangible ingredients of security, including the identification of the people with the State (legitimacy) and of people with each other (integration). These complex and delicate state-making and nation-building processes have also been impacted by international forces, especially in the context of postcolonialism and globalisation.[37]

What Azar and Moon term as integration is referred to by Barry Buzan as 'the variable of sociopolitical cohesiveness': Buzan also accords primary explanatory power to this variable – which he considers the defining feature in the distinction between 'strong' and 'weak' states – and he relates this difference to the time available to states to complete the processes of state-making and nation-building.[38] Interestingly, in addition to a country's historical depth, Buzan also speaks of the importance of states' founding ideologies. Describing the essence of the State, he refers to a triangle whose three points are: the physical base of the State (effective sovereignty, international consensus on territorial limits); the institutional expression of the State (consensus on political rules of the game but also on the scope of state institutions); and the idea of the State (implicit social contract and ideological consensus pertaining to a given society).[39] All three elements are key to determining the strength or weakness of a polity: a state whose founding ideology isn't shared, or is contested, is weaker and more vulnerable, especially to threats to its own identity.

The countries of the GCC, often no more than a few decades past independence, and usually having socially exclusive rather than shared founding ideologies, fit the description of Buzan's weak states and are very vulnerable to threats against their own national identity.

In fact, the concept of 'ontological security' – the need of a state to have a distinctive and consistent sense of self and to have that sense affirmed by others – appears particularly relevant to Saudi Arabia and the GCC states, as May Darwich points out.[40] Unlike other Arab states, where nationalism was based on ethnic elements combined with territorial affinities related to the struggle against colonialism, the GCC states were not born out of a struggle for national self-determination, but under the protection of an external power. Monarchs of the GCC have, in the past, appealed more frequently to tribal and religious identities, rather than nationalism, to reinforce their domestic legitimacy.[41] For instance, when the al-Saud family established the Kingdom of Saudi Arabia through armed conquest over several different tribes, they described the endeavour as a religiously motivated liberation of territory from a perceptibly un-Islamic form of governance, and quickly adopted a doctrine that was deeply socially exclusive as their founding ideology.[42] The new state lacked a national identity that could fuel what Buzan calls 'the idea of a state': the ruling family gave its name to the kingdom, becoming a unique national symbol, a process encouraged in the public discourse, from education to the media.[43] In fact, all the GCC ruling families, though to varying degrees, were instrumental in the very foundation of the countries, or, as it has been argued, 'at the heart of the emergent state-building project'.[44] While this strong centralisation facilitates a tighter control over the discourse on 'legitimacy' as defined by Azar and Moon, the same centralisation is an obstacle to what they call 'integration', i.e. sociopolitical cohesiveness.[45] In other words, in a strongly vertical system with ontological insecurity, deep polarisation and divisions at the horizontal level can develop into an institutionalised lack of integration and, ultimately, become sociopolitical vulnerabilities.

Sociopolitical vulnerabilities, especially a lack of integration and of a strong idea-of-a-state, often result in contested legitimacy and group fragmentation.[46] In the GCC countries, a political economy revolving around the rentier model has blended with these, crystallising major inequalities and imbalances.[47] Although data on the GCC countries are often outdated or unavailable, clear trends highlighting such inequalities and imbalances can still emerge. While these vulnerabilities are shared, at the structural level, by all six Gulf monarchies, on a more detailed look some indicators present key differences from one country to another.

Indeed, the GCC countries could be divided into two groups: Saudi Arabia/Oman/Bahrain, having lower gross domestic product (GDP) per capita and higher unemployment levels, and the UAE/Kuwait/Qatar, with the highest GDP per capita and lowest unemployment ratio.[48] Another obvious difference is size: in 2020, Saudi Arabia had a population of over 34 million people, while the other GCC countries registered between 1.6 million (Bahrain) and 9.7 million (the UAE) in the same year.[49] Finally, the percentage of foreigners in the total population is also relevant: data from 2019 show that foreign nationals make up the majority of the population in Bahrain, Kuwait, Qatar, and the UAE (and more than 80 per cent of the population in Qatar and the UAE), while they represent less than one-third of the population in Saudi Arabia and Oman.[50] Still, some key trends remain the same across the region. for example, the private sector in the GCC countries has been, for decades, dependent on foreign labourers and disregarded by nationals, whose majority work in the public sector.[51] The preference for a public sector, undemanding job is closely related to a culture of entitlements correlated with citizenship: for decades GCC citizens have been entitled to a cradle-to-grave welfare system in exchange for political quiescence.[52] In this sense political and economic status are very closely interrelated, as more benefits are granted to groups that are closer to the rulers or play a role in patrimonial politics.

Patronage networks are formed across specific groups, tribes, or sects, thus crystallising sociopolitical fragmentation within nations.[53] This unequal access to opportunities and benefits institutionalises cleavages among ethno-sectarian segments within the social fabric, one of the main sociopolitical vulnerabilities of the GCC countries. This is valid when looking at the sectarian divide in countries such as Saudi Arabia or Bahrain but also other types of divides such as that between citizens and *bidoons* (from the Arabic for 'without' – meaning those without citizenship, apolidi) in Kuwait. By alienating segments of the society, often knowingly, GCC regimes fuel existing structural socioeconomic vulnerabilities, paving the way for the politicisation of internal fault lines.

These sociopolitical and socioeconomic vulnerabilities inform decision-makers' perceptions, even if leaders may choose to ignore or exploit them to preserve their hegemonic position in the short term, despite weakening overall regime and State stability in the long term.

Categorising threats: a wider perspective

Categorising threats by nature, type, and dimension is necessary to perform an effective threat analysis. The most basic distinction operated in security studies scholarship is that between external and internal threats, but this simplistic categorisation does not fit the post-2011 reality of the GCC countries. While the literature on the security of the developing world argues that the insecurity from which these states suffer emanates to a substantial degree from within their boundaries rather than from outside,[54] the history of the foreign and defence policies of GCC countries is one that constantly shows consideration of two external threats, namely Iraq and Iran, as the two main sources of danger to the monarchies.[55] Furthermore, ideologies such as Iraq's pan-Arabism and Iran's Khomeinism were considered grave threats by the GCC regimes in the 1960s and 1980s respectively.[56] Constructivists then opened up the scholarly debate to consider the existence of threats that weren't exclusively external or internal in their nature, something that indeed applies very well to a region where transnationalism is strong, and security interdependence solid. However, threats were still only predominantly categorised within two dimensions: material and ideational.

The introduction of new types of threats is owed particularly to the work of Barry Buzan, who distinguished among five types: military, economic, societal, ecological, and political.[57] While political and military threats had already been more commonly discussed, economic, societal, and ecological threats were somehow new concepts in the early 1990s. Buzan himself pointed out the difficulty of determining, for example, the threshold of what is acceptable in the economic realm – based on an inherent instability of the liberalised market economy – and what is a threat.[58] Societal threats can also be ambiguous to consider but are substantially relevant to the GCC countries and to all other 'weak states', i.e. states with a contested founding ideology or a divisive identity. This type of threat has acquired key relevance since the 1990s, as most of the conflicts showed a strong societal element, descending often into civil war.[59] Civil wars have been particularly common in the MENA region, where sectarian and ethnic violence adds to the gravity of these conflicts. Finally, the term 'ecological threat' equally covers natural disasters and man-made phenomena such as global warming, pollution, and poisoning.

To Buzan, any formulation of a security agenda that doesn't take into account these multiple dimensions would be partial, as 'five sectors do not operate in isolation from each other … all are woven together in a strong web of linkage'.[60] For example, ecological threats can trigger societal or economic ones – such as when desertification threatens the resources of a country or endangers the livelihood of a community – and societal threats can easily spill over into military and political threats. Some scholars convincingly argued that a severe drought, substantially eroding the economic conditions of Syria, is to be included in the broad set of factors triggering the conflict that erupted there in 2011.[61]

The idea of widening the scope of security has also slowly found its way into security thinking in the GCC countries.[62] In 2002 Prince Naef bin Ahmed al-Saud, a colonel in the Saudi armed forces with responsibility for the strategic planning in the kingdom, delineated as assets to be protected by Saudi security policy 'territorial integrity, economic wellbeing, cultural values and fundamental beliefs, and the system of government'.[63] Viewed through Buzan's lens, the document warns against military, economic, societal, and political threats. In addition, the author is concerned with both external and internal threats, which he considers closely linked, and he makes explicit reference to regional stability as a key value of the country's security calculus. For example, he cites the repercussions of Saddam Hussein's possible fall, specifically 'either a fragmented Iraq or the emergence of a new regime in Baghdad committed to redrawing its borders', as a 'threat in the making'.[64] Arguing that change in other countries can impact regional stability, the document underlines the security interdependence of the Gulf as a regional security sub-complex. It is interesting also to explore the centrality of cultural factors – protecting Wahhabi Islam as the source of national identity and monarchical legitimacy – as crucial to shaping Saudi (societal) stability, a word used almost as a synonym for security. Also quite relevant is the reference to the threats to Saudi Arabia's economic assets, trade routes, and offshore oilfields, vulnerable because dependent on the safety of the sea. In a 2014 study, Nawaf Obaid, a long-time special counsellor to Saudi ambassadors and the Royal Court, shaped his own suggestions for a new Saudi defence doctrine.[65] Obaid argues that it should focus on threats both to Saudi Arabia – border security, terrorist acts, and jihadist ideology – and to the wider region, by protecting the country's international status and its strategic partnerships.[66] Obaid's work also includes Iraq and Iran as traditional sources of military and political threats. Finally, Obaid makes a distinction between threats emanating from conventional and those from asymmetrical warfare, i.e. terrorism. Defining the latter as the most important security threat throughout the Gulf for the foreseeable future, Obaid describes it as both an endogenous threat, related to the economically and socially disenfranchised population prey to extremist rhetoric, and an exogenous one, in the form of operations sponsored by hostile powers to destabilise GCC governments.[67] Similar documents from the early 2000s relating to other GCC countries – such as some authored by security officials from the UAE and Kuwait – unfolded along very similar lines.[68]

In addition to providing an idea of the security priorities of the GCC countries in the 2010s, all of these documents also elaborate, explicitly or implicitly, on the growing transnationalism of threats – which makes boundaries between internal and external threats increasingly blurred – without, however, offering a specific systematisation to conceptualise this interrelation analytically. Even the area studies literature has only marginally addressed this question of interconnectedness, failing to look at threats comprehensively, in their multi-layered and multi-dimensional nature, consolidated after 2011.[69]

In fact, as Kristian Ulrichsen argued in 2017, the 'outbreak of the Arab Spring in 2011 and regional responses to the broader political upheaval across the Middle East and North Africa gave urgency to the porous relationship between internal and external security'.[70] Drawing attention to globalisation as an accelerator of transnationalism, Ulrichsen further argues that the rise of cross-boundary oppositional movements and non-state actors has highlighted how 'the internal and external dimensions of security in the Gulf were interconnected and bound together in the 2000s as never before'.[71] As such, rather than arguing that threats should be categorised only as external or internal, it seems more fitting to speak also of intermestic threats. The term 'intermestic' has been employed only by a few scholars, including Victor Cha, who defines intermestic issues as the 'interpenetration of foreign and domestic issues'.[72] Intermestic threats are here defined as threats that have a mixed external and internal nature, such as those moved by exogenous motives but spreading internally and having domestic implications or, vice versa, those that have endogenous stimuli but repercussions on international security. They are thus different from external threats, those originated from external sources that affect international security, and internal threats, those that have endogenous roots and affect internal security.

Hypothesising on prioritisation

Not many scholars have worked on proposing clear and testable hypotheses about how states prioritise among different kinds of threats. The area literature has found a consensus that, particularly in the GCC, priority is accorded to regime security, but refrained from offering detailed assumptions on which types of threat can potentially be more salient in that context.[73] Except when a state actually brandishes military force against another state, or possesses a clear aggregate power advantage and hostile intentions, it is indeed a complex task to identify the gravest and most imminent threat to a regime. The matter becomes less clear in an environment such as the MENA region, where threats are multi-dimensional and emanate simultaneously but from different sources.

One form of guidance comes from Gregory Gause, who provides a testable hypothesis on which threat is likely to be perceived as the most dangerous to stability, working to prove his theory with ample historical references.[74] With specific reference to Saudi Arabia, Gause considers cases when two types of threat, external attack and internal destabilisation, happen simultaneously and yet are de-linked. He contends that in many instances after the 1990s, leaders seem to perceive the domestic destabilisation threat as more serious and immediate than the classic power capabilities threat. His reference is that if military power considerations dominated Saudi alignment behaviour, one would have expected to see Riyadh balancing against Iraq at the outset of the 1980s and at the end of the Iran–Iraq war. Instead, the

Saudis balanced against Iran, the state exhibiting the greater degree of hostile intention towards the Saudi regime, despite Iran's not having embraced the military posture to back that hostility up.[75] Even after the end of the war and until the invasion of Kuwait, Saudi Arabia continued its alignment with Iraq against Iran, despite the relative increase in Iraqi power compared to Iran's.[76]

Indeed, while reference to Iraq's invasion of Kuwait is frequently used in the region to argue that it should be no surprise that GCC leaders worry about the military power of their neighbours, Gause's work validated the hypothesis that GCC leaders in fact prioritise domestic threats to regime stability, especially if they originate abroad or are abetted by foreign actors. These kinds of threats, as described by Gause, are what this book calls intermestic threats. The hypothesis, which will be tested in the empirical chapters, is that they are seen as particularly salient because of the strength of trans-border political identities and the multitude of transnational links that have historically made borders in the Gulf region particularly porous.

Notes

1 An excellent overview of the different schools of thought in the field of security studies can be found in Myriam Dunn Cavelty and Thierry Balzacq (eds), *Routledge Handbook of Security Studies* (London: Routledge, 2016).
2 Emanuel Adler, 'Seizing the Middle Ground: Constructivism in World Politics', *European Journal of International Relations* 3:3 (1997), 319–363.
3 Roland Paris, 'Human Security: Paradigm Shift or Hot Air?', *International Security* 26:2 (2001), 87–102.
4 Alan Collins, *Contemporary Security Studies* (Oxford: Oxford University Press, 2016).
5 Buzan, *People, States and Fear*, 4.
6 Alexander Wendt, 'Anarchy Is What States Make of It: The Social Construction of Power Politics', *International Organization* 46:2 (1992), 391–425 (393).
7 Buzan, *People, States and Fear*, 6.
8 *Ibid.*
9 Ehteshami and Hinnebusch, 'Foreign Policymaking in the Middle East'.
10 Andreas Krieg, 'Gulf Security Policy after the Arab Spring', in Khalid Almezaini and Jean-Marc Rickli (eds), *The Small Gulf States: Foreign and Security Policies before and after the Arab Spring* (London: Routledge, 2016).
11 Priess, 'Balance-of-Threat Theory'; Ayoob, *The Third World Security Predicament*.
12 Barry Buzan, 'New Patterns of Global Security in the Twenty-First Century', *International Affairs* 67:3 (1991), 431–451 (432–433).
13 Buzan, *People, States and Fear*, 134.
14 Wæver, *Securitization and Desecuritization*, 6.

15 Gause, 'Balancing What?', 276.
16 Ulrichsen, *The Changing Security Dynamics*, 15.
17 *Ibid.*, 278.
18 James Fearon, 'Rationalist Explanations for War', *International Organization* 49:3 (1995), 379–414; Robert Powell, 'War as a Commitment Problem', *International Organization* 60:1 (2006), 169–203.
19 Fred Lawson, 'Neglected Aspects of the Security Dilemma', in Rex Brynen, Bahgat Korany, and Paul Noble (eds), *The Many Faces of National Security in the Arab World* (London: Palgrave Macmillan, 1993).
20 Jervis, *Perception and Misperception*.
21 *Ibid.*
22 Michael Williams, '(In)Security Studies, Reflexive Modernization and the Risk Society', *Cooperation and Conflict* 43:1 (2008), 57–79.
23 Alexander Wendt, *Social Theory of International Politics* (Cambridge: Cambridge University Press, 1999), 163.
24 Jeremy Jones and Nicholas Ridout, *A History of Modern Oman* (Cambridge: Cambridge University Press, 2015).
25 Johan Eriksson and Erik Noreen, 'Setting the Agenda of Threats: An Explanatory Model', Uppsala Peace Research Papers 6 (2002).
26 Robin Hogarth and William Goldstein, *Judgment and Decision Making: An Interdisciplinary Reader* (Cambridge: Cambridge University Press, 1996).
27 Margaret Hermann and Joe D. Hagan, 'International Decision Making: Leadership Matters', *Foreign Policy* 110, special edn, *Frontiers of Knowledge* (Spring 1998), 124–137.
28 A comprehensive description of the process of policy-making in the Gulf monarchies and the centrality of the leaders appears in Gregory Gause, 'Understanding the Gulf States', *Democracy* 36 (2015), https://democracyjour nal.org/magazine/36/understanding-the-gulf-states/ (accessed 29 July 2023).
29 *Ibid.*, 3.
30 Lewis Snider, 'Comparing the Strength of Nations: The Arab Gulf States and Political Change', *Comparative Politics* 20:4 (1988), 461–484.
31 Mazhar al-Zo'by and Birol Başkan, 'Discourse and Oppositionality in the Arab Spring: The Case of the Muslim Brotherhood in the UAE', *International Sociology* (2014), 401–417 (402).
32 David Roberts, 'Qatar and the Muslim Brotherhood: Pragmatism or Preference?', *Middle East Policy* 21:3 (2014), 84–94; David Roberts, 'Mosque and State: The United Arab Emirates' Secular Foreign Policy', *Foreign Affairs*, 18 March 2016, https://www.foreignaffairs.com/united-arab-emirates/mosque-and-state (accessed 26 July 2023); Christopher Davidson, 'The UAE, Qatar, and the Question of Political Islam', in Krieg, *Divided Gulf*.
33 Helle Malmvig, 'Power, Identity and Securitization in Middle East: Regional Order after the Arab Uprisings', *Mediterranean Politics* 19:1 (2014), 145–148.
34 For example see Justin Gengler, 'The Political Economy of Sectarianism in the Gulf', Carnegie Endowment for International Peace (2016), https://carnegieen dowment.org/files/Gengler_Sectarianism_Final.pdf (accessed 19 July 2023).

35 Fabien Nathan, 'Natural Disasters, Vulnerability and Human Security', in Hans Günter Brauch, Úrsula Oswald Spring, John Grin *et al.* (eds), *Facing Global Environmental Change: Environmental, Human, Energy, Food, Health and Water Security Concepts*, Hexagon Series on Human and Environmental Security and Peace 4 (Berlin: Springer-Verlag, 2009).

36 Edward Azar, and Chung-in Moon, 'Third World National Security: Toward a New Conceptual Framework', *International Interactions* 11:2 (1984), 103–135.

37 Bahgat Korany, 'Strategic Studies and the Third World: A Critical Evaluation', *International Social Science Journal* 38:4 (1986), 547–562 (547–546).

38 Buzan, *People, States and Fear*, 82.

39 *Ibid.*

40 May Darwich, 'The Ontological (In)security of Similarity: Wahhabism Versus Islamism in Saudi Foreign Policy', *Foreign Policy Analysis* 12 (2016), 469–488.

41 Neil Partrick. 'Nationalism in the Gulf States', Kuwait Programme on Development, Governance and Globalisation in the Gulf States, London School of Economics (2009), Research Paper 5, https://eprints.lse.ac.uk/55257/1/Patrick_2009.pdf (accessed 26 July 2023).

42 Abdullah Hamid Al-Din, 'Hawiyya Waṭniyya Sa'ūdiyya' (Saudi National Identity), *Al-Hayat* (2014), http://alhayat.com/Opinion/Abdullah-hameed-Al-Deen/4700740 (accessed 9 May 2019).

43 *Ibid.*

44 Partrick, 'Nationalism in the Gulf States'.

45 Azar and Moon, 'Third World National Security', 115.

46 Ulrichsen, *Insecure Gulf*, 64.

47 Hertog, 'The Sociology of the Gulf Rentier Systems'.

48 A similar classification appears in Steffen Hertog, 'Arab Gulf States: An Assessment of Nationalisation Policies', GLMM Research Paper 1 (2014), Migration Policy Centre, https://hdl.handle.net/1814/32156 (accessed 26 July 2023).

49 *Ibid.*

50 'Fair Migration: Setting an ILO Agenda', International Labour Conference, 103rd Session, Report I(B), International Labour Organization, 2020, https://www.ilo.org/wcmsp5/groups/public/---ed_norm/---relconf/documents/meetingdocument/wcms_242879.pdf (accessed 26 July 2023).

51 Hertog, 'The Sociology of the Gulf Rentier Systems'.

52 Steffen Hertog, 'The Private Sector and Reform in the Gulf Cooperation Council', Kuwait Programme on Development, Governance and Globalisation in the Gulf States, London School of Economics and Political Science (2013), Research Paper 6, https://eprints.lse.ac.uk/54398/1/Hertog_2013.pdf (accessed 26 July 2023).

53 Hertog, 'The Sociology of the Gulf Rentier Systems'.

54 Mohammed Ayoob and Chai-Anan Samudavanija, 'Leadership and Security in Southeast Asia: Exploring General Propositions', in Mohammed Ayoob and Chai-Anan Samudavanija (eds), *Leadership Perceptions and National*

Security: The Southeast Asian Experience (Singapore: Institute of Southeast Asian Studies, 1989), 256.

55 See for instance Long and Koch, *Gulf Security in the Twenty-First Century*.

56 Michael Barnett, 'Sovereignty, Nationalism, and Regional Order in the Arab States System', *International Organization* 49:3 (1995), 479–510.

57 Buzan, *People, States and Fear*.

58 *Ibid.*

59 Mirjam Sørli, Nils Petter Gleditsch, and Håvard Strand, 'Why Is There So Much Conflict in the Middle East?', *Journal of Conflict Resolution* 49:1 (2005), 141–165.

60 Buzan, 'New Patterns of Global Security', 433.

61 Peter Gleick, 'Water, Drought, Climate Change, and Conflict in Syria', *Weather, Climate, and Society* 6:3 (2014), 331–340.

62 Given the impossibility of accessing Defence White Papers or National Security Strategies from the GCC countries, as those are not published, the author has researched studies authored by either government or security officials, or advisors thereof.

63 Naef bin Ahmed Al-Saud, 'Underpinning Saudi National Security Strategy', *Joint Force Quarterly* (2002), 124–130.

64 *Ibid.*, 126.

65 Nawaf Obaid, 'A Saudi Arabian Defense Doctrine', Defense and Intelligence Projects, Belfer Center for Science and International Affairs (Cambridge, MA: President and Fellows of Harvard College, 2014), https://ciaotest.cc.colum bia.edu/wps/isp/0031181/f_0031181_25247.pdf (accessed 20 July 2023).

66 Interestingly, the objectives outlined in Obaid's paper have been largely repeated by HRH Navy Captain (Ret.) Prince Sultan bin Khalid Al-Faisal Al Sa'ud in his speech 'Analyzing and Assessing Saudi Arabian Defense Strategy', given on 6 October 2015 at the National Council on US–Arab Relations, Washington, DC.

67 Obaid, 'A Saudi Arabian Defense Doctrine', 11.

68 Musallam Al Rashedi, 'The UAE National Security Strategy in the 21st Century', thesis (United States Marine Corps, School of Advance Warfighting, Marine Corps University, 2005); Badea A. Al-Raqum, 'A New Approach for Kuwait's National Defense Strategy', Strategy Research Project (Carlisle, PA: US Army War College, 2001).

69 Kristian Ulrichsen is among the very few who have written about all of the different threats mentioned here and how external and internal threats are connected. See Kristian Ulrichsen, 'Internal and External Security in the Arab Gulf States', *Middle East Policy* 16:2 (2009), 39–58; and Kristian Ulrichsen, 'Links between Domestic and Regional Security', in Ulrichsen, *The Changing Security Dynamics*.

70 Ulrichsen, 'Links between Domestic and Regional Security', 27.

71 *Ibid.*, 23.

72 Victor Cha, 'Globalization and the Study of International Security', *Journal of Peace Research* 37:3 (2000), 391–403 (391).

73 Steven David, 'Explaining Third World Alignment', *World Politics* 43:2 (1991), 233–256.

74 Gause, 'Balancing What?'.

75 A quite comprehensive account of the history of Saudi support for Iraq in the 1980s can be found in Ghazi Algosaibi, *The Gulf Crisis: An Attempt to Understand* (London: Kegan Paul, 1993), 28–29.

76 Aaron Karp, 'Military Procurement and Regional Security in South Asia', *Contemporary Asia* (1998), 334–362.

Part I

Bahrain, Saudi Arabia, and the UAE:
The elusive quest for a security alliance

3

Bahrain

The impact of the Arab Spring

The protests taking place on the long wave of the Arab Spring in Bahrain were qualitatively and quantitatively different from those happening in other GCC countries: they were inscribed in a historically contentious sectarian context, involved a higher proportion of the citizen population than any other country affected by the Arab Spring, and were more entangled with regional politics than in any other GCC country.[1]

The first major protest, organised via Facebook, took place on 14 February 2011 – dubbed Day of Rage – with dozens of marches gathering approximately 6,000 people.[2] This was already a significant beginning for the smallest GCC country, with only around 1.2 million inhabitants. Protests then continued to take place every day, even amid violent crackdowns, and a national strike called in solidarity with protesters for the following week was joined by almost 80 per cent of Bahraini citizens.[3] In March protests escalated, extending to areas predominantly inhabited by Sunni Bahrainis and to locations within reach of the royal palace, at times clashing with counterprotests, mostly comprising Sunni loyalists.[4] Some of the demonstrators had become openly anti-monarchical, with thousands chanting 'Down with the King', and the main Shi'a opposition party, al-Wefaq, had taken political lead of the movement.[5] Sheikh Isa Qassim, a top Bahraini Shi'a cleric also linked to al-Wefaq, became the movement's inspriational lead. On 13 March 2011, the Bahraini King, Hamad bin Isa al-Khalifa, put in a request for assistance from the GCC Peninsula Shield Forces: the following day about 1,200 units from the Saudi Royal Guard and 800 police officers from the UAE entered Manama under the umbrella of the Peninsula Shield Forces, deployed to guard some of the country's critical infrastructure, while Bahraini forces cracked down on the protests.[6] The King declared a three-month state of emergency, and the Pearl Monument, the symbolic centre of the movement, was demolished. Sporadic protests would continue well into the first anniversary of the Spring in February 2012 – with over 100,000 people joining a demonstration ahead of the Formula 1 Grand Prix hosted in Manama in April – but the major wave of the Bahraini Arab Spring was over.[7] On the tenth anniversary of the protests, 14 February 2021, a small and underwhelming march took place in Manama, amid a hefty deployment of security forces.

The Bahraini Arab Spring was characterised by two main elements. One was the failed attempt led by Bahrain's Crown Prince to work out a political solution through dialogue with parliamentary groups. This endeavour was fatally undermined by other royals – especially the all-powerful Prime Minister, in office since the country's independence in 1971. This camp claimed that the protesters' demands, for the creation of a new power-sharing mechanism and a constitutional monarchy with legislative powers to elected parliamentarians, were a very direct threat to the control of the al-Khalifa royal family, and to the privileged access of Sunni Bahrainis to political and economic power.[8] In fact, the dominant view within the regime was that the Shi'a opposition was attempting to exploit the protests to corner the leadership into the systemic changes to the country's power structures that were being demanded by the demonstrators to the country's power structures, and that these changes would erode the power of the ruling establishment and irreversibly weaken their authority.[9] In this sense, the regime viewed the Arab Spring not as a stand-alone wave of genuine popular protest, but as an opportunity for Shi'a opposition to continue their decades-long fight against the Sunni regime's legitimacy, directly linked to the 1990s insurgency.[10] The disbandment of al-Wefaq in 2016 and the life sentence passed on its leader, Ali Salman, in 2018 sealed the lid on a political approach to Shi'a opposition in Bahrain.

The second element was the regionalisation of the crisis. The countries of the GDD pledged $20 billion to assist Bahrain (and Oman), issued statements that hinted at foreign countries' (meaning Iran) plotting with protesters to undermine Bahrain's stability, and joined a Peninsula Shield operation.[11] The Peninsula Shield operation was strongly criticised by the Iranian Ministry of Foreign Affairs and by the Supreme Leader of the Iranian Revolution, Grand Ayatollah Ali Khamenei, who stated that the 'victory of the people of Bahrain was inevitable'.[12] This Iranian involvement was instrumentalised by the regime, who framed the protests as exogenous, and the opposition as masterminded by Iran.[13] This sustained narrative denied the endogenous roots of dissent – socioeconomic inequality and sociopolitical marginalisation – which had turned into chronic structural vulnerabilities over the decades. In fact, Bahrain's 'minority rule' system, whereby members of a minority sociopolitical group (the Sunni royal family) rule through an authoritarian approach over a different socio-political majority

(Shi'a Bahrainis), rests on a number of divide-and-rule tactics, including targeted coercion and patronage, aimed at preventing cross-societal opposition and preserving regime security.[14]

The magnitude and prolonged duration of the Bahraini protests, and the presence of popular, well-organised hardliner and anti-monarchical opposition groups were significant elements in influencing the regime's hyper-securitised outlook after 2011. Hyper-securitisation was applied first and foremost to Iran, seen as an existential, multi-dimensional threat to an even greater extent than in Saudi Arabia. When Bahrain normalised relations with Israel in 2020, it was primarily seeking extra deterrence against Iran, as Manama focused on establishing technical cooperation on cybersecurity and air defence, as well as further intelligence cooperation, with Mossad operatives active in the Bahraini kingdom.[15] Nonetheless, hyper-securitisation was also applied to Qatar and, to a lesser extent, to Islamists. Indeed, Bahrain quickly joined Saudi Arabia and the UAE against Qatar in both intra-GCC crises, and was the only country to resist the reconciliation with Qatar after the al-Ula Summit in 2021. It would take a year-and-a-half of ongoing skirmishes before the Qatari and Bahraini leaders would meet in person at the Jeddah Summit of July 2022, when Bahrain finally removed Qatar from the no-travel list. The two countries have a conflictual shared past. Bahrain's ruling family, the al-Khalifa, ruled over large parts of present-day Qatar until they were ousted by the al-Thani tribe, with the support of Britain, in the nineteenth century.[16] The Bahraini–Qatari rivalry was also at the core of both states' decisions not to join the proposed Federation of Arab Emirates as members, alongside the Trucial States, or present-day UAE.[17] Territorial disputes, including that over control of the Hawar islands, marred the bilateral relations, especially until they were settled by the International Court of Justice in 2001.[18] In 1996, Qatar accused Bahrain of participating in a counter-coup against Sheikh Hamad bin Khalifa al-Thani, aimed at restoring the rule of his pro-Saudi father.[19] Relations improved in the 2000s, with a number of ambitious joint ventures and Bahrain's King defining ties with Qatar as 'excellent'.[20] In 2011, the Bahraini regime was extremely irked when Qatari media Al Jazeera English aired a documentary on the protests in Manama (titled *Shouting in the Dark*) that was profoundly critical of the regime. When Qatar tried to broker negotiations between the Government and the main Shi'a opposition bloc, al-Wefaq, Manama accused Doha of attempting to destabilise Bahrain.[21] This accusation was strongly renewed at the time of the first intra-GCC crisis in 2014, when Bahraini authorities publicly accused Qatar of harming its national security by offering citizenship to some Bahraini nationals. The Interior Ministry's Undersecretary for Nationality, Passports and Residence Affairs, Rashid bin Khalifa Al-Khalifa, then declared that Qatar had 'targeted specific families and singled out a particular category of people'.[22] This particular category, Bahraini officials claimed privately, was that of Sunni tribes, which formed part of the regime's core constituency.

A second consequence of the weakness experienced by the Bahraini regime during the Arab Spring was an even greater need to seek comprehensive protection under the Saudi–Emirati umbrella. Riyadh and Abu Dhabi had been the two major players in the Peninsula Shield intervention to rescue the Bahraini Government in 2011. After the protests, the Government, which had already been dependent on revenues from the Saudi ARAMCO-controlled Abu Saʿfah oil field for decades, needed additional financial backing from both Riyadh and Abu Dhabi. On top of the $10 billion aid package in 2011, Bahrain was granted another one for the same amount in 2017.[23] This growing debt to Riyadh and Abu Dhabi increased their leverage in the small kingdom. Bahrain already traditionally subscribed to foreign policy initiatives promoted by Saudi Arabia, and consistently toed the Saudi line in regional politics.[24] After the Arab Spring, Manama also fell under greater Emirati influence in both domestic and regional affairs.

Bahrain and the 'Shi'a threat'

Bahrain's perceptions of Iran are intrinsically related to the Government's relations with its Shi'a citizens, slightly improving when the Bahraini Shi'a communities were more acquiescent, and rapidly deteriorating as the communities became more restive.[25] Since the 2011 uprising, in fact, Bahrain–Iran relations have entered a downward spiral, with no improvements after the 2021 strategic pause in regional escalation.

Although official data are not available, scholars believe that as much as 60 per cent of the Bahraini population is Shi'a.[26] Despite being the majority, for decades Bahraini Shi'a have conveyed a sense of both institutionalised and informal discrimination by the Government. Shi'a citizens are informally cut off from several positions in the public sector, the country's largest employer, and specific positions within the security sector. Interestingly, security sector jobs are instead generously awarded to naturalised Sunni foreigners, in a move thought to be about altering the sectarian balance of the country in favour of the Sunnis as much as about creating a security sector more prone to repress Shi'a.[27] More generally, levels of unemployment and underemployment are disproportionally high among Shi'a.[28] These socioeconomic inequalities are linked to institutionalised sociopolitical marginalisation, starting with the country's foundational myth. Bahraini Arab Shi'a consider themselves the true original inhabitants of Bahrain and often represent the al-Khalifa as 'foreign usurpers'.[29] Court-supported historians instead describe the al-Khalifa as a pacifying force, ending a period of inse-curity and barbarism.[30] These divisions extend also to symbolic questions such as the National Day: while it officially falls in December, when King Hamad's father became emir of an independent Bahrain in 1971, the oppo-sition has long called to have it in August, the day that Britain officially withdrew from Bahrain.[31]

As a marginalised group, Bahraini Shi'a became a closely knit commu-nity that relied on informal, often religious, networks for material support. While there are no official Bahraini religious guides, many Bahraini Shi'a fol-low local scholars, such as Sheikh Isa Qassim, Sheikh Mohamed Mahfouz, and Sheikh Abdulla Ghurayfi.[32] However, they also follow foreign scholars, including Iran's Grand Ayatollah Ali Khamenei – who subscribes to the doc-trine of Wilayat al-Faqih, granting political authority and legitimacy to the religious establishment – and Iraq's Ayatollah Ali Al-Sistani, who instead rejects Wilayat al-Faqih.[33]

The religious connection to Iran is made more complicated by the fact that territorial control over Bahrain has been historically contested by Persian and Arab polities.[34] The Arab al-Khalifa tribe conquered the islands in 1783, after a century of Persian Safavid presence.[35] Iranian claims to the sovereignty of Bahrain continued during the British protectorate and inten-sified in the 1950s, when the Oil Nationalization Act officially designated Bahrain Iran's fourteenth province for the purpose of oilfield exploitation.[36] After the British withdrawal, the Shah of Iran reluctantly accepted Bahraini independence in 1971 following regional and international negotiations.[37] However, sporadic Iranian claims on Bahrain persisted, including in a 2007 editorial in *Kayhan*, a newspaper with ties to the Supreme Leader, and in a 2009 speech by Ali Akbar Nateq Nuri, working in Khamenei's office.[38] Calls to restore Iranian rule over Bahrain intensified after Manama nor-malised relations with Israel in 2020. In 2021, Iranian authors released a documentary (*The Fourteenth Province*) and a book (*The Unforgivable Sin: Separating Bahrain from Iran and the Fake Referendum*) arguing that Bahrain's declaration of independence in 1971 was masterminded by the USA against the will of Bahrainis.

In this context, the Bahraini regime has consistently accused the IRGC of trying to export the Islamic revolution, especially in the aftermath of 1979. These fears escalated in 1981 when an organisation calling itself the Islamic Front for the Liberation of Bahrain (IFLB) attempted to overthrow the al-Khalifa rule to establish a 'free Islamic order'.[39] The organisation was led by Hadi al-Mudarrisi, who claimed to be Ayatollah Khomeini's repre-sentative in Bahrain, and received support and training in terms of ideol-ogy, leadership, media, logistics, and military matters from the IRGC.[40] The IFLB was disbanded with the arrest of seventy-three Gulf Arab nationals, including Bahrainis, Saudis, one Kuwaiti and one Omani, but these events left a mark on decision-makers.[41] Indeed, the Bahraini Government accused Iran of being behind the protests taking place in the country between 1994 and 1999 via a proxy named Hezbollah al-Bahraini, and accused al-Wefaq spiritual leader Sheikh Isa Ahmed Qassim of complicity.[42]

Al-Wefaq's formal entry into Parliament in 2006, and the subsequent constraint of its activism in the institutional space, initially helped to defuse tensions between the Shi'a communities and the regime.[43] Interestingly, the second half of the 2000s was also a period of improved ties with Iran. In 2008, the two countries began negotiations over Iranian export of natural gas to Bahrain and a possible $4 billion Bahraini investment in the sector.[44] In 2010, maritime border negotiations, stalled since 1993, resumed.[45] In June of the same year, Bahrain's Foreign Minister, Khalid bin Ahmed al-Khalifa, stated that his Government 'totally reject[ed]' the underlying anti-Iranian sentiment of Bahraini News Agency reports accusing Tehran of seeking to expand its power and influence in the region.[46] Then, the Arab Spring came.

Ascertaining the exact level of Iranian involvement within Bahrain's protests is problematic, and Shi'a activists have long argued that the ruling al-Khalifa family exaggerates Iranian influence to tarnish calls for democratisation.[47] Without subscribing to the official narrative that Iran was the movement's sole and major mastermind, the perception that Iran has exploited the protests to extend its influence in Bahrain was ubiquitous in Manama's leadership circle and even among some opposition figures.[48] These perceptions were aroused by a number of factors, such as the involvement of the Islamic Action group, led by former IFLB leader Hadi al-Modarresi. Then, in June 2011, Shi'a theologian Mehdi Khalaji, while advocating for Iranian support for the opposition, described Sheikh Isa Qassim as a 'religious representative of Khamenei' and stressed that Khamenei had described Qassim as 'a star in the sky of Shi'a'.[49] Finally, a number of Shi'a clerics, identifying themselves as 'followers of Grand Ayatollah Khamenei in Bahrain', wrote to the Supreme Leader in March 2011 soliciting his help.[50]

By 2014, a few radicalised groups akin to a low-intensity insurgency-like movement had started employing sophisticated improvised explosive devices against the Bahraini security forces. In 2015 Bahrain Public Security Chief, Major-General Tariq Al-Hassan, described a new militia called Saraya al-Ashtar, stating: 'There are clear similarities between the tactics, techniques and procedures used in manufacturing the explosives found in Bahrain and those used by IRGC proxy groups, particularly Kata'eb Hezbollah, in Iraq and Afghanistan.'[51] Saraya al-Ashtar (also known as Al-Ashtar Brigades) is, alongside other similar organisations, such as Saraya al-Mukhtar and Saraya al-Muqawama al-Shabiya, included on the blacklists of terrorist organisations issued by the Saudi-led quartet in the context of the 2017 intra-GCC crisis. Its leaders, Ahmad Hasan Yusuf and Alsayed Murtadha Majeed Ramadhan Alawi, were both designated in 2017 as terrorists by the US State Department, and linked to the IRGC.[52] From 2013 onwards, the Bahraini Government has reported small-scale attacks and seizures every year of weapons supplied by Iran.[53] Security officials saw this armed diffuse resistance as an Iranian scheme. In 2016, the Commander-in-Chief of the Bahrain Defence Force, Field Marshal Khalifa bin Ahmed al-Khalifa, stated to a delegation of parliamentarians from the European Parliament visiting Manama that:

> Iran uses cultural centre and mosques to disseminate the ideology of Wilayat al-Faqih and recruit potential candidates for opposition movements. Then, it strengthens their leadership, through operational training and further theological study in Iran and then sets up a network of underground cells responding to the IRGC.[54]

As argued by Steve Wright, 'Iran is seen by the government of Bahrain as an external party to domestic politics within the country and one which works against developing a common national identity.'[55] In other words, Iran is seen to exploit the country's most significant socioeconomic and sociopolitical vulnerabilities, inscribed even in its foundational myth, one of sectarian disenfranchisement. In this sense, after 2011 the Bahraini leadership has consistently perceived Iran as a political threat, able and willing to challenge the regime's identity and stability, and the integral functioning of the institutions and borders. There is a clear (asymmetric) military dimension to the prception of this threat, allegedly conveyed by underground Bahraini cells intent on triggering an anti-monarchical insurgency on behalf of Tehran. Thus, while the UAE, and even Saudi Arabia after 2019, engaged in a strategic pause dialogue with Iran, Bahrain refused to attend even the multilateral Baghdad Conference for Cooperation and Partnership of 2021, then signed a defence memorandum of understanding and a deal to purchase Israeli drones and anti-drone systems in 2022. The Bahraini perceptions of the 'Iran threat' had remained unequivocally acute throughout the post-Arab Spring decade.

Bahrain and the 'Islamist threat'

Formed in 1984, al-Minbar is the political arm of a social organisation called al-Islah, running charity, educational, and social programmes in Bahrain since 1941.[56] Unlike other Brotherhood-affiliated groups in the GCC, many of al-Minbar's members were not from North Africa but Bahraini Hawala, a sociopolitical group of Sunni Arab merchants who migrated to Persia before returning to the Arabian Peninsula's eastern shore.[57] The society's political traction was initially meagre, and in 1973, Minbar leader Abdulrahman Al-Jowder won only seventy-three votes in the very first Bahraini parliamentary elections.[58] A turning point for the political profiling of the society was their posture against the 1990s Bahraini uprisings, which inaugurated a persistent loyalist trend by the group.[59]

Sunni Islamist groups such as al-Minbar and the Salafi al-'Asalah Society have proven to be highly useful allies to the government, providing an avenue of leverage within the Sunni communities in a context of contentious relations with the Shi'a communities. In Parliament, the support of the al-Minbar for Government policies has been, often, crucial to offset opposition parties and, especially, the Shi'a party al-Wefaq. For example, al-Minbar has consistently supported the necessity to respect the role of the fully royally appointed Consultative Council (Shura), which has the same authority as the elected chamber, the Council of Representatives (Nuwab).[60] Al-Minbar is also closely connected to some members of the al-Khalifa family: one of the King's uncles, 'Isa bin Muhammad al-Khalifa, a former labour and social affairs minister, was involved in the establishment of al-'Islah, and ran it between 1963 and 2013.[61]

The convergence between the Government and the main Islamist parties, both al-Minbar and al-'Asalah, has become particularly salient after the Arab Spring. In 2011, al-Minbar and al-'Asalah helped organise a mass countermobilisation, which they defined as a 'national unity front to defend Bahraini stability and the al-Khalifa rule', and denounced protesters as Iranian agents.[62] In February 2013, al-Minbar boycotted the National Dialogue to protest against the hostile attitude of al-Wefaq, and criticised the ruling family for responding too softly to Shi'a dissent.[63]

The amicable approach of the Government towards al-Minbar stands in stark contrast to the Saudi and Emirati aggressive campaigns against the Brotherhood in Egypt and elsewhere, highlighting a markedly different perception. And yet Manama's growing dependence on both Saudi Arabia and the UAE after 2011 meant that the declaration of the Muslim Brotherhood as a terrorist organisation by Riyadh and Abu Dhabi in 2014 posed new dilemmas for the Bahraini ruling family.[64] Al-Minbar had long highlighted the differences between themselves and more oppositional Brotherhood-affiliated groups elsewhere in the region, and again in 2014 the society's chairman declared to the press: 'All eyes of the voters are on us as they say we are the Muslim Brotherhood, which is not right. It is the ideology that we follow, but we do not have the organisation in Bahrain – neither do we support it.'[65] In fact, al-Minbar has close connections with Kuwait's branch of the Muslim Brotherhood and, to a lesser extent, Egypt's.[66] Abdulrahman

Jowder had studied in Cairo – where he met the Brotherhood leadership, including leading ideologue Hassan al-Banna – and was also a founding member of the Kuwait-based International Islamic Charity Organization, the original nucleus of the Kuwaiti Brotherhood-affiliated party.[67] However, the Government embraced al-Minbar's argument. In March 2014 Bahrain's Foreign Minister, Khaled bin Ahmed al-Khalifa, commented that his Government was not labelling al-Minbar a terrorist organisation because the group had not acted against the security of the country, distinguishing between the international Muslim Brotherhood organisation and its domestic branch.[68] Later the same day the minister issued a clarification via his official Twitter account, falling back in line with the Saudi–Emirati narrative: 'The Muslim Brotherhood movement is a global movement with a single approach ... and will be dealt with according to the law of each country and the covenants to which it is party.'[69]

Despite this rhetorical teetering, in practice the Government took steps partially to rein in al-Minbar in 2014. Ahead of the parliamentary elections that year, an electoral reform was implemented to redraw the boundaries of electoral districts, affecting also the strongholds of the Sunni Islamist formations; consequently, al-Minbar only retained one seat in the Council of Representatives.[70] Al-Minbar was also impacted by legislation passed in May 2016 attempting to separate religion and politics – i.e. banning any preacher from being a member in any political society or engaging in political activities.[71] Then, in May 2017, Bahrain's Foreign Minister declared: 'We consider the Muslim Brotherhood a terrorist group and anyone who shows sympathy with them will be tried.'[72] However, the declaration was not conducive to a crackdown on al-Minbar members in Bahrain. Indeed, the fact that the statement was given by the Foreign Minister rather than the Interior Minister may suggest that, as in 2014, the words were addressed to the international affiliates of the Muslim Brotherhood, rather than to the domestic organisation. On its official Twitter account, al-Minbar reacted by reiterating that it is a 'national institution ... not subject to any external dictates', and voicing support for the regime.[73]

By tracing the evolution of al-Minbar's relations with the Bahraini Government, especially after 2011, it can be argued that this group isn't perceived as a threat with the capability and intent to undermine the regime's stability and identity, or the integrity of the country's boundaries and the functionality of its institutions. However, despite supporting Government interests, al-Minbar is still perceived as posing at least three latent risks. One – internal – risk is about their potential to try and rally a Sunni elite opposition, perhaps by leveraging their loyalism to enter the game of royal factionalism within Bahrain's ruling family.[74] Another is the risk that al-Minbar's activity might jeopardise Bahrain's regional relations. The

Saudi–Emirati efforts to ban the Muslim Brotherhood cannot be overlooked by Bahrain, given its increased dependence upon the two fellow GCC countries. Alienating Riyadh and Abu Dhabi to protect al-Minbar, thus calling into question the investments pledged by those two capitals, vital to the Bahraini state budget, could have highly destabilising consequences for regime stability. A final risk is that Islamists might utilise the newfound space for anti-Shi'a rhetoric to galvanise Sunni extremism in the local discourse for political gains, and for this to spiral out of control.[75] During the momentum of jihadist groups in the region, Sunni extremism escalated dangerously in Bahrain. As early as 2012 the press started reporting on delegations of al-'Asalah members of parliament (MPs) heading into Syria to provide 'donations sent by the Bahrainis' to the Islamist Suqour al-Sham Brigades, later renamed as the Islamic Front.[76] One prominent al-'Asalah MP, Abdelhalim Murad, was even accused of facilitating the passage of hundreds of Bahrainis to fight against Bashar al-Assad's forces.[77] Jihadist groups such as Daesh, extremely hostile to the royal family, attracted some Sunni officers on the security forces – where anti-Shi'a narratives were historically strong – and few notable Bahrainis.[78] These included Mohammed Isa al-Binali, former lieutenant in the Bahraini police force; Ali Yousif al-Binali, killed fighting in Syria in May 2014; and their relative Turki al-Binali.[79] Turki al-Binali first joined Daesh in Libya in 2013 and subsequently joined the group in Syria, becoming one of its top clerics and propagandists.[80] Even before joining the group, al-Binali was active as a jihadi propagandist, posting on social media; giving sermons in Bahrain, Libya, and Tunisia; and protesting outside the American embassy in Manama while waving pictures of Osama bin Laden and banners of al-Qa'ida.[81] However, the Bahraini Government hesitated for years to deploy a full crackdown, revoking his citizenship only in 2016. This was probably out of fear of jeopardising al-Khalifa's support base, of which the al-Binali family represents a key pillar, being a numerous and influential clan, prominent in commerce and with ties to the ruling family.[82] And yet, given the tense sectarian relations within Bahrain, Sunni extremism getting out of control could lead to major political violence and related instability.

Bahrain's security priorities after 2011

The post-2011 regional polarisation led to the upsurge of sectarianism, fuelled by a power fight between Saudi Arabia and Iran, and deeper fault lines between pro-Islamist and an anti-Islamist camps within the Sunni communities, boosting hyper-securitisation in sociopolitically diverse Bahrain. The Bahraini Government opted for a 'securitisation of the Shī'a problem',[83] and has been pushed into re-examining its relations with Islamist groups, even risking the erosion of the regime's traditional loyalist base. Overall, the Bahraini regime's security priorities between 2011 and 2021 could be described in two separate phases. The first phase, between the 2011 uprising and the disbanding of al-Wefaq in 2016, was one in which the gravest threat perceived came from the Shi'a opposition, made even more formidable by its intermestic connection to Iran in the regime's perceptions. The second phase, which began in 2016, is one in which the regime felt more insulated from internal or intermestic threats and focused on strengthening relations with external backers, especially Saudi Arabia and the UAE, even at the risk of having to re-examine the composition of its domestic loyalist base.

The first phase was strongly defined by a sectarian divide-and-rule strategy, pushed by powerful figures within the ruling family such as the Royal Court Minister, Khalid bin Ahmed al-Khalifa, and his brother, the Minister of Defence and Commander-in-Chief of the Bahrain Defence Force, Khalifa bin Ahmed al-Khalifa – together known as the 'Khawalid' – who sidelined more conciliatory figures such as the Crown Prince.[84] According to a prominent former al-Wefaq MP, the extensive crackdowns that followed 'morally crushed the opposition'.[85] Bahrain's signing of the Abraham Accords normalising relations with Israel in 2020, and the signing of the follow-up security agreement, are further evidence of the regime's hard-line posturing vis-à-vis the Shi'a restive communities – viciously opposed to relations with Israel – and vis-à-vis Iran. As COVID-19 disproportionately hit Shi'a Bahrainis first, Manama resorted to accusing Iran of 'biological aggression', covering up the spread of the virus in the Islamic Republic and failing to stamp the passports of Bahraini Shi'a on pilgrimage to Iranian holy sites.[86] It might be surprising that the Bahraini regime persisted in embracing such a lack of sociopolitical cohesiveness – a major vulnerability – instead of trying to create a unified, inclusive national identity, which is key to sustainable political stability. The geopolitical context, and the intermestic nature of the Shi'a threat in the regime's perceptions, are relevant factors in explaining this choice to embrace divisiveness over a shared national identity. Resource scarcity also plays a role, as it limits the regime's ability to deploy large-scale co-optation in exchange for political loyalty, as typical of other rentier economies.[87] Most importantly, a divisive strategy has also prevented the establishment of a significant cross-sectarian opposition that would overwhelm the regime, depriving it of its main 'otherisation' argument for pushback.[88]

On the other hand, the 'otherisation' of Shi'a also made relations between the regime and Sunni constituents more sensitive and problematic. Initially, it provided Sunni loyalist constituents, including Islamists, with greater negotiating power. For example, the Bahraini regime had to maintain a cautious approach towards Islamists, despite Saudi and Emirati pressures after 2014, so as not to alienate Sunni political societies, such as al-Minbar. Ultimately, the regime chose to run these risks and prioritise the external security dimension. Ahead of the 2014 parliamentary elections the Government redrew electoral boundaries in a way that penalised Sunni Islamists, and al-Minbar only won one seat. A 2016 law banning any preacher from being a member of any political society targeted not only Shia Islamists, but Sunni ones, too. As a result, the tightly controlled 2018 elections confirmed the political retreat of Sunni Islamists, with al-Minbar failing to win a single seat for the first time since its creation. Interestingly, the redistricting ended up 'favoring pragmatic businessmen and tribal leaders ready to support the regime's policies'.[89]

This was an attempt by the regime to redefine its loyalist base while strengthening its traditional core, focusing on Sunni tribes and urbanised elites. For instance, Manama strongly prioritised the risk emanating from Qatar's alleged attempt financially to lure members of influential Sunni tribes into relocating to Doha and acquiring Qatari nationality.[90] The regime had to cater to these prominent tribes, such as the al-Binali, and then attempted to expand its circle of interlocutors. Appointing two non-royal Sunni, Adel bin Khalifa al-Fadhel and Tariq al-Hasan, to high-profile positions leading the National Security Agency and the Public Security Forces respectively, can be seen as an attempt to give more stakes in the state to other Sunni tribes.[91] At the same time, the regime tried to look towards urban elites, predominantly Sunni but also Shi'a, as a potential new loyalist constituency, to play off against rural, Islamist-leaning groups.[92] In 2014, the post of Minister of Industry, Commerce and Tourism was given to Zayed bin Rashid al-Zayani, from one of the most prominent business families in Bahrain. This process was accelerated by Crown Prince Salman bin Hamad, who replaced the controversial veteran Prime Minister Khalifa bin Salman after his death in 2020. The new Prime Minister promoted the largest cabinet reshuffle in the country's history in 2022, creating a government with only three ministers from the ruling al-Khalifa family – the fewest ever – and nine ministers from the Shi'a urban elite. Mohammed Mubarak bin Daina, hailing from another business family, was appointed Minister of Oil.

Amid this security-first approach, the Bahraini leadership remained unable to address the country's major socioeconomic vulnerabilities, largely fuelled by rising unemployment, scarce investment, and inflation.[93] As non-regional investors were hesitant to inject liquidity into the country, State finances became 'depleted by a combination of high expenses on security and political stability'.[94] While economic inequality might be especially evident in the Shi'a areas of the country, these challenges are damaging not to the Shi'a communities alone, but also to rural Sunni communities.[95]

Hence, the risk of a cross-sectarian, economically motivated dissent cannot be disregarded. In this context, the economic fallout linked to the COVID-19 pandemic was dramatic, with the economy contracting by 5.8 per cent in 2020 and by an additional 2.1 per cent in the first months of 2021.[96] Sanitary restrictions took a heavy toll on three major sectors of the local economy: tourism, retail trade, and logistics.[97] The COVID-19 stimulus package to the private sector was worth 7 per cent of the GDP, pushing debt from 101 per cent to 129 per cent of the GDP.[98] Relying exclusively on bailouts from regional partners such as Saudi Arabia and the UAE is hardly a sustainable approach. For one, it triggers conflicts of interest as, for example, the UAE's development plans are in direct competition to Bahrain's in key sectors such as financial technology, or fintech. Moreover, it can further reinforce fault lines in domestic politics, as regional allies attempt to export their own security blueprints to Bahrain. Ultimately, the root of the kingdom's ontological insecurity remains the risk that its longstanding divide-and-rule strategy could backfire amid a polarised context, activating its sociopolitical and socioeconomic vulnerabilities, with the simultaneous shrinking of its loyalist base.

Notes

1 Toby Matthiesen, *Sectarian Gulf: Bahrain, Saudi Arabia, and the Arab Spring that Wasn't* (Stanford: Stanford University Press, 2013).
2 Stephen Zunes, 'Bahrain's Arrested Revolution', *Arab Studies Quarterly* 35:2 (2013), 149–164 (154).
3 Mahmoud Cherif Bassiouni, Migel Rodley, Bardia Al-Awadhi, Philippe Kirsch, and Mahnoush H. Arsanjani, 'Report of the Bahrain Independent Commission of Inquiry, presented in Manama, on 23 November 2011', www.bici.org.bh/BICIreportEN.pdf (accessed 17 September 2022).
4 *Ibid.*, 116
5 Zunes, 'Bahrain's Arrested Revolution', 156.
6 Louër, 'Sectarianism and Coup-Proofing Strategies in Bahrain', *Journal of Strategic Studies* 36:2 (2013), 245–260.
7 Zunes, 'Bahrain's Arrested Revolution', 157.
8 Bassiouni *et al.*, 'Report of the Bahrain Independent Commission of Inquiry'.
9 Interview by the author of a Bahraini diplomat, London, 3 July 2017; interview by the author of a Bahraini MP, Manama, 2 November 2016.
10 Munira Fakhro, 'The Uprising in Bahrain: An Assessment', in Sick and Potter, *The Persian Gulf at the Millennium*.
11 'Bayan sadir 'an al-dawra al-thamina ba'da al mi'a lil majlis al-wizari' (statement of the 118th session of the ministerial council), www.gcc-sg.org/indexb18f.html?action=Sec-Show&ID=316 (accessed 23 November 2021).

12 Mitra Amiri, 'Iran Objects to Foreign Troops in Bahrain', Reuters, 15 March 2011, www.reuters.com/article/us-iran-bahrain-troops-idUSLDE72E02N20110315 (accessed 23 August 2022).

13 Matthiesen, *Sectarian Gulf*.

14 A definition of a minority rule is offered in Oded Haklai, 'A Minority Rule over a Hostile Majority: The Case of Syria', *Nationalism and Ethnic Politics* 6:3 (2000), 19–50. While Bahrain keeps data on its sectarian demographics a closely guarded secret, academic studies largely agree that Bahraini Shi'a represent between 55 and 60 per cent of the population. See for instance Justin Gengler, 'Segregation and Sectarianism: Geography, Economic Distribution, and Sectarian Resilience in Bahrain', in *Countering Sectarianism in the Middle East* (Washington, DC: RAND Corporation, 2019), 41. The divide-and-rule strategy has been traced back to the very inception of the state: Omar Hesham Al-Shehabi, 'Contested Modernity: Divided Rule and the Birth of Sectarianism, Nationalism, and Absolutism in Bahrain', *British Journal of Middle Eastern Studies* 44:3 (2017), 333–355.

15 Elham Fakhro and Tareq Baconi. 'A Shared Vision: Security Convergence between the Gulf and Israel', *Journal of Palestine Studies* (2022), 50–55.

16 Zahlan, *The Making of the Modern Gulf States*, 11.

17 *Ibid.*

18 Krista Wiegand, 'Bahrain, Qatar, and the Hawar Islands: Resolution of a Gulf Territorial Dispute', *Middle East Journal* 66:1 (2012), 79–96 (94).

19 'Life Sentences for Qatari Coup Plotters', BBC News, 29 February 2000, http://news.bbc.co.uk/1/hi/world/middle_east/660887.stm (accessed 26 August 2022).

20 'US Embassy Cables: King of Bahrain Discusses Jordan, Saudi Arabia and Israel/Palestine', *Guardian*, 16 February 2005, www.theguardian.com/world/2011/apr/07/bahrain-jordan?cat=world&type=article (accessed 23 August 2022).

21 'Bahrain TV Plays Tapes Showing Qatar's Role in 2011 Crisis', Gulf News, 17 June 2017, https://gulfnews.com/news/gulf/bahrain/bahrain-tv-plays-tapes-showing-qatar-s-role-in-2011-crisis-1.2045153 (accessed 26 August 2022).

22 'Bahrain Accuses Qatar of Luring Citizens to Switch Nationality-Agency', Reuters, 7 August 2014, www.reuters.com/article/bahrain-qatar-naturalisation-idINL6N0QD4Q320140807 (accessed 17 September 2022).

23 Eckart Woertz, 'Bahrain's Economy: Oil Prices, Economic Diversification, Saudi Support, and Political Uncertainties', Barcelona Centre for International Affairs (2018), https://www.cidob.org/en/publications/publication_series/notes_internacionals/n1_189/bahrain_s_economy_oil_prices_economic_diversification_saudi_support_and_political_uncertainties (accessed 30 July 2023); Glen Carey and Matthew Martin, 'In Saudi Shadow, One Troubled Gulf State Seeks an Investor Reset', Bloomberg, 26 March 2018, www.bloomberg.com/news/articles/2018–03–26/in-saudi-shadow-one-troubled-gulf-state-seeks-an-investor-reset (accessed 24 August 2022).

24 'Little Bahrain Turns to Its Neighbors for Help, Again', Stratfor, 6 September 2018, https://worldview.stratfor.com/article/little-bahrain-turns-its-neighbors-help-again (accessed 24 August 2022).

25 'Bahrain's Sectarian Challenge', Middle East Report 40, International Crisis Group (2005), https://www.crisisgroup.org/middle-east-north-africa/gulf-and-arabian-peninsula/bahrain/bahrains-sectarian-challenge (accessed 30 July 2023).

26 Justin Gengler, 'Al-Fātiḥ Wa Al-Maftūḥ: The Case of Sunni–Shi'i Relations in Bahrain', in Justin Gengler, *Group Conflict and Political Mobilization in Bahrain and the Arab Gulf: Rethinking the Rentier State* (Bloomington: Indiana University Press, 2015).

27 Louër, 'Sectarianism and Coup-Proofing Strategies in Bahrain'; interview by the author of a researcher on the team of the Bassiouni report, Kuwait City, 11 December 2018.

28 Laurence Louër, 'The Politics of Labor Policy Reform in Bahrain', *Gulf Affairs* (2015), 9–12, https://sciencespo.hal.science/hal-03459681/document (accessed 30 July 2023).

29 Gengler, 'Al-Fātiḥ Wa Al-Maftūḥ', 40.

30 *Ibid.*, 42.

31 *Ibid.*

32 Sajjad Rizvi, 'Political Mobilization and the Shi'i Religious Establishment (Marja'iyya)', *International Affairs* 86:6 (2010), 1299–1313.

33 On Wilayat al-Faqih, see Rainer Brunner and Werner Ende (eds), *The Twelver Shia in Modern Times* (Leiden: Brill, 2000).

34 Steven Wright, 'Iran's Relations with Bahrain', in Gawdat Bahgat, Anoushiravan Ehteshami, and Neil Quilliam (eds), *Security and Bilateral Issues between Iran and Its Arab Neighbours* (London: Palgrave Macmillan, 2017), 61.

35 *Ibid.*

36 Majid Khadduri, 'Iran's Claim to the Sovereignty of Bahrayn', *American Journal of International Law* 45:4 (1951), 631–647.

37 *Ibid.*

38 Simon Mabon, 'The Battle for Bahrain: Iranian–Saudi Rivalry', *Middle East Policy Council* 19:2 (2012), 84–97.

39 Hasan Tariq Alhasan, 'The Role of Iran in the Failed Coup of 1981: The IFLB in Bahrain', *Middle East Journal* 65:4 (2011), 603–617 (605).

40 *Ibid.*, 603.

41 Interview by the author of a Bahraini diplomat, London, 3 July 2017; Wright, 'Iran's Relations with Bahrain', 69.

42 Adam Hanieh, 'Bahrain', in Paul Amar and Vijay Prashod (eds), *Dispatches from the Arab Spring: Understanding the New Middle East* (Minneapolis: University of Minnesota Press, 2013), 71.

43 Frederic Wehrey, *Sectarian Politics in the Gulf* (New York: Columbia University Press, 2013), 92.

44 'Bahrain to Press on with Iran Gas Deal', *Financial Times*, 24 October 2008, www.ft.com/cms/s/0/d590232a-a162-11dd-82fd-000077b07658.html#axzz1RvTNGCJK (accessed 23 August 2022).

45 'Iran, Bahrain to Review Border Issues', Fars News Agency, 25 May 2010, http://english.farsnews.com/newstext.php?nn=8903040735 (accessed 23 August 2022).

46 Habib Toumi, 'Shaikh Khalid Receives Iran's Ambassador to Bahrain', Gulf News, 22 June 2010, http://gulfnews.com/news/gulf/bahrain/shaikh-khalid-receives-iran-s-ambassador-to-bahrain-1.644721 (accessed 23 August 2022).

47 Frederic Wehrey, David E. Thaler, Nora Bensahel, *et al.*, 'Arab Perceptions of the Iranian Threat', in *Dangerous but Not Omnipotent: Exploring the Reach and Limitations of Iranian Power in the Middle East* (Washington, DC: RAND, 2009), 129–152 (150); interview by the author of a prominent Bahraini Shi'a activist, London, 19 September 2018.

48 Interview by the author of a researcher on the team of the Bassiouni report, Kuwait City, 11 December 2018; interview by the author of a prominent Bahraini Shi'a activist, London, 19 September 2018; interview by the author of a Bahraini diplomat, London, 3 July 2017; interview by the author of a Bahrain-based senior researcher at the International Institute for Strategic Studies, Skype, 17 April 2019.

49 Mehdi Khalaji, 'Iran's Policy Confusion about Bahrain', Washington Institute for Peace, 27 June 2011, www.washingtoninstitute.org/templateC05.php?CID=3376 (accessed 23 August 2022).

50 *Ibid.*

51 'Bahrain Says Seizes Explosives Meant for Use in Saudi Arabia', Reuters, 18 June 2015, www.reuters.com/article/uk-bahrain-saudi-explosives-idUKKBN0OY0Y720150618 (accessed 17 September 2022).

52 'State Department Terrorist Designations of Ahmad Hasan Yusuf and Alsayed Murtadha Majeed Ramadhan Alawi', website of the US Department of State, 17 March 2017, https://tinyurl.com/w5zz42re (accessed 17 September 2022).

53 Michael Knights and Matthew Levitt, 'The Evolution of Shia Insurgency in Bahrain', *Combating Terrorism Center* 11:1 (2018), https://ctc.westpoint.edu/evolution-shia-insurgency-bahrain/ (accessed 30 July 2023).

54 Remarks by Commander-in-Chief of the Bahrain Defence Force, Field Marshal Sheikh Khalifa bin Ahmed Al Khalifa, to a delegation of parliamentarians from the European Parliament, 2 November 2016, Manama.

55 Wright, 'Iran's Relations with Bahrain'. 79.

56 Baquer al-Najjar, *Al-Harakat al-Diniyya fi al-Khalij al-Arabi* (*Religious Movements of the Gulf*) (Beirut: Dar al-Saqi, 2007), 30–45.

57 Wehrey, *Sectarian Politics in the Gulf*, 59.

58 Adam Hanieh, 'Bahrain', 73.

59 Abbas Mirza al-Mirshid and Abd al-Hadi al-Khawaja, *Al-Tanzimat wa al-Jama'iyyat al-Siyyasiyya fi al-Bahrain* (*Reforms and Political Organizations in Bahrain*) (Bahrain: n.p., 2008), 185.

60 *Ibid.*

61 Among a number of sources, this information is cited in J. E. Peterson, 'Bahrain: Reform, Promise, and Reality', in Joshua Teitelbaum (ed.), *Political Liberalization in the Persian Gulf* (New York: Columbia University Press, 2009), 165; and Marc Valeri, 'Islamist Political Societies in Bahrain: Collateral Victims of the 2011 Popular Uprising', in Hendrik Kraetzschmar and Paola Rivetti (eds), *Islamists and the Politics of the Arab Uprisings: Governance, Pluralisation and Contention* (Edinburgh: Edinburgh University Press, 2018), 176.

62 Elisheva Machlis, 'Al-Wefaq and the February 14 Uprising: Islam, Nationalism and Democracy – the Shiʿi–Bahraini Discourse', *Middle Eastern Studies* 52:6 (2016), 978–995 (985).

63 Valeri, 'Islamist Political Societies'.

64 'UAE Lists Muslim Brotherhood as Terrorist Group', Reuters, 15 November 2014, www.reuters.com/article/us-emirates-politics-brotherhood/uae-lists-muslim-brotherhood-as-terrorist-group-idUSKCN0IZ0OM20141115 (accessed 16 September 2022).

65 Ali Ahmed, quoted in Alex MacDonald, 'Sunni Islamists Could Face Uphill Struggle in Bahrain Elections', *Middle East Eye*, 20 November 2014, www.middleeasteye.net/in-depth/features/sunni-islamists-could-face-uphill-struggle-bahrain-elections-1404489268 (accessed 16 September 2022).

66 Baquer al-Najjar, *Al-Harakat*, 33.

67 *Ibid.*

68 الإسلامية المؤتمر الصحفي المشترك لمعالي وزير الخارجية مع سعادة وزير المواصلات في جمهورية باكستان, الخبر تفاصيل (The Joint Press Conference of His Excellency the Minister of Foreign Affairs with His Excellency the Minister of Communications of the Islamic Republic of Pakistan), Ministry of Foreign Affairs of the Kingdom of Bahrain's official website, 20 March 2014, www.mofa.gov.bh/ Defa ult. aspx?tabid=8266&language=ar-BH&ItemId=4008 (accessed 30 August 2022).

69 Ibrahim Hatlani, 'Bahrain between Its Backers and the Brotherhood', Carnegie Endowment for International Peace (20 May 2014), http://carnegieendowm ent.org/sada/55653 (accessed 30 August 2022).

70 Valeri, 'Islamist Political Societies'.

71 'Bahrain MPs Ban Mixing of Politics and Religion', Gulf News, 18 May 2016, https://gulfnews.com/news/gulf/bahrain/bahrain-mps-ban-mixing-of-politics-and-religion-1.1830097 (accessed 30 August 2022).

72 'Bahrain FM: Muslim Brotherhood is a Terrorist Group', Al Jazeera, 6 July 2017, www.aljazeera.com/news/2017/07/bahrain-fm-muslim-brotherhood-terrorist-group-170706140931861.html (accessed 30 August 2022).

73 أمين عام 'المنبر': قناة الجزيرة تستخدم أسلوب التدليس لتحقيق انتصارات إعلامية زائفة (Secretary General of Al-Manbar: Al-Jazeera Uses Fraud to Achieve False Media Victories), Al Watan News, 6 July 2017, http://alwa tann ews.net/ arti cle/ 723 520?rss= 1 (accessed 30 August 2022).

74 Interview by the author of a member of Bahrain's Consultative Council (Shura), London, 6 November 2018.

75 Ahmed Al-Rawi, 'Sectarianism and the Arab Spring: Framing the Popular Protests in Bahrain', *Global Media and Communication* 11:1 (2015), 25–42.

76 A report on a Tunisian television show in early 2014 featured an interview with a Bahraini fighter in Syria who claimed to have received direct funding from two al-'Asalah MPs, including former society head Sheikh Adil al-Ma'wda. The report can be watched in full at www.youtube.com/watch?v=XxWt_GpY LpY&feature=youtu.be (accessed 30 August 2022).

77 المنامة: جدل بعد زيارة نواب بحرينيين لسوريا (Manama: Controversy after the Visit of Bahraini Deputies to Syria), CNN Arabic, 6 August 2012, http://archive.arabic.cnn.com/2012/middle_east/8/6/Bahraini-BMs-Syria/ (accessed 30 August 2022).

78 Interview by the author of a prominent Bahraini Shi'a activist, London, 19 September 2018; interview by the author of a Bahraini professor of Gulf politics, Skype, 11 February 2019.

79 Cole Bunzel, 'The Kingdom and the Caliphate: Duel of the Islamic States', Carnegie Endowment for International Peace (2016), https://carnegieen dowment.org/files/Brief-Bunzel-Duel_of_The_Islamic_States.pdf (accessed 19 July 2023).

80 *Ibid.*

81 Ala'a Shehabi, 'Why Is Bahrain Outsourcing Extremism?', *Foreign Policy*, 29 October 2014, https://foreignpolicy.com/2014/10/29/why-is-bahrain-outsourcing-extremism/ (accessed 30 August 2022).

82 Interview by the author of a member of Bahrain's Consultative Council (Shura), London, 6 November 2018.

83 Justin Gengler, 'Royal Factionalism, the Khawalid, and the Securitization of "the Shi'a Problem" in Bahrain', *Journal of Arabian Studies* 3:1 (2013), 53–79.

84 *Ibid.*; interview by the author of a prominent Bahraini Shi'a activist, London, 19 September 2018.

85 These remarks were part of a speech delivered by a former al-Wefaq MP at a closed-door roundtable held in London, 30 November 2018.

86 Nafisa Eltahir and Lisa Barrington, 'Bahrain Accuses Iran of "Biological Aggression", Gulf States Try to Curb Coronavirus', Reuters, 12 March 2020, www.reuters.com/article/us-health-coronavirus-saudi-travel-idUSKBN20Z03K (accessed 30 August 2022).

87 Interview by the author of a Bahraini professor of Gulf politics, Skype, 11 February 2019.

88 Justin Gengler, 'Are Bahrain's Sunnis Still Awake?', Carnegie Endowment for International Peace (June 2012), http://carnegieendowment.org/sada/?fa= 48650 (accessed 23 August 2022).

89 Valeri, 'Islamist Political Societies', 176.

90 Interview by the author of a Bahrain-based senior researcher at the International Institute for Strategic Studies, Skype, 17 April 2019; interview by the author of a member of Bahrain's Consultative Council (Shura), London, 6 November 2018.

91 Interview by the author of a Bahraini professor of Gulf politics, Skype, 11 February 2019.

92 Speech delivered by a former al-Wefaq MP, closed-door roundtable, London, 30 November 2018.

93 Abdulrahman Al-Fawwaz, 'Foreign Direct Investment and Economic Stability: The Case of Arab Peninsula', *Advances in Social Sciences Research Journal* 5:8 (2018), 251–263; Hanan Naser, 'Financial Development and

Economic Growth in Oil-Dependent Economy: The Case of Bahrain', dissertation (University of Munich, 2018).

94 Interview by the author of an official from Bahrain's Ministry of Foreign Affairs, Riyadh, 5 March 2022.

95 Interview by the author of an expert from the Bahraini think tank DERASAT, Riyadh, 5 March 2022.

96 World Bank Group, 'COVID-19 Pandemic and the Road to Diversification', *Gulf Economic Update*, August 2021, https://www.worldbank.org/en/country/gcc/publication/gulf-economic-update-covid-19-pandemic-and-the-road-to-diversification (accessed 30 July 2023).

97 Sebastian Shehadi, 'How Manama's Movement away from Oil Is Paying Dividends', *Investment Monitor*, 19 July 2021, https://investmentmonitor.ai/analysis/manama-bahrain-move-oil-paying-dividends (accessed 17 September 2022).

98 World Bank Group, 'COVID-19 Pandemic'.

4

Saudi Arabia

The impact of the Arab Spring

The security perceptions of the Saudi regime were influenced heavily by the events of the Arab Spring and changed significantly in the ten years after 2011. While protests in the kingdom were also driven by socioeconomic vulnerabilities, the regime's security policies over the following ten years showed the prioritisation of sociopolitical vulnerabilities. This became more prominent after the enthronement of King Salman in 2015 and the appointment of his son Mohammad bin Salman to the position of Crown Prince in 2017. The Saudi leadership then introduced significant economic reforms with Vision 2030 – published in 2016 – but these were actively weakening rentierism and did not focus on providing short-term economic gains to the population. Instead, the regime focused more prominently on assertively confronting political threats emanating from Iran, the Muslim Brotherhood, and their supporters – especially Qatar and Turkey. The core objective was to invent a new (hyper-) nationalism – traditionally weakened by tribal, sectarian, or religious allegiances – in the pursuit of greater ontological security.

Just three days after large-scale protests started in Bahrain in February 2011, protests began in the Shi'a-majority Eastern Province of Saudi Arabia, home to the bulk of Saudi Arabia's oil resources and three key commercial and industrial ports – King Abdul Aziz Port, Jubail Port, and King Fahad Industrial Port – and location of the State-owned energy major ARAMCO, the kingdom's most strategically valuable company.[1] Demonstrations were encouraged, inspired, and at times coordinated by Shi'a clerics such as the influential scholar Nimr al-Nimr.[2] In February 2011 a letter entitled 'Declaration of National Reform' was signed by 119 activists from across the different sociopolitical communities, demanding the establishment of a federal system to give greater authority to local governments, and an elected parliament (i.e. National Assembly), eyeing the institution of a constitutional monarchy.[3] In early March, a diverse range of youth protest groups coalesced into a movement called the Free Youth Coalition, calling for a nationwide 'Day of Rage' on 11 March 2011. The prospect of nationwide protests raised the level of concern for the regime, and King Abdullah bin Abdulaziz al-Saud met with some of the Shi'a leaders, promising financial packages worth $130 billion to tackle youth unemployment and a rampant housing crisis, all in the attempt to convince them to withdraw support from the planned protests.[4] When the day arrived, amid a large deployment of security forces, only a few dozen people took the streets, and only in al-Ahsa, Safwa, 'Awamiyya, and Qatif.[5] A week later, thousands of Saudi youths protested in the Eastern Province in solidarity with Bahraini Shi'a, calling for the withdrawal of the Peninsula Shield from the country.[6] Sporadic rallies continued for months, with limited confrontation between protesters and security forces, until a rally in 'Awamiyya in October 2011 escalated, with dozens wounded.[7] After this violent incident the Saudi Ministry of Interior released a statement accusing the protesters of acting 'at the behest of a foreign country seeking to undermine the security and stability of the homeland'.[8] It was the first time Saudi authorities openly connected the demonstrators with a 'foreign country', i.e. Iran. On their part, protesters themselves started openly to question the legitimacy of their rulers in Riyadh: responding to the Ministry of Interior's statement, Nimr al-Nimr remarked in a sermon that:

> We are not loyal to other countries or authorities, nor are we loyal to this country. What is this country? The regime that oppresses me? The regime that steals my money, sheds my blood, and violates my honor? What does a country mean? The regime? The ruling clan? The soil? I don't know what a country means. Loyalty is only to Allah! We have declared, and we reiterate, that our loyalty is to Allah, not the Saud clan.[9]

In November, the burial of two protesters killed by the police in earlier demonstrations brought 20,000 people onto the streets of Qatif in the largest demonstration in the Eastern Province since the uprising of 1979.[10] Demonstrators chanted against the regime and chanted 'Death to al-Saud'.[11] Tensions flared up again in early 2012, around the first anniversary of the uprising in Bahrain, and erupted in violent clashes after the arrest of Nimr al-Nimr in July 2012.[12] And yet, given the prominent role played by al-Nimr in the regime's perceptions of the Arab Spring, his arrest symbolically closed the first and major phase of the event.

A Shi'a cleric who openly questioned the foundational myth of the kingdom and occasionally advocated for the secession of the Eastern Province, Nimr al-Nimr had a long history of connections to Iran and of outspoken criticism of the Saudi regime. By the late 1970s he had joined the transnational

Shi'a movement led by Iraqi-Iranian cleric Mohammed Mahdi al-Shirazi, which was at the forefront of the 1980s protests in Kuwait, Bahrain, and Saudi Arabia.[13] In the aftermath of the uprisings, al-Nimr went into exile in Iran, where he subsequently became one of the key representatives for the movement's revolutionary political leader, Muhammad Taqi al-Mudarrisi, in Saudi Arabia.[14] The Saudi regime saw al-Nimr's leadership in the Eastern Province as clear evidence of Iranian involvement.[15]

While the logistical or financial support, as well as the political coordination alleged by the Saudi regime between Iran and the protesters has not been proven, there were strong demonstrations of moral and media support from Iran. Protests in Saudi Arabia were widely covered by the Iranian-sponsored Arabic-language Al Alam channel, Lebanese Hezbollah's Al Manar, and Iraq's Ahlul Bait TV.[16] These displays of solidarity were largely instrumental in the Saudi regime's confirmation of external influence over the protest movements, and its embrace of the rhetoric of Iran's interference in the domestic affairs of both Bahrain and Saudi Arabia, as part of the IRGC's mission to export the Khomeinist revolution to the region.[17] This framing was employed by the State to delegitimise the protesters' legitimate grievances, while raising the spectre of an Iranian takeover of the Eastern Province's oilfields with the help of local Shi'a strengthened the loyalty of the Sunni majority to the regime.[18] Saudi officials consistently acknowledged the legitimate grievances of the Saudi Shi'a communities, but Iran's agenda to exploit such grievances to cause instability and extend its influence in Saudi Arabia is never questioned.[19]

In fact, Saudi Shi'a – estimated at between 1.5 and 2 million people, or around 10 per cent of the citizenry – have long complained of systematic, structural discrimination in religious practice, government employment, and business, and overall marginalisation in political, economic, and social terms.[20] Shi'a religiosity has been repressed though arbitrary mosque closures, and the prohibition of public gatherings and rituals. The Saudi educational system, imbued with Wahhabi thought, long tolerated and, at times, promoted anti-Shi'ism. Shi'a lamented the unfairness of the judicial system, since Shi'a courts' jurisdiction has been traditionally limited both geographically, only operating in local courts of the Eastern Province, and thematically, only dealing with family law. A lack of economic opportunities and viable employment options relegated many areas in the oil-rich Eastern Province to socioeconomic underdevelopment. Shi'a have been underrepresented in or excluded from sensitive government agencies – such as the Ministry of Interior, the National Guard, and the Ministry of Defence – police forces, the Royal Court, the cabinet, the diplomatic corps, and governorates' institutions. This institutionalised, structural inequality and marginalisation are the sociopolitical and socioeconomic vulnerabilities of Saudi Arabia.

In fact, the Arab Spring influenced the threat perceptions and security thinking of the Saudi regime for many years after 2011. Riyadh saw Iran taking advantage of protests in Saudi Arabia, Bahrain, Iraq, and Yemen to strengthen and expand its influence. After 2011, the Saudi regime felt encircled by Iranian encroachment, and turned to hyper-securitisation. Regaining control became synonymous with pushing back against the Arab Spring, which had empowered actors outside the Saudi orbit. This was the thinking behind Saudi Arabia's joining forces with the other members of the quartet against Qatar in 2014 and 2017, vocally accusing Qatar of funding 'terrorist groups' – chiefly, the Muslim Brotherhood – and supporting Iran as well as Iranian-backed militias in the region.[21] In fact, Riyadh's concern with Doha was the latter's refusal to align with Saudi geopolitical preferences, and its systematic embrace of policies and actors that were directly opposite to Saudi interests. In other words, the Saudi regime clearly saw Qatar's policies as undermining its own efforts to reinstate a regional status quo that would minimise external and intermestic threats to the kingdom, especially those posed by two winners of the Arab Spring: Iran and the Islamists.

In this context, a transformative element was the dramatic shift in the key security partnership for Riyadh: that with the United States.[22] In his obsession to secure his leadership domestically, Crown Prince Mohammad bin Salman had started a campaign against dissidents that ultimately resulted in the killing of Saudi journalist and US resident Jamal Khashoggi in Istanbul in 2018. The event became an international scandal, as the Central Intelligence Agency attributed the political responsibility of the killing to Mohammad bin Salman, threatening his international standing. When the administration led by Donald Trump, which had close ties with Riyadh, refused to respond to missile and drone attacks against critical Saudi oil infrastructures in Abqaiq and Khurais in 2019, attributed to Tehran, Riyadh questioned the soundness of the decades-old US deterrence umbrella vis-à-vis Iran.[23] This perception was severely aggravated in 2021, as Democratic President Joe Biden – who was extremely critical of Mohammad bin Salman – took office and withdrew US military hardware from the kingdom. Subsequently, Saudi Arabia embraced a different approach vis-à-vis Iran, combining limited direct engagement in de-escalation talks, with the scramble to strengthen the deterrence umbrella by diversifying security partnerships internationally and regionally.[24] Indeed, this urge towards diversification also encouraged Riyadh to seek reconciliation with Qatar at the 2021 al-Ula summit, and Turkey the following year, as a weakened Brotherhood ceased to be seen as threat in Riyadh.[25] Ten years after the Arab Spring, the Saudi regime had been relatively successful in consolidating its internal stability through a mixture of coercion and hyper-nationalism, but was significantly more vulnerable to external threats, especially from Iran.

Saudi Arabia and the 'Shi'a threat'

Despite the abundance of public and private statements from Saudi officials identifying Iran as a major threat, especially after 2011, the characterisations of this threat oscillated between perceiving Iran as an internal threat, intent on destabilising the kingdom from within, and an external threat, damaging the regional interests of Saudi Arabia, described 'both in terms of balance of power and as a transnational ideological threat'.[26] In a 2014 study, Nawaf Obaid, a long-time special counsellor to Saudi ambassadors and the Royal Court, wrote that 'Saudi Arabia perceives Iran as the main threat to regional stability'.[27] In 2016, Prince Sultan bin Khalid Al-Faisal al-Saud, former Commander of the Royal Saudi Naval Forces Counter-Insurgency Special Operations Task Force, wrote that 'serious risks and threats as a result of the pervasive and corrosive influence of Iran in our region – and in particular on Saudi Arabia – amount to a conventional threat and present a clear danger to our national security'.[28] In 2018 Crown Prince Mohammad bin Salman remarked in an interview that 'Iranians, they're the cause of problems in the Middle East, but they are not a big threat to Saudi Arabia. But if you don't watch it, it could turn into a threat.'[29]

The Islamic Revolution's leader Ayatollah Ruhollah Khomeini wrote and spoke with deep-seated hostility about Saudi Arabia, defining the Saudis in his testament as 'not worthy of being in charge of the hajj and Kaaba affairs'.[30] This was going to remain a key theme in bilateral relations and a cause of extreme concern for the Saudi rulers, who view their guardianship of the holy places as an integral part of their legitimacy mix and national identity.[31] Since 1979, Saudi Arabia had felt it was 'facing a radical, militaristic and expansionist Iran that leverages Shi'a disenfranchisement, local power vacuums and a vast and growing network of well-armed and well-trained proxies to export its Islamic Revolution throughout the Middle East'.[32] Indeed, the Saudi perceptions of Iran are still influenced by Saudi collective memory of the Islamic Revolution, when the IRGC established the Office of Liberation Movements with the explicit purpose of supporting revolutionary groups in the Gulf, including the Organization of the Islamic Revolution and Hezbollah al-Hijaz.[33] The Organization of the Islamic Revolution was established in 1979 by Shi'a clerics – such as Hassan al-Saffar, Tawfiq al-Saif, and Jafar al-Shayeb – in the aftermath of a short-lived uprising that had spread in Saudi Arabia's Eastern Province to protest poor living conditions and religious discrimination.[34] Hezbollah al-Hijaz, founded in 1987, was a more militant group, vowing to overthrow the Saudi rulers by violence and establish an Islamic Republic after the Iranian model, which received training from the IRGC and Lebanese Hezbollah.[35] The attempted coup of 1981 by the IRGC-supported Islamic Front for the Liberation of Bahrain (IFLB) had substantially alerted the Saudi regime, which regarded Bahrain as an extension of its national security space.[36]

Iraq's invasion of Kuwait and the death of Khomeini created the conditions for a partial rapprochement between Saudi Arabia and Iran and, subsequently, a less conflictual period between the Saudi regime and Shi'a clerics. This lasted until 2009, when a violent clash between Shi'a pilgrims and the security forces during a religious celebration in Medina turned the frustrations of the Shi'a communities into outright animosity against the regime.[37] The Saudi authorities reacted to the Medina incident with arbitrary detentions, mosque closures, the prohibition of public display of Shi'a rituals and gatherings, and movement restriction measures.[38] A diplomatic cable from the US consulate in Dhahran dated November 2010 highlighted the mounting frustration, 'turning to hopelessness and exasperation' in the Shi'a communities of the east.[39] The spark of the Arab Spring was sufficient to ignite the protests fully. The Saudi regime saw the 2011 Shi'a uprisings in Bahrain and Saudi Arabia as a repeat of the pre-1990s past, which had left a long-lasting mark on the Saudi collective memory.[40] The 2011 demonstrations, centred around the same issues, were the largest witnessed since then. Like in the 1980s, Shi'a protests in Saudi Arabia and Bahrain were linked, resting on a web of people-to-people and social ties, with both directly questioning the legitimacy of the royal families and the State itself. Indeed, the potential success of the uprising in Bahrain was perceived by the Saudi regime as a major boost for its own opposition, and a threat to the Saudi regime's survival.[41] For this reason, Riyadh launched the Peninsula Shield intervention in Bahrain, contributing 1,200 security officers.[42] While Iran's direct involvement in the Saudi and Bahraini uprisings remains to be proven, events provided an opportunity for Iran to present itself as the patron of disgruntled Shi'a minorities and extend its political influence.[43]

The Saudi regime perceived Iranian strategy in the kingdom to be following a familiar model: the establishment of proxy militias and political factions, indoctrinated in Khomeinism, weakening the State from within.[44] From Riyadh's point of view, this happened with Hezbollah in Lebanon, and the Hasd al-Shabi (or Popular Mobilization Units, PMU) and political factions such as the Islamic Supreme Council of Iraq (ISCI) and the Islamic Dawa Party, in post-Saddam Iraq.[45] King Abdullah of Jordan then famously described this geopolitical belt connecting Lebanon, Syria, Iraq, and Iran under Iranian influence as a Shi'a 'crescent'.[46] Seen from Riyadh the crescent had long resembled a 'full moon' when taking into consideration Iran's perceived ambitions in Yemen, which, to Saudi Arabia, were 'not about foreign policy, but about national security'.[47] Already involved in a military conflict against Saudi Arabia since 2009, the Shi'a-aligned Zaydi rebel group known as Houthis took advantage of the street protests that toppled the

Yemeni regime in 2011 to conquer large swathes of Yemen, including the capital, Sanaa, in 2014.[48] Then Alireza Zakani, a confidant of the Supreme Leader, boasted that 'three Arab capitals [Beirut, Damascus, and Baghdad] have already fallen into Iran's hands and belong to the Iranian Islamic Revolution, and Sana'a is the fourth'.[49] The ascension of Mohammad bin Salman to the royal palaces in Riyadh came with an attempt to push back on this Iranian encirclement. In 2015 Saudi Arabia launched a new military offensive against the Houthis with UAE backing.[50] In 2017, Mohammad bin Salman exerted pressures on Lebanon's Prime Minister Saad Hariri, leader of the Saudi-aligned Sunni formation Future Movement, to resign in protest at Iranian influence over Beirut, and offered support to Iraqi political factions, including Shi'a cleric Moqtada al-Sadr, in exchange for their taking the distance from Tehran.[51] Yet, the strategy failed on all fronts. The war in Yemen failed to weaken the Houthis' territorial grip, resulting in hundreds of missile and drone attacks against Saudi territory and critical infrastructures over the following years.[52] After intervention from French President Emmanuel Macron, Hariri withdrew his resignation and Lebanon remained under the control of Iranian ally Hezbollah, which fared well in 2022 elections.[53] Moqtada al-Sadr rejected Saudi support and became the leading political actor, preventing the reappointment of Saudi-supported Prime Minister Mustafa al-Kadhimi after the 2021 elections in Iraq.[54]

Mohammad bin Salman's pushback strategy included moving against the Iran nuclear deal, or JCPOA, seen through the lens of this perceived regional expansion. From a Saudi perspective, by lifting comprehensive economic sanctions, the agreement provided Iran with more economic resources to be reinvested in its regional proxies.[55] For this reason, Saudi officials such as Turki al-Faisal voiced concerns that regional dossiers had not been discussed in the framework of the negotiations, and that GCC states had not been invited to the negotiating table.[56] The widespread perception was that global powers – first and foremost the United States – had ignored GCC concerns, driven by the objective of recreating the 1970s twin pillar policy relying on both Iran and Saudi Arabia as the two regional powers to secure the Gulf, and thus creating an equilibrium that would allow the fatigued United States to retrench from its decades-long role of security guarantor.[57] After 2016, Riyadh joined forces with Abu Dhabi and Tel Aviv to encourage US President Donald Trump – who had spoken against the JCPOA in his electoral campaign and had appointed anti-Iran hawks such as Secretary of State Mike Pompeo – to undo the deal.[58] Trump embraced a sanctions-centred 'maximum pressure' campaign against Iran and withdrew the USA from the JCPOA in 2018.[59] However, this Saudi approach also failed, given the US choice not to respond to the 2019 Iran-attributed attacks against Saudi Arabia and the UAE, and the subsequent decision by the US administration led by Democratic President Joe Biden to launch negotiations for a JCPOA revival in 2021. Ten years after the Arab Spring, Riyadh had failed to contain the external dimension of the Iran threat.

Domestically, the Saudi regime secured itself more effectively. Riyadh decided to hand exemplary punishment to those identified by the regime as leaders of the Saudi Shi'a revolts and, in January 2016, Nimr al-Nimr was executed for terrorism.[60] In response, Iranian mobs stormed the Saudi embassy in Tehran and the general consulate in the city of Mashhad; accusing Iranian authorities of failure in protecting its diplomatic premises, Saudi Arabia broke diplomatic relations with Iran. In the summer of 2017 the Saudi authorities moved in to bulldoze Nimr al-Nimr's home town, 'Awamiyya, where fighting between the security forces and small militant groups had never fully stopped.[61] Neither of these developments reignited Shi'a protests or raised the level of the threat against the regime.

At the same time, the Saudi leadership also attempted a more conciliatory approach towards the politically inactive Shi'a communities, including in the context of countering jihadist groups such as Daesh and their sectarian strategy. Since its establishment in 2014 in Mosul, Daesh had predominantly targeted the Shi'a communities, often quoting Wahhabi preachers, including from Saudi Arabia, in justification of their anti-Shi'a positions.[62] Between 2014 and 2016, dozens of attacks by Daesh targeted the Shi'a-majority Eastern Province. The aim was to provoke a violent reaction from Shi'a communities against the Saudi Government and to 'ignite a sectarian civil war' in order to thrive in the ensuing chaos and weaken the functional integrity of the kingdom's institutions.[63] The regime reacted to this sectarian strategy: King Salman dispatched Crown Prince Mohamed bin Nayef to Qatif to offer condolences, and referred to Shi'a worshippers who had prevented a second attack as 'martyrs' and 'heroes'.[64] Shi'a funerals were broadcast in full on Saudi television, and the attack was condemned by several clerics as well as the Grand Mufti, Abdul Aziz ibn Abdullah al-Sheikh.

The Saudi regime consistently viewed I—an- and Shi'a-aligned groups as a full-fledged threat, having the intent and capabilities to damage the functional integrity of the Saudi borders and its institutions, as much as its political stability and monarchical identity. They havce also been perceived as a quintessential intermestic threat, originating from abroad but having developed a strong internal dimension, threatening the regional interests of the Saudi regime and its internal stability. The Saudi regime attempted to address these internal and external dimensions simultaneously, but ineffectively. The asymmetric missile and drone attacks added a military dimension to the threat. An economic dimension emerged in its focus on the oil-rich Eastern Province and critical infrastructures more broadly. The potential for sectarian-flavoured disruptions to the Saudi national fabric, underestimated by the regime, shows a societal dimension.

Saudi Arabia and the 'Islamist threat'

The Saudi regime's perceptions of the Muslim Brotherhood varied greatly over the decades as a function of both domestic and regional dynamics, with regime–Brotherhood relations going from accommodation to competition.[65] These oscillations through cycles of conflict and reconciliation mirror closely the Saudi leadership's perceptions of the group.

Similarly to other GCC countries, the Brotherhood arrived in the kingdom in the 1950s and 1960s, introduced as thousands of members fled persecution at the hands of Arab nationalist regimes in Syria, Egypt, and beyond.[66] In the kingdom they joined together in an informally structured movement self-named Islamic Awakening (al-Sahwa al-Islamiyya) or Sahwa, which over time became heavily contaminated by local Wahhabi tradition. Members of the Brotherhood affiliated to the Sahwa initially developed cooperative relations with the Government and with the Wahhabi clerical establishment, to counter the ideological threat coming from Arab socialism and nationalism via media and education work, as well as social activities.[67]

The deployment of American troops on Saudi soil, engaged against Iraq's invasion of Kuwait in 1991, provided the context for a turning point in the relations between the Sahwa and the Saudi regime. Sahwa members launched nationwide petitions against the presence of foreign troops on Muslim soil and, more generally, the regime's alliance with the United States.[68] The regime reacted through mass arrests and a repression campaign between 1994 and 1995, effectively driving the movement underground.[69] When released from prison in the late 1990s, some of the Sahwa leaders, such as Abdallah al-Hamid and Abd al-Aziz al-Qasim, engaged again in discourses of political reform, calling for the establishment of a constitutional monarchy.[70] The movement's mobilisation capacity became apparent in the first municipal elections of the kingdom's modern history in 2005, when Sahwa-backed candidates won with very high percentages in most districts.[71] The Interior Minister at the time, Prince Nayif bin Abdulaziz, who identified the Brotherhood as the 'source of all evil in the Kingdom', spearheaded new arrest campaigns.[72] At the same time, the regime enlisted some other Sahwa clerics in the ideological fight against al-Qa'ida, who had launched a bombing campaign in the kingdom in the early 2000s.[73]

The same dynamics were at play during the Saudi Arab Spring, especially as protests against corruption spread to the central conservative region of Qassim.[74] While a few prominent 'constitutionalist' Sahwa figures, such as Salman al-'Awda, openly supported calls for reforms, most clerics condemned protests as a sign of degeneration towards westernisation and disloyalty to the kingdom.[75] The reluctance to grow into a full-scale opposition force is linked to the fact that 'Sahwa members have for years been co-opted by the regime and been embedded into the State, leveraging its resources to grow in power and influence'.[76]

Sahwa clerics were more active in their support for the Arab Spring regionally – especially in North Africa, as well as in Syria and Yemen – and welcomed the Muslim Brotherhood's rise to power in Egypt, while denouncing the Saudi regime's counterrevolutionary policies.[77] In particular, in 2013 a petition was circulated on social media with hashtags such *as al-malik la yomathilani* (the King does not represent me), heavily criticising the Saudi financial and political support for Egyptian General Abdel Fattah al-Sisi.[78] Sahwa clerics also joined the social media campaign showing the four-finger gesture, symbolising solidarity with the Muslim Brotherhood supporters massacred in the Rabaa al-Adawiya square by the Egyptian military in August 2013.[79] However, the regime did not step back from its anti-Brotherhood policies and, on the contrary, designated the Muslim Brotherhood as a terrorist organisation in March 2014, criminalising all shows of support for it.[80] At the same time, there were convergences between Sahwa clerics and other regime policies, especially those that countered Iran and the Shi'a, such as support for the Bahraini regime, the Syrian opposition, and the war in Yemen.[81] Prominent preachers Salman al-Awda, Muhammad al-Arifi, and Awad al-Qarni publicly praised the King for fighting Iran and Iranian-backed forces in Yemen, whom they identified as 'Rawafid' (rejectionist, a derogatory term to indicate Shi'a).[82] The Iranian threat was thus successfully employed by the regime to silence Islamist dissent and strengthen Sunni unity around itself. Indeed, in 2015, King Salman held a series of meetings with a number of leaders affiliated with the Muslim Brotherhood – such as Rachid Ghannouchi, the leader of the Islamist Ennahda Party in Tunisia; Abdul Majeed Zindani, the leader of al-Islah Party in Yemen; and Khaled Meshaal, the former leader of Hamas – in the attempt to co-opt them into Saudi Arabia's regional network.[83]

With this attempt failing, Islamists were to emerge as a major target for the regime and, especially, Mohammad bin Salman. His 2016 all-encompassing vision for Saudi Arabia, Vision 2030, featured a social liberalisation programme at its core.[84] This would result, over the course of the following two years, in the introduction of cinemas, music and entertainment events, the clampdown of the religious and morality police – the Committee for the Promotion of Virtue and the Prevention of Vice, or *muṭṭawwiʿa* – and, finally, the end of the ban on women driving.[85] Social reforms were, for Mohammad bin Salman, a fundamental political tool to win over the allegiance of the overwhelmingly young Saudi population; to strengthen the connection between the youth and the regime and the latter's legitimacy, questioned during the Arab uprisings; and in the hope that societal liberalisation would neutralise calls for political liberalisation.[86] Social reforms accelerated once Mohammad bin Salman officially became Saudi Arabia's Crown Prince in June 2017, and, in parallel, the Government launched a new and large-scale crackdown on Sahwa clerics. The 2017 intra-GCC crisis provided the context to arrest those clerics accusing them of being 'agents of Qatar'.[87] In September 2017, the Crown Prince signed the first round of arrests for twenty clerics and religious scholars, including Salman al-Awda and Awad al-Qarni, and, a year later, State prosecutors demanded the death penalty for both.[88] The Saudi regime saw Sahwa clerics' opposition to social liberalisation as highly detrimental to its legitimacy, given the millions-strong following of these clerics, and hence perceived them as actors in a political threat to the identity and stability of the regime.[89] Mohammad bin Salman built his own narrative on Islamism by linking the Muslim Brotherhood to more militant, more radical, and even jihadi groups. He claimed that his policies and reforms represented a return to pure Islam, corrupted by Islamists since Juhayman bin Sayf al-Otaibi had led around 500 insurgents to seize the Grand Mosque in Mecca in 1979, protesting against the al-Saud's policies of modernisation and westernisation, decrying the presence of non-Muslim troops on sacred Saudi soli, and asking for the overthrow of the royal family.[90] The presence of non-Muslim, US troops in Saudi Arabia was also a central argument in the 1990s for Osama bin Laden's strategy to cultivate Saudi Arabia as a fundraising and recruitment ground for al-Qa'ida, including fifteen of the nineteen hijackers involved in the 9/11 attacks.[91] Jihadist ideas continued to show traction within Saudi Arabia during al-Qa'ida's 2003–2009 campaign in the Arabian Peninsula (AQAP), and then with Daesh, which, according to estimates by the Ministry of Interior, had attracted over 2,000 Saudi recruits to Iraq by 2016.[92] In its narratives, the Saudi regime created a link between non-violent Islamists and jihadi groups when describing their common goal to establish a Caliphate with Islam's holiest sites at its core, thus challenging the religious credentials of the Saudi regime, a key element of its ontological security.[93] In 2018, the Crown Prince also stated to the *New York Times* that the Brotherhood was always the basis of terrorism, saying 'If you look at Osama bin Laden, you will find that he was a Muslim Brother. If you look at al-Baghdadi of IS, you will find that he too was a Muslim Brother. In reality, if you look at any terrorist, you will find that they were a Muslim Brother.'[94] The Sahwa's inability to mobilise a significant reaction within Saudi Arabia to the regime's repression campaign and its efforts to create a political convergence between the Brotherhood and jihadism eased Riyadh's threat perceptions regarding Islamists.

The progressive weakening of the movement regionally was equally significant to the same effect. With Qatar expelling key figures from the Egyptian Brotherhood after the 2014 intra-GCC crisis, the Egyptian regime felt confident of having crushed the Islamist opposition at home.[95] Securing the Egyptian regime was a crucial goal for Riyadh. Then Qatar progressively scaled back its support for the organisation after the 2017 crisis, and finally with the reconciliation process leading up to the 2021 al-Ula summit.[96] That same year, Brotherhood-affiliated parties suffered a crushing electoral defeat in Morocco and were ostracised from political life during a soft coup by Tunisian president Kais Saied, supported by Riyadh and Abu Dhabi.[97] The external dimension of the Islamist threat had been significantly downsized.

In sharp contrast with the fully co-opted official Wahhabi establishment, the Saudi regime long saw the Muslim Brotherhood as 'competing for allegiance among the Gulf populations and challenging the religious legitimacy of the Saudi state'.[98] In this sense, Islamists did pose a political threat to the regime's identity, especially after their political empowerment in several MENA countries in 2011. The Saudi regime, especially after 2016, responded with full-on repression, indicating both the severity with which it regarded the threat to security, and its indifference to the possible societal dimension of such a confrontation, namely the sociopolitical risk of deepening the fault lines between regime supporters and the large numbers of Islamists in the kingdom.

Saudi Arabia's security priorities after 2011

What stands out in the analysis of Saudi security thinking is the predominantly intermestic nature of the perceptions of all the dangers examined. This speaks of strong underlying vulnerabilities weakening the State from within and creating enabling conditions for exogenous dangers to develop an internal dimension. Saudi Arabia indeed suffers from ontological insecurity, i.e. the vulnerability of the State's identity.[99]

Prominent scholars such as May Darwich explain this vulnerability by looking back at the history of the foundation of the Saudi kingdom.[100] The embryonic core of the kingdom was formed when Mohammad Ibn Saud, a ruler from Najd, joined Mohammad 'Abd al-Wahab, a co-regionalist religious leader and theologian, to establish a political entity in 1732. Between the nineteenth and twentieth centuries, the army led by Ibn Saud slowly but surely expanded its territorial control through military annexations, while Mohammad 'Abd al-Wahab's network of religious preachers, diffused thorough the Peninsula, provided religious legitimacy and ideological ammunition to Ibn Saud to entrench such control.[101] Saudi Arabia's foundational myth is therefore one of conquest over disparate regional identities.[102] Najdi tribal elites were at the centre of the kingdom's emerging power, while other tribes were forcefully integrated.[103] As the conquerors' ideology, Wahhabism was imposed over the conquered regions as a key ingredient of the new regime's identity.[104] Given its fundamentalist views, and its inherent exclusivist nature, Wahhabism alienated non-Wahhabi Sunnis and Shi'a, defined as deviant in the orthodoxy, in the Eastern Province, the more liberal Hijaz, and also the tribal south.[105] In regions distant from the centres of authority, with a relatively homogeneous population and the presence of a local elite, such as the Eastern Province and Qassim, strong regional identities also fuelled opposition and created the conditions for mobilisation, including in 2011.[106]

From the 1950s to the 1970s, Saudi kings have attempted to shape the regime's self-identity in opposition to sweeping pan-Arabism, through pan-Islamism.[107] In fact, King Faisal bin Abdulaziz al-Saud, who ruled from 1964 to 1975, was the first Saudi ruler to assume the title of Custodian of the Two Holy Mosques and to establish a number of national and supranational institutions to promote cooperation in the Muslim world under Saudi leadership, such as the Organisation of Islamic Cooperation and the Muslim World League.[108] In this context, Iran's Islamic revolution undermined the Saudi leadership of the entire Muslim world, claiming a stronger authority over the Shi'a communities.[109] The Saudi regime and Wahhabi clerical establishment joined forces in responding to Iran's claims to pan-Islamist leadership, by highlighting the distinctiveness of a demonised 'Other', Shi'a.[110] The inevitable sectarian tune of the political operation has reinforced the Shi'a sense of marginalisation from the 1980s onwards, 'compromising the sense of Saudi national identity'.[111]

Pan-Islamism was also employed against tribalism, to limit the tribes' capability to mobilise against the regime.[112] The Saudi tribal landscape features over 100 tribes ranging from several hundred to millions of members, increasingly able to forge networks and reinforce tribal identity through new communications technology and media.[113] While the tribes have mostly focused on apolitical sectors of public life to avoid reprisals from the regime, they have shown the capacity to coordinate in local elections.[114] Indeed, the Saudi regime consistently regarded independent tribal organisation and the tribes' growing sociopolitical influence as counterproductive to the regime's efforts to create a new nationalism.[115]

In this context, creating a new form of nationalism was a major goal for King Salman and, especially, Mohammad bin Salman.[116] The Saudi regime embraced a hybrid strategy vis-à-vis the Shi'a communities, combining a repressive crackdown approach to crush political dissent with limited top-down concessions in exchange for political quiescence. The regime sought a recalibration of the official discourse, away from sectarianism and towards national cohesion and a limited engagement of the Shi'a communities.[117] King Salman appointed three civil society leaders from Shi'a communities to the Shura Council.[118] The King Abdulaziz Center for National Dialogue launched a programme to enhance national cohesion focused on the Eastern Province under the name 'Naseej'.[119] The Government channelled over $64 million to the reconstruction of 'Awamiyya, bulldozed to deprive dissident groups of safe havens.[120] However, overtures to Saudi Shi'a still appear very limited: a law criminalising hate speech and discrimination on the basis of sect, ethnicity, and tribal background has met resistance in the Shura Council, and no Shi'a has yet been appointed to the Council of Senior Scholars, as a judge in the national courts, or to a high-ranked position in the security forces.[121] To a certain extent, the regime also employed a hybrid strategy vis-à-vis tribes. On one hand, it stepped up its rentier approach to tribes, by introducing specific financial contributions.[122] The regime also appropriated elements and symbols of tribal identities from the pre-Islamic period (known by the derogatory term as 'Jahiliyyah'), such as the archaeological Nabatean heritage of al-Ula, into its new formula for a national identity.[123] At the same time, the regime also stepped up interference in tribal affairs, for example, by appointing Interior Ministry delegates to tribes; more often choosing a rival to the tribe's acknowledged leader; or creating an alternative, explicitly pro-Government centre of power within the tribe, also weakening a tribe's ability to act as an independent check on governmental power.[124]

This has been complemented by several moves to deprive the Wahhabi clerical establishment of any power to determine what it means to be Saudi.[125] Instead, the regime centralised this power and offered a new top-down version of hyper-nationalism centred around Vision 2030. Launched in April 2016, Vision 2030 was an ambitious programme to reform the Saudi economy – away from overdependence on oil and rentierism – and to modernise Saudi society by socially empowering the liberal youth. By focusing on incentivising the private sector, including by launching megaprojects, and carefully scaling back benefits by introducing new taxes and cutting subsidies on fuel, gas, electricity, and desalinated water, the Saudi regime demonstrated it wouldn't shy away from attempts to redefine the rentier social contract.[126] It was significant that, for example, VAT was tripled from 5 to 15 per cent amid the collapse of oil prices in 2020, at a politically sensitive time, as the Government introduced severe restrictions on movement in order to contain the spread of COVID-19. The 2022 rebound of oil prices, provoked by Russia's invasion of Ukraine, was certainly instrumental in doubling down on public investments in the Saudi real economy, but this wasn't to respond to specific socioeconomic grievances.

Ten years after the Arab Spring, the Saudi regime had been relatively successful in consolidating its internal stability, but was struggling to redefine the perameters of its ontological security top-down, through a mixture of coercion and hyper-nationalism.

Notes

1 For a full account of protests in the Eastern Province see Toby Matthiesen, 'A "Saudi Spring"? The Shi'a Protest Movement in the Eastern Province 2011–2012', *Middle East Journal* 66:4 (2012), 628–659.

2 *Ibid.*, 635.

3 An English translation of the Declaration of National Reform is available at 'A Call from Saudi Intellectuals to the Political Leadership', *Jadaliyya*, 28 February 2011, www.jadaliyya.com/Details/23744/A-Call-From-Saudi-Intellectuals-to-the-Political-Leadership (accessed 33 August 2022).

4 Frederic Wehrey, 'The Forgotten Uprising in Eastern Saudi Arabia', Carnegie Endowment for International Peace (2013), https://carnegieendowment.org/files/eastern_saudi_uprising.pdf (accessed 23 July 2023).

5 *Ibid.*

6 Matthiesen, 'A "Saudi Spring"?'.

7 *Ibid.*

8 *Ibid.*, 645.

9 An English translation of the sermon is available at 'Saudi Ayatollah Nimr Al-Nimr Dares Saudi Regime to Attack Iran and Declares: We Are Loyal to Allah, Not to Saudi Arabia or Its Royal Family', MEMRI, 17 October 2011, www.memri.org/reports/saudi-ayatollah-nimr-al-nimr-dares-saudi-regime-attack-iran-and-declares-we-are-loyal-allah (accessed 23 August 2022).

10 Matthiesen, 'A "Saudi Spring"?', 650.

11 *Ibid.*

12 Wehrey, 'The Forgotten Uprising'.

13 Toby Matthiesen, 'The World's Most Misunderstood Martyr', *Foreign Policy*, 8 January 2018, https://foreignpolicy.com/2016/01/08/the-worlds-most-misunderstood-martyr/ (accessed 23 August 2022).

14 *Ibid.*

15 Interview by the author of a member of the Saudi Shura Council, Riyadh, 9 March 2022.

16 Matthiesen, 'A "Saudi Spring"?', 633.

17 Abdulkhaleq Abdullah, 'Ar-rabi'a al arabi: Wijhat nazar min al khalij al arabi' ('The Arab Spring: A Point of View from the Arabian Gulf), *Al Mustaqbal Al Arabi* 391 (2011), 117–128; Bernard Haykel, 'Saudi Arabia vs the Arab Spring', *Project Syndicate*, 16 August 2011, www.project-syndicate.org/commentary/saudi-arabia-vs--the-arab-spring (accessed 23 August 2022).

18 See for instance Madawi Al-Rasheed, 'Sectarianism as Counter-Revolution: Saudi Responses to the Arab Spring', *Studies in Ethnicity and Nationalism* 11:3 (2011), 513–526.

19 Interview by the author of a senior Saudi diplomat, Brussels, 13 June 2022; interview by the author of a member of the Saudi Shura Council, Riyadh, 9 March 2022.

20 For a comprehensive overview of the grievances of Saudi Shi'a, see 'The Shiite Question in Saudi Arabia', Middle East Report 45, International Crisis Group (2005), https://www.crisisgroup.org/middle-east-north-africa/gulf-and-arabian-peninsula/saudi-arabia/shiite-question-saudi-arabia#:~:text=From%20Sa udi%20Arabia's%20establishment%20in,to%20improve%20inter%2Dsectar ian%20relations (accessed 31 July 2023).

21 Neil Quilliam, 'The Saudi Dimension: Understanding the Kingdom's Position in the Gulf Crisis', in Krieg, *Divided Gulf*, 109–126.

22 Muddassir Quamar, 'Saudi Arabia's Strategic Partnership with the United States: Fraying at the Margins?', *Strategic Analysis* (2022), 1–14.

23 *Ibid.*

24 *Ibid.*

25 Speech by a senior official for the Saudi Foreign Ministry at a closed-doors roundtable of the European Council on Foreign Relations, 10 June 2021.

26 Gregory Gause, 'The Foreign Policy of Saudi Arabia', in Raymond Hinnebusch and Anoushiravan Ehteshami (eds), *The Foreign Policies of Middle East States*, 2nd edn (Boulder, CO: Lynne Rienner, 2014), 191.

27 Obaid, 'A Saudi Arabian Defense Doctrine'.

28 Sultan bin Khalid Al-Faisal, 'Clear and Present Danger', in David DesRoches (ed.), 'GCC Security amid Regional Crises', *Gulf Affairs*, Oxford Gulf & Arabian Peninsula Studies (OXGAPS) (2016), 24.

29 'Crown Prince Mohammed bin Salman Talks to *TIME* about the Middle East, Saudi Arabia's Plans and President Trump', *TIME*, 5 April 2018, http://time. com/5228006/mohammed-bin-salman-interview-transcript-full/ (accessed 23 August 2022).

30 'Excerpts from Khomeini Speeches', *New York Times*, 4 August 1987, www. nytimes.com/1987/08/04/world/excerpts-from-khomeini-speeches.html (accessed 23 August 2022).

31 Hasan Kosebalaban and Mohammed Ayoob (eds), *Religion and Politics in Saudi Arabia: Wahhabism and the State* (Boulder, CO: Lynne Rienner, 2009).

32 Ali Shihabi, 'The Iranian Threat: The Saudi Perspective', London School of Economics and Political Science blog, 15 June 2018, https://blogs.lse. ac.uk/mec/2018/06/15/the-iranian-threat-the-saudi-perspective/ (accessed 23 August 2022).

33 Louër, *Transnational Shiite Politics: Religious and Political Networks in the Gulf* (New York: Columbia University Press, 2008), 179.

34 Toby Jones, 'Rebellion on the Saudi Periphery: Modernity, Marginalization, and the Shia Uprising of 1979', *International Journal of Middle East Studies* 38:2 (2006), 213–233.

35 Toby Matthiesen, 'Hizbullah al-Hijaz: A History of the Most Radical Saudi Shi'a Opposition Group', *Middle East Journal* 64:2 (2010), 179–197.

36 Louër, *Transnational Shiiite Politics*, 139–143.

37 Wehrey, *Sectarian Politics in the Gulf*, 109.

38 '2010 Report on International Religious Freedom: Saudi Arabia', website of the US Department of State (2010), www.state.gov/j/drl/rls/irf/2010/ (accessed 23 August 2022).

39 'Eastern Province Shia Frustrated', diplomatic cable, US Consulate in Dhahran, *Wikileaks*, 1 November 2009, https://wikileaks.org/plusd/cables/09DHAHR AN266_a.html (accessed 23 August 2022).

40 Jones, 'Rebellion on the Saudi Periphery'.

41 This connection was often reiterated by primary sources, including in an interview by the author of a former Saudi diplomat held in London on 19 May 2018 and in a speech delivered by a Saudi scholar and director of a Riyadh-based think tank with ties to the Saudi regime during a closed-door roundtable held in London, 20 September 2018.

42 Simon Mabon, 'The End of the Battle for Bahrain and the Securitization of Bahraini Shi'a', *Middle East Journal* 73:1 (2019), 29–50.

43 Anoushiravan Ehteshami, 'The Foreign Policy of Iran', in Hinnebusch and Ehteshami, *The Foreign Policies of Middle East States*, 283–309.

44 Comments by a senior Saudi royal at a closed-doors roundtable, Berlin, 16 September 2022.

45 Ehteshami, 'The Foreign Policy of Iran'.

46 'Jordan's Abdullah Concerned Iraq May Tilt toward Iran', MSNBC, 8 December 2004, www.nbcnews.com/id/6679939/ns/world_news-mideast_n_ africa/t/jordans-abdullah-concerned-iraq-may-tilt-toward-tehran/#.XIfWb8_ 7S9a (accessed 23 August 2022).

47 Saudi analyst quoted in Ginny Hill and Gerd Nonneman, 'Yemen, Saudi Arabia and the Gulf States: Elite Politics, Street Protests and Regional Diplomacy', briefing paper, Chatham House (2011), 9, www.chathamhouse.org/sites/ default/files/public/Meetings/Meeting%20Transcripts/120511yemen.pdf (accessed 20 July 2023). The expression 'full moon' was employed by a confidant of Mohammad bin Salman in 'Young Prince in a Hurry', *Economist*, 9 January 2016, www.economist.com/briefing/2016/01/09/young-prince-in-a-hurry (accessed 31 July 2023).

48 Hokayem and Roberts, 'The War in Yemen'.

49 Quoted in Dina Esfandiary and Ariane Tabatabai, 'Yemen: An Opportunity for Iran–Saudi Dialogue?', *Washington Quarterly* 39:2 (2016), 155–174 (158).

50 Thomas Juneau, 'Iran's Policy towards the Houthis in Yemen: A Limited Return on a Modest Investment', *International Affairs* 92:3 (2016), 647–663.

51 'Saudi Arabia Forcibly Detained Lebanon's Prime Minister, Sources Say', *Washington Post*, 10 November 2017, www.washingtonpost.com/opinions/ global-opinions/saudi-arabia-forcibly-detained-lebanons-prime-minister-sources-say/2017/11/10/b93a1fb4-c647–11e7–84bc-5e285c7f4512_story. html?utm_term=.f9c537e23e33 (accessed 23 August 2022); 'Iraqi Shi'ite

Leader Sadr Makes Rare Visit to Saudi Arabia', Reuters, 30 July 2017, www.reuters.com/article/us-saudi-iraq-cleric/iraqi-shiite-leader-sadr-makes-rare-visit-to-saudi-arabia-idUSKBN1AF0UN (accessed 23 August 2022).

52 Anthony Cordesman, 'The Strategic Implications of the Strikes on Saudi Arabia', Center for Strategic and International Studies (2019), www.csis.org/analysis/strategic-implications-strikes-saudi-arabia (accessed 31 July 2023).

53 David Daoud, 'Lebanon Just Had an Election. Its Result? Curb the Optimism', Atlantic Council, 31 May 2022, www.atlanticcouncil.org/blogs/menasou rce/lebanon-just-had-an-election-its-result-curb-the-optimism/ (accessed 23 August 2022).

54 Kjetil Selvik and Iman Amirteimour, 'The Big Man Muqtada al-Sadr: Leading the Street in Iraq under Limited Statehood', *Third World Thematics* (2021), 1–18.

55 David Schenker, 'The Shift in Saudi Foreign Policy', Policy Analysis, Washington Institute for Near East Policy, 10 February 2016, www.washingt oninstitute.org/policy-analysis/view/the-shift-in-saudi-foreign-policy (accessed 23 August 2022).

56 Steven Erlanger, 'Saudi Prince Criticizes Obama Administration, Citing Indecision in Mideast', *New York Times*, 15 December 2013, www.nytimes.com/2013/12/16/world/middleeast/saudi-prince-accuses-obama-of-indecision-on-middle-east (accessed 23 August 2022).

57 Gause, *The International Relations*, 16–25.

58 Ahmadian, 'Iran and Saudi Arabia'.

59 *Ibid.*

60 'Sheikh Nimr al-Nimr: Saudi Arabia Executes Top Shia Cleric', BBC, 2 January 2016, www.bbc.co.uk/news/world-middle-east-35213244 (accessed 23 August 2022).

61 'Inside the Saudi Town that's Been under Siege for Three Months by Its Own Government', *Independent*, 4 August 2017, https://tinyurl.com/24dkv3zf (accessed 17 September 2022).

62 Bunzel, 'The Kingdom and the Caliphate'.

63 Bilal Sabab, 'Can the House of Saud Survive ISIS?', *Foreign Affairs*, 11 June 2015, www.foreignaffairs.com/articles/2015-06-11/can-house-saud-survive-isis (accessed 23 August 2022).

64 *Ibid.*

65 Stéphane Lacroix, *Awakening Islam: The Politics of Religious Dissent in Contemporary Saudi Arabia* (Cambridge, MA: Harvard University Press, 2011).

66 *Ibid.*, 38.

67 *Ibid.*, 39.

68 Hrair Dekmejian, 'The Rise of Political Islamism in Saudi Arabia', *Middle East Journal* 48:4 (1994), 627–643 (631).

69 *Ibid.*, 642.

70 Stéphane Lacroix, 'Is Saudi Arabia Immune?', *Journal of Democracy* 22:4 (2011), 48–59.

71 Hendrik Jan Kraetzschmar, 'Electoral Rules, Voter Mobilization and the Islamist Landslide in the Saudi Municipal Elections of 2005', *Contemporary Arab Affairs* 3:4 (2010), 515–533.

72 Lacroix, *Awakening Islam*.

73 Lacroix, 'Is Saudi Arabia Immune?', 53.

74 These protests remain underexplored, but some information is available in Stéphane Lacroix, 'Saudi Islamists and the Arab Spring', research paper, Kuwait Programme on Development, Governance and Globalisation in the Gulf States, London School of Economics and Political Science (2014), https://eprints.lse.ac.uk/56725/1/Lacroix_Saudi-Islamists-and-theArab-Spring_2014.pdf (accessed 31 July 2023).

75 Stéphane Lacroix, 'Is Saudi Arabia Immune?'.

76 Interview by the author of a former Saudi diplomat, London, 19 May 2018.

77 Marc Lynch, 'Gulf Islamist Dissent over Egypt', *Foreign Policy*, 18 August 2013, https://foreignpolicy.com/2013/08/18/gulf-islamist-dissent-over-egypt/ (accessed 23 August 2022).

78 Madawi al-Rasheed, 'From Cooperation to Collision: Saudi Arabia and Its Islamists', *Sharq Forum*, 17 November 2017, www.sharqforum.org/2017/11/17/from-cooperation-to-collision-saudi-arabia-and-its-islamists/ (accessed 23 August 2022).

79 Lacroix, 'Saudi Islamists and the Arab Spring', 25.

80 'Saudi Arabia Designates Muslim Brotherhood Terrorist Group', Reuters, 7 March 2014, www.reuters.com/article/us-saudi-security-idUSBREA260SM20140307 (accessed 23 August 2022).

81 Raihan Ismail, 'The Saudi 'Ulama and the Syrian Civil War', in Amin Saikal (ed.), *The Arab World and Iran* (New York: Palgrave Macmillan, 2016), 83–102.

82 See various quotes in Angus McDowall, 'Yemen Strikes Boost Saudi Nationalism and Sectarianism', Reuters, 10 April 2014, http://in.mobile.reuters.com/article/idINL6N0WX4U720150410?irpc=932. (accessed 23 August 2022).

83 Ali al-Arian, 'Is Saudi Arabia Warming up to the Muslim Brotherhood?', Al Jazeera, 29 July 2015, www.aljazeera.com/news/2015/7/29/is-saudi-arabia-warming-up-to-the-muslim-brotherhood (accessed 23 August 2022).

84 See the full text of Vision 2030 at http://vision2030.gov.sa/en (accessed 31 July 2023).

85 The connection among social liberalisation, the crackdown against Sahwa clerics, and the narrative against Qatar is developed in Quilliam, 'The Saudi Dimension'.

86 Interview by the author of an official from the Saudi Ministry of Foreign Affairs, Riyadh, 6 March 2022.

87 Mustafa Menshawy and Simon Mabon, 'The Muslim Brotherhood Faultline in Saudi–Qatari Relations: Domestic Divisions and Regional Rivalry', *Insight Turkey* 23:4 (2021), 51–62.

88 *Ibid*.

89 Interview by the author of a member of the General Secretariat of the Council of Senior Scholars, London, 14 August 2018.

90 Robert Lacey, *Inside the Kingdom: Kings, Clerics, Modernists, Terrorists, and the Struggle for Saudi Arabia* (London: Penguin, 2009).

91 Thomas Hegghammer, *Jihad in Saudi Arabia: Violence and Pan-Islamism since 1979* (Cambridge: Cambridge University Press, 2010).

92 US Bureau of Counterterrorism, 'Country Report on Terrorism 2017: Saudi Arabia', website of the US Department of State, www.state.gov/j/ct/rls/crt/index.htm (accessed 13 August 2022).

93 Obaid, 'A Saudi Arabian Defense Doctrine', 11.

94 Quoted in Mohamed Mokhtar Qandil, 'The Muslim Brotherhood and Saudi Arabia: From Then to Now', Washington Institute for Near East Policy, 18 May 2018, www.washingtoninstitute.org/policy-analysis/muslim-brotherhood-and-saudi-arabia-then-now (accessed 23 August 2022).

95 Nicola Pratt and Dina Rezk, 'Securitizing the Muslim Brotherhood: State Violence and Authoritarianism in Egypt after the Arab Spring', *Security Dialogue* 50:3 (2019), 239–256.

96 Francois Burgat, 'Is the Era of Islamists Coming to an End?', *Middle East Eye*, 25 October 2021, www.middleeasteye.net/opinion/era-islamists-coming-end (accessed 23 August 2022).

97 *Ibid.*

98 Guido Steinberg, 'The Gulf States and the Muslim Brotherhood', Project on Middle East Political Science, 9 March 2014, https://pomeps.org/the-gulf-states-and-the-muslim-brotherhood (accessed 17 September 2022).

99 Darwich, 'The Ontological (In)security of Similarity'.

100 Tim Niblock, *Saudi Arabia: Power, Legitimacy and Survival* (London: Routledge, 2006).

101 Alexei Vasiliev, *The History of Saudi Arabia* (London: Saqi, 2000).

102 *Ibid.*

103 Joseph Kostiner, 'Transforming Dualities: Tribe and State Formation', in Philip Shukry Khoury and Joseph Kostiner (eds), *Tribes and State Formation in the Middle East* (Oakland: University of California Press, 1991).

104 Ayoob and Kosebalaban, *Religion and Politics in Saudi Arabia*.

105 *Ibid.*

106 Sultan Alamer, 'Beyond Sectarianism and Ideology: Regionalism and Collective Political Action in Saudi Arabia', in Madawi Al-Rasheed (ed.), *Salman's Legacy: The Dilemmas of a New Era in Saudi Arabia* (Oxford: Oxford University Press, 2018), 97–117.

107 *Ibid.*

108 Hegghammer. *Jihad in Saudi Arabia*, 17.

109 Niblock, *Saudi Arabia*, 55.

110 *Ibid.*, 57.

111 'Eastern Province Shia Frustrated', diplomatic cable, US Consulate in Dhahran, *Wikileaks*, 1 November 2009, https://wikileaks.org/plusd/cables/09DHAHRAN266_a.html (accessed 13 August 2022).

112 *Ibid.*, 117.

113 Sebastian Maisel, 'The New Rise of Tribalism in Saudi Arabia', *Nomadic Peoples* 18:2 (2014), 100–122.

114 *Ibid.*, 116.

115 Telephone interview by the author of a Saudi diplomat, 5 December 2017; interview by the author of a Saudi analyst of strategic affairs, Prague, 21 February 2020; interview by the author of an official from the Saudi Ministry of Foreign Affairs, Riyadh, 6 March 2022.

116 Gadi Hitman, 'Saudi Arabia's Wahhabism and Nationalism: The Evolution of Wataniyya into Qawmiyya', *Digest of Middle East Studies* 27:1 (2018), 79–96.

117 Simon Mabon, 'Eastern Saudi Arabia: Is De-Sectarianization a Byproduct of Vision 2030?', commentary, *Istituto Studi di Politica Internazionale*, 10 September 2020, www.ispionline.it/en/pubblicazione/eastern-saudi-arabia-de-sectarianization-byproduct-vision-2030-27324 (accessed 13 August 2022).

118 'Mother of Saudi Killed Preventing ISIS Attack Appointed to Shoura Council', Al Arabiya, 3 December 2016, https://english.alarabiya.net/en/features/2016/12/03/Mother-of-Saudi-who-fought-off-ISIS-attack-appointed-to-Shoura-coun cil.html (accessed 23 August 2022); 'Dr Yousef bin Trad Al-Saadoun, Nabih bin Abdulmohsen Al-Ibrahim Appointed as Members of Shura Council', Saudi Press Agency, 26 February 2018, www.spa.gov.sa/viewfullstory.php?lang= en&newsid=1729619 (accessed 23 August 2022).

119 ' "Naseej" Increases Social Cohesion', *Saudi Gazette*, 10 May 2016, www.saudigazette.com.sa/article/164674 (accessed 13 August 2022).

120 Mabon, 'Eastern Saudi Arabia'.

121 Antonella Caruso, 'Saudi Arabia Still Treats Shiites as Second-Class Citizens', *Foreign Policy*, 11 May 2021, https://foreignpolicy.com/2021/05/11/moham med-bin-salman-mbs-saudi-arabia-still-treats-shiites-second-class-citizens/ (accessed 23 August 2022).

122 Jon Alterman, 'Ties that Bind: Family, Tribe, Nation, and the Rise of Arab Individualism', Center for Strategic and International Studies, 2 December 2019, www.csis.org/analysis/ties-bind-family-tribe-nation-and-rise-arab-indivi dualism (accessed 17 September 2022).

123 Interview by the author of a Saudi analyst of strategic affairs, Prague, 21 February 2020.

124 Alterman, 'Ties that Bind'.

125 Hitman, 'Saudi Arabia's Wahhabism and Nationalism'.

126 'The "New" Saudi Arabia, where Taxes Triple and Benefits Get Cut', Forbes, 15 May 2020, www.forbes.com/sites/thebakersinstitute/2020/05/13/the-new-saudi-arabia-where-taxes-triple-and-benefits-get-cut/?sh=4cadf6ba2a22 (accessed 23 August 2022).

5

The United Arab Emirates

The impact of the Arab Spring

In the ten years after the Arab Spring, the UAE fully embraced hyper-securitisation. The peculiar element is that it did so without experiencing a full threat to the regime resulting from street protests. In fact, the UAE's security calculus had a strong regional dimension for the entire decade, reflecting itss self-perception as a medium-sized regional power, rather than a small state in an insecure region.

The UAE did not experience a full chapter of the Arab Spring, and no street protests were held in the country.[1] The isolated instances of dissent were met with full repression, mixed with some degree of co-optation, such as enlarging the electoral college to 129,000 voters – which still constituted only 12 per cent of the citizen population –signing a $2.7 billion agreement to help poorer nationals pay off outstanding loans; boosting welfare benefits by up to 20 per cent; and granting huge public sector pay increases, in some cases up to 100 per cent.[2] From the beginning, the UAE regime's perceptions vis-à-vis the Arab uprisings were particularly alert to the issue of political Islam, both domestically and regionally.

In 2011, 133 Emiratis – including academics, former government officials and Federal National Council (FNC) members, journalists, and activists – signed a petition addressed to the UAE President Khalifa bin Zayed al-Nahyan and the members of the Supreme Council, the body that includes all rulers of the seven emirates, asking that the FNC be given more authority, including legislative powers and the ability to hold officials accountable, and for the introduction of universal suffrage.[3] Five people among the signatories were subsequently arrested in April 2011, sentenced to several years for 'publicly insulting the UAE's leaders' and 'undermining national security', and then pardoned the next day.[4] The five activists included Ahmed Mansoor, an engineer and blogger; Nasser bin Ghaith, an economist and university lecturer at Sorbonne Abu Dhabi; and online activists Fahad Salim Dalk, Ahmed Abdul-Khaleq, and Hassan Ali al-Khamis. Both

Ahmed Mansoor and Nasser bin Ghaith would then be arrested again between 2015 and 2017, and both would be given harsh prison sentences for their criticism of the Emirati regime.[5] Despite the State's demonstrative quick reaction, the first petition was followed by increased online and offline activities. Civil society organisations, of different sociopolitical motivations, published statements calling for an FNC with full oversight and legislative powers. Among those organisations was the Reform and Social Guidance Association (al-Islah), a group close to the Muslim Brotherhood.[6] The regime embraced a different and specific approach towards those dissidents with ties to al-Islah. In December 2011 seven of al-Islah's active members were permanently stripped of their citizenship and charged with 'involvement in actions that pose a threat to national security, and connections to organisations and individuals on the terror watch list'.[7] The arrests marked only the beginning of the crackdown on al-Islah. By the end of 2012, ninety-four alleged members of the group had been arrested, with sixty-nine of them sentenced to between seven and fifteen years in prison.[8] Among them was Mohammed al-Mansoori, the deputy chairman of al-Islah and a former president of the Jurists' Association. Until 2010, he had also been a legal advisor to the Government of Ras al-Khaimah, one of the seven UAE emirates.[9] Another high-profile detainee was Sultan bin Kayed al-Qasimi, chairman of al-Islah and cousin of Saud bin Saqr al-Qasimi, the Emir of the northern emirate of Ras al-Khaimah: arrested in April 2012, he was sentenced to ten years in prison.[10] Given his position, al-Qasimi was perceived as a special liability by the Abu Dhabi leadership, and his arrest underlined the special attention paid by the regime towards Islamists specifically linked to the northern emirates.[11]

While Islamists initially joined forces with liberal pro-democracy activists, this loose coalition quickly collapsed under the weight of different expectations, drivers and modi operandi. Liberals seemed to lose steam soon after sending off the March 2011 petition, indicating lack of grassroots support for challenging the State to grant political liberalisation in the UAE, where a generous welfare state and general positive economic conditions, depending on a network of patronage and clientelism with the rulers, discouraged dissent.[12] In a classic feature of rentier systems, citizens rarely resort to challenging the governments managing their rents, unless their stake in those rents is challenged.[13] Neither were liberals organised into a proper movement, as political parties or societies are outlawed in the UAE.[14] Conversely, al-Islah, registered as a social non-governmental organisation, followed the highly centralised and hierarchical organisational structure traditional of Muslim Brotherhood affiliates, and was the oldest, largest, and best organised society in the UAE.[15] This longevity, together with the organisation's effective internal structure, represented significant and risky political capabilities from the Government's point of view.[16] In fact, Islamist dissidents in the Gulf and their quintessentially political grievances, more strongly motivated by ideological questions of political legitimacy than by material demands, represent an exception to rentier state theory.[17] Arguably, it was this ideological dimension, together with al-Islah's organisational capacity, that contributed to the Emirati regime's heightened antigonism against the group in the context of the activism taking place in 2011.

All these different elements considered, it is worth reiterating the limited nature of the dissidence phenomenon in the UAE in 2011. The petitions represented the momentum of the events, and no major street protests took place in the country. The crackdown that the Government launched in response may therefore appear disproportionate, and the fact that it was focused on al-Islah is crucial in tying it back to the larger issue of Government–Islamist relations. Overall, for the UAE leadership the 2011 events represented, first and foremost, an unwelcome challenge to the status quo. If such a challenge was on a small scale at the domestic level, it was thoroughly disruptive at the regional level. In fact, the Arab Spring signalled the regionalisation of national security for Abu Dhabi. There was a greater emphasis on proactive approaches to regional security and on 'not awaiting threats to reach the UAE's borders or internal space'.[18] Regional stability became a primary concern for the UAE leadership in the face of the crumbling of friendly regimes in Egypt; Tunisia; Yemen; and, especially, Bahrain. The UAE participated in several GCC meetings in the early days of March 2011, and Abu Dhabi was the only other member state, beyond Saudi Arabia, to commit ground personnel to a Peninsula Shield mission supporting the Bahraini regime's forces. While Saudi Arabia sent approximately 1,200 armed forces, the UAE sent around 800 police officers, who remained in the country for months.[19] This was a significant commitment, especially relative to that of Saudi Arabia, which had a vital interest in shutting down protests in Bahrain and could count on a much larger security force. Moreover, the UAE joined Saudi Arabia, Kuwait, and Qatar in committing $20 billion to Oman and Bahrain, the two GCC countries most affected by protests.[20] From Abu Dhabi's viewpoint, the old order had shown its vulnerabilities, and these vulnerabilities could easily be leveraged by hostile players, such as Islamists and their supporters: chiefly, in the regime's perceptions, Qatar and Turkey.

This explains why the UAE was, together with Saudi Arabia, at the forefront of the intra-GCC crises of 2014 and 2017.[21] Mohammad bin Zayed al-Nahyan, then Abu Dhabi's Crown Prince, tightened a strategic alliance with Mohammad bin Salman after the latter became Deputy Crown Prince of Saudi Arabia in 2015. Together, the two were a major driving force behind the assertive foreign and security policies to push back against the Islamists and Iran regionally. Despite being a small state by all measures, the UAE was as much in the driving seat as Saudi Arabia.[22] The roots of this assertiveness are to be found as much in the threat perceptions of the Emirati regime vis-à-vis Iran and the Islamists as in the UAE's self-image as a medium-sized regional player. Indeed, the UAE's security calculus in the ten years after the Arab Spring had a double dimension. Internally, its priority was preserving the unity of the seven emirates' Federation. At the same time, Abu Dhabi also pursued a newly prominent place within the post-2011 regional order, which it helped shape.

The UAE and the 'Shi'a threat'

The UAE's perceptions of Iran and the threats it may pose via Shi'a proxies are informed by the history of bilateral engagement as much as by the nature of Government–Shi'a relations within the Emirates. Amid the 1979 Islamic revolution, the UAE leadership shared with its neighbours some concerns about Ayatollah Khomeini's hegemonic ambitions and Tehran's encouragement of Emirati Shi'a to revolt against the Government.[23] In fact, this didn't happen, establishing a perception of loyalty in the Government vis-à-vis Emirati Shi'a.[24]

Although statistical data from official sources not available, Shi'a citizens are estimated to represent approximately 15 per cent of the UAE's citizen population and live predominantly in the northern emirates.[25] Over time, governing authorities have pursued political strategies to provide these communities with a stake in the regime's stability.[26] For instance, State authorities routinely finance Shi'a mosques; attend Shi'a religious celebrations; and engage in a rhetoric to promote, with some success, harmonious Sunni–Shi'a relations.[27] The Islamic studies curriculum in the UAE is based exclusively on Sunni schools of thought, yet it is not openly discriminatory against Shi'a beliefs.[28] The status of Emirati Shi'a stands in stark contrast with the institutionalised marginalisation suffered by Shi'a communities in Bahrain and Saudi Arabia, but Emirati Shi'a do face some unofficial discrimination with regard to positions deemed as sensitive, such as diplomatic or high-ranking posts within the armed forces and State security.[29] By contrast, the level of economic inclusiveness of the communities is, on average, high. For example, several Shi'a families belong to the country's rich merchant elites and run some of the biggest business conglomerates in Dubai, such as Alfardan, Al Sayegh, Galadari, and Al Yousuf LLC.[30] This absence of major socioeconomic and sociopolitical vulnerabilities is a key element explaining why the Emirati Government does not perceive Iran as capable of upsetting the UAE's domestic stability. The focus, in fact, has long been on Iran's regional policies as an external threat.

Describing Iran's regional policies, Emirati policy-makers would always start from 1971, when, as soon as the British left, the Shah occupied three small Gulf islands that were meant to become jointly administered by Iran and the UAE.[31] The dispute that ensued brought into the open Iranian perceptions of the UAE as an illegitimate British creation.[32] Having failed to solve the dispute via the International Court of Justice and the United Nations, this has remained relevant for decades.[33] When Iran's Foreign Minister Javad Zarif suggested in 2013 that Iran should 'talk to the UAE and remove any misunderstanding about the islands', the idea was dismissed by IRGC's Major General Mohammad Jafari, who invoked national security.[34] This disagreement provides a window onto the strategic significance of the islands, which are 'Iran's lock to close the Strait of Hormuz, a major geostrategic asset for a hegemonic power'.[35] Although Iranian threats to close the Strait never materialised, Iran's military presence in Abu Musa allows Tehran to control a shipping route through which pass a fifth of the world's oil supplies, while also projecting militarily the major Iranian port of Bandar Abbas, hosting critical infrastructures.[36]

In fact, UAE leaders have long viewed Iran as a predatory power, with the then Crown Prince Mohammad bin Zayed al-Nahyan describing Iran's desire to acquire a nuclear deterrent as an instrument to pursue the re-establishment of 'a Persian empire in the twenty first century' and 'emirates' in the Muslim world in 2009.[37] The 2011 protests in Bahrain and the Houthi takeover of Sana'a fitted these perceptions, encouraging the UAE to intervene with a security force in Manama in 2011 and join the 2015 Saudi-led military operations in Yemen.[38] While the UAE focused its operations on the south of Yemen, military and diplomatic resources were also deployed against the Houthis. The signing of the nuclear deal between the P5+1 and Iran in July 2015 was received amid this background in Abu Dhabi, and in close alignment with the perceptions of Bahraini and Saudi leaders. The UAE Foreign Minister al-Nahyan argued that Tehran was exploiting the good faith of the international community and the financial resources provided by the lifting of nuclear-related sanctions in order to fund destabilising activities in the region.[39] The UAE Ambassador to the USA, Yousef al-Otaiba, was an active and effective voice in convincing the Trump administration to withdraw from the JCPOA in May 2018.[40] Opposition to the JCPOA and Iran's regional policies was particularly strong in Abu Dhabi, which is the decision-maker on foreign and security policy. The leaders of Sharjah – the most conservative of the emirates, often closely aligned to Riyadh – shared these perceptions.[41] On the other hand, economic considerations have largely driven a different reaction in Dubai, Iran's most important regional trade partner, and, to a certain extent, in Ras al-Khaimah, also enjoying good commercial relations with Iran.[42] Dubai officials believed that it was in their best interest to secure their flourishing economic relations through the accommodation of Iran rather than outright confrontation. The JCPOA, with the removal of nuclear-related sanctions, was deemed useful to that purpose. Asked if it was time to lift sanctions against Iran, after the 2013 interim nuclear agreement, the ruler of Dubai, Mohammed bin Rashid al-Maktoum, stated: 'I think so and give Iran a space ... everybody will benefit.'[43]

Indeed, Dubai has traditionally provided concrete economic opportunities to its large Iranian community, which was traditionally heavily involved in exporting and re-exporting goods to Iran.[44] The UAE became less hospitable towards this community, with many experiencing difficulties buying property, receiving loans, and extending residence permits between the Arab Spring in 2011 and the beginning of the strategic pause in late 2019. After the start of a bilateral engagement between Iran and the UAE in late 2019, and the recommencement of nuclear talks to revive the JCPOA in 2021, the Iranian community was back in business, and the UAE became again the re-export hub for Iran to the point of being referred to colloquially as the 'Iranian Amazon'.[45] This was of great benefit to the economy of Dubai specifically, as it had been substantially affected by the international sanctions introduced against Iran in response to Tehran's development of a nuclear programme in the early 2000s and then again under US 'maximum pressure' between 2016 and 2020.[46]

However, this cyclical economic engagement with Iran never indicated a reduction in the Emirati perception of threat vis-à-vis Tehran. For the ten years following the Arab Spring, Iran was always seen as an external threat in Abu Dhabi. Economic engagement was rather a tool in the toolbox to pair some enticement with containment of the threat, as the UAE also aligned solidly with the USA and, after 2020, even Israel, to deter Tehran. In signing the Abraham Accords, the UAE was in fact looking for 'an extra layer of deterrence' against Iran.[47] Within the framework of the Accords, the UAE aId Israel began cooperating on cyber-security and air defence after the UAE suffered missile and drone attacks against Emirati and international tankers in Emirati territorial waters in 2019, attributed by Abu Dhabi to Iran. The 2019 attacks crucially affected the security perceptions of the Emirati regime. On one hand, a lack of reaction from the USA solidified the perception of a US disengagement from the MENA region and determined a decline in Emirati trust towards the USA's ability to serve as a security guarantor.[48] These events pushed the UAE to diversify its security partnerships, including by normalising relations with Israel. At the same time, they also pushed the Emirati leadership to diversify its strategy vis-à-vis Iran by coupling engagement with containment. The two sides began a gradual bilateral engagement with maritime security talks, then expanding to potential cooperation in renewable energy and a memorandum of understanding on environmental security cooperation. Most importantly, as mentioned earlier, the UAE became again a major re-export hub for Iran, providing breathing room to an economy severely under pressure from sanctions. In 2022, the UAE sent its ambassador back to Iran, after he had been withdrawn after the storming of Saudi diplomatic seats in Iran in 2016.

Considering the numerous elements in the multi-dimensional relations between the UAE and Iran, unpacking the UAE leadership's security perceptions vis-à-vis the Islamic Republic is a complex exercise. In Abu Dhabi Iran is certainly perceived as a threat, but of a quintessentially external nature. There is very limited concern that Iran may be challenging the regime's stability from within the Emirates, via the expat or local Shi'a communities. The preoccupation, heightened after the Arab Spring and its aftermath, is with Iran's capability to threaten the stability, identity, borders, and functional integrity of the regional order, and the UAE's position in it. This is inextricably linked to the ambitions of the UAE as a medium-sized regional player. Via its strategic relationship with Saudi Arabia, the UAE played a prominent role in Bahrain, Yemen, and the Qatar crisis; Abu Dhabi also was seen as a force to reckon with in Oman and North and Eastern Africa, and a relevant political interlocutor in Syria, Iraq, Turkey, and Afghanistan. The UAE worked to rebuild a regional order and become a pillar within it, and Iran could threaten this strategy significantly. The Iranian threat as seen in the UAE thus has a clear political and also military dimension, in the form of direct confrontations between the Houthis – considered an Iranian proxy – and the UAE armed forces in Yemen, as well as the threat of ballistic missiles launched against the UAE. Iran remains an external threat, as the UAE feels insulated internally from a lack of socioeconomic and sociopolitical vulnerabilities.

The UAE and tle 'Islamist threat'

The perceptions of the UAE leadership around the Arab Spring were largely impacted by its view of political Islam, particularly as embodied by the Muslim Brotherhood and its affiliates, including al-Islah. The history of the relations between the UAE Government and the Islamists before 2011 is crucial in highlighting the reasons why political Islam was the focus of the UAE's attention after the Arab Spring. At the domestic level, Islamists have been perceived as leveraging the State's vulnerabilities in a way that threatened the integrity and functioning of the UAE Federation and Abu Dhabi's undisputed leadership of it. This alleged agenda is also perceived to be part and parcel of a region-wide strategy, in a full overlap between the regional and domestic domains of security.

As in other GCC countries, many of the teachers recruited for the nascent Emirati schooling systems in the 1960s were Egyptian Brotherhood members fleeing anti-Islamist President Nasser.[49] The society Jamiyyat Al-Islah (Society of Reform) was formed shortly afterwards, in 1974, and has had some kind of existence in the Emirates since.[50] Because the Government intended to use the Islamist group as a bulwark against Arab nationalists – who, in those years, were publicly attacking the legitimacy of the Gulf rulers for their alliance with the West – al-Islah initially received support from some of the UAE leaders, including donations from Dubai's ruler Rashid bin Sa'id al-Maktoum and land from Abu Dhabi's ruler Zayed bin Sultan al-Nahyan.[51] In these early days, al-Islah focused on disseminating conservative Islamic values and arguing against cultural contamination, both from leftist ideologies such as pan-Arabism and, later, western liberalism.[52] Individual affiliates rose through the ranks of the Emirati bureaucracy. Saeed Abdullah Salman, a founding member of the society, was the UAE's first Minister for Housing in 1971, and then Minister of Education and Chancellor of the UAE University in 1979.[53] Another member, Mohammed Abdel-Rahman al-Bakr, became Minister of Justice and Islamic Affairs and Endowments in 1977.[54] Crucially, Sultan bin Kayed al-Qasimi, the same person who would then head the society and be arrested after 2011, was head of the Curriculum Division in the UAE for seven consecutive years, from 1977 to 1983. From such positions of influence, al-Islah managed to have a deep impact on Emirati youth, and it was such a level of influence that attracted the authorities' concerns from the end of the 1980s, as the need to contrast pan-Arabism had become less pressing.

In 1994, the UAE Government replaced members of al-Islah's Board of Directors with Government appointees, and downsized the work of the society's branches in Dubai, Ajman, and Fujairah.[55] The Ras al-Khaimah branch escaped such provisions because of the protection provided by the ruler of the Emirates at the time, Saqr bin Mohamamd al-Qasimi, who was sympathetic to the organisation.[56] The Government wanted to minimise opposition to its plans to turn the UAE into a modern economy largely influenced by western models of multi-culturalism and globalisation, and was alerted by an Egyptian security services investigation claiming that al-Islah had pledged allegiance to the Brotherhood's General Guide in Egypt and its pan-Islamist cause.[57] Since then, senior members of the Abu Dhabi ruling family, including then Crown Prince Mohammed bin Zayed, de facto leader of the country between 2014 and 2022, and his brothers Hamdan bin Zayed (Deputy Prime Minister) and Hazza bin Zayed (State Security Department Director), have consistently referred to al-Islah members as the 'standard bearers for an essentially foreign ideology'.[58]

Additionally, as the UAE authorities have long drawn an ideological connection between the Muslim Brotherhood and jihadi groups, the crackdown on al-Islah worsened in the early 2000s after the 9/11 attacks, when it emerged that two of the nineteen hijackers were Emirati citizens, that more than half of the hijackers flew directly out of Dubai to the United States, and that the UAE banking system had been used by hijackers to launder funds.[59] The events of 9/11 were a true shock for the Emirati leadership as they risked seriously damaging US–UAE relations, with long-lasting potential implications for the UAE's security. Subsequently, the Government boosted a securitarian approach, both against jihadi organisations and against non-violent Islamists. In the early 2000s, over 250 people linked to al-Islah were arrested or removed from their positions within the State institutions or bureaucracy, educational institutions, or civil society organisations.[60]

In a 2004 meeting with US officials, Mohammed bin Zayed noted that 'We are having a (culture) war with the Muslim Brotherhood in this country', referring to the Islamists' use of their opposition to liberalisation to delegitimise the Islamic credentials of the Government.[61] Mohammad bin Zayed, sympathetic to political Islam before being educated at the British military college of Sandhurst, is often described as having a strong personal hostility against political Islam and an inflated perception of its political strength and subversive intent.[62] Such a perception may also be linked to the fact that the bulk of Emirati Brotherhood supporters are located in the northern emirates, where economic inequality with respect to the other emirates is stark, and the average per-capita GDP is less than a third of that in Abu Dhabi.[63] This structural socioeconomic vulnerability provides political ammunition for al-Islah to argue against the effectiveness of Abu Dhabi as the leader of the Federation.[64] Moreover, there were longstanding links between the Emir of the northern emirate of Ras al-Khaimah, Saud bin Saqr al-Qasimi, and the local al-Islah branch. Al-Qasimi had shielded the organisation from the crackdowns of the 1990s and 2000s, even when in direct opposition to and defiance of Abu Dhabi's provisions, and had contacts with symbols of Islamist movements worldwide.[65] Interestingly, many of the signatories of the 2011 petitions belonged to Ras al-Khaimah's largest tribe.[66] These factors amplified Abu Dhabi's leaders already hyper-vigilant perception of al-Islah as targeting the integrity and functioning of the UAE Federation and Abu Dhabi's undisputed leadership of it.

Such longstanding hostility of the Emirati regime towards the Brotherhood mounted between the end of 2011 and 2012, when Brotherhood affiliates tried to seize the political opportunities offered by the Arab Spring. As mentioned, al-Islah members were involved in the dissidence demonstrations in the UAE itself. Al-Islah was labelled as a terrorist organisation, and branches in Dubai, Fujairah, and Ras al-Khaimah were effectively dismantled in

2012.[67] Attorney General Ali Salim al-Tunaiji announced that 'the country's national security was under threat from a group of people with ties to foreign organisations and agendas', a clear reference to the international Muslim Brotherhood.[68] During the GCC National and Regional Security Conference run by the Bahrain Center for Strategic, International, and Energy Studies in January 2012, Dubai police chief General Dahi Khalfan stated: 'The Muslim Brotherhood is a security threat to the Gulf, and is no less dangerous than Iran.'[69]

Once the regime felt it was secure against Islamist opposition domestically, after 2013 it focused on the regional dimension. Abu Dhabi substantially supported on the ground, logistically and financially, anti-Islamist actors all around the region.[70] It focused on countering the Brotherhood's electoral victories in Egypt and Tunisia, and their battlefield victories in Libya, Syria, and Yemen.[71] As mentioned, in 2014 and 2017 Abu Dhabi led the charge against Qatar, perceived as a major sponsor of the Brotherhood. Emirati relations with Turkey, Qatar's closest ally after 2011, deteriorated.[72] This hostility against the Brotherhood relented only with the progressive weakening of the movement regionally: as the Egyptian regime felt confident of having crushed Islamist opposition domestically, Qatar agreed to scale back its support for the organisation after the 2021 al-Ula summit, and Brotherhood-affiliated parties suffered a crushing electoral defeat in Morocco and were ostracised from political life during a soft coup that same year by Tunisian President Kais Saied, supported by Riyadh and Abu Dhabi.[73] In this context, the UAE also sought de-escalation with Turkey, with Mohammad bin Zayed announcing a \$10 billion fund for investing in Turkey during a high-level meeting with Turkish President Recep Tayyip Erdoğan in November 2021.[74]

The full-scale response and harsh rhetoric of the UAE Government towards domestic Islamist dissent, and the unprecedented level of UAE engagement in countering Brotherhood expansion regionally, show the strict interrelation between the domestic and regional level in the Emirati leadership's perception of security, viewing political Islam as a proper intermestic threat after 2011: a threat originating from – and linked to – the regional Muslim Brotherhood, but with an internal relevance. This threat perception has a clear-cut political dimension, as the Brotherhood was treated as posing a direct danger to the regime's stability until at least 2013. While the scarcity of supporters in the UAE and the tough repressive response of the Government would suggest that al-Islah is hardly capable of threatening the existence of the State, al-Islah was thought to be capable of exploiting what could arguably be the country's main sociopolitical and socioeconomic vulnerabilities, the unequal balance of power amongst the seven emirates. The anti-modernisation, anti-globalisation, and anti-westernisation stances of al-Islah add an economic and social dimension to the threat perceived, as even a relative empowerment could be damaging to the UAE's globalised economy – in particular for Dubai, whose wealth largely depends on its internationalisation – while Islamist conservative ideology could potentially disrupt social cohesiveness by pitting more conservative Emiratis against the more globalised local elites.[75] The Emirati regime saw the same threats as relevant to the regional order it sought to create – and, to a certain extent, lead – after 2011. The political, economic, and societal characteristics of this order were directly in opposition to the model offered and pursued by Islamists in the region. Countering the Brotherhood until its regional project ceased to be a credible alternative was thus a priority in the UAE's security calculus for the ten years following the Arab Spring.

The UAE's security priorities after 2011

At their core, the UAE's security priorities after 2011 were about pursuing a stable regional order, with the UAE at its core, in the face of major ideological forces sweeping through the region. In order to do that, the Emirati regime focused on its key latent sociopolitical vulnerability: preserving the unity of the seven emirates' Federation.

When the UAE was formed in 1971, the leaders of the seven emirates of Abu Dhabi, Ajman, Dubai, Fujairah, Ras al-Khaimah, Sharjah, and Umm al-Quwain had to overcome numerous challenges to the difficult task of unifying the state.[76] It took two decades for the military to unify and for Abu Dhabi to become the official capital.[77] The emirates have distinct ruling families such as the al-Nahyan (Abu Dhabi), the al-Maktoum (Dubai), the al-Qasimi (Sharjah and Ras al-Khaimah), the al-Nuaimi (Ajman), the al-Mu'alla (Umm Al Quwain), and the al-Sharqi (Fujairah). Formally, the UAE's highest constitutional authority is the Federal Supreme Council, where each ruler has one vote, as ruling families hesitate to surrender power or autonomy. In fact, the actual political weight of the seven rulers has been profoundly divergent. The inequality in the distribution of power mirrors the vast inequality in the distribution of wealth. In the face of a chronic lack of reliable statistics, which also highlights the sensitivity of the issue, regional affairs scholar David Roberts has calculated that in the period from 2004 to 2014, Abu Dhabi, holding the vast majority of the UAE's oil and gas reserves, accounted for an average of 55.9 per cent of the state's GDP; Dubai contributed 28.6 per cent; Sharjah 4.7 per cent; and the northern emirates respectively 1.7 per cent (Ras al-Khaimah), 1 per cent (Ajman), 0.6 per cent (Fujairah), and 0.2 per cent (Umm al-Quwain).[78] Indeed, the northern emirates have struggled consistently with issues of unemployment as well as water and power outages, unknown in Abu Dhabi, which, in turn, has long been subsidising them.[79] This socioeconomic inequality may also be one of the biggest vulnerabilities of the Federation. In 2011 dissent was more widespread in the northern emirates than in any other area of the UAE. Indeed, the Government issued a $1.5 billion investment package specifically dedicated to the area, intended to tackle potential causes for animosity against the capital.[80] Abu Dhabi increased its outreach to northern emirates youth to have them employed as staff in the federal institutions, including the army and other security forces, where nationalism is more naturally strengthened, in a way further centralising loyalties towards Abu Dhabi as the leader of the Federation. Abu Dhabi's bailout of Dubai after the 2008 global economic collapse came with the decrease of the latter's political clout, depriving the Federation of a second political pole.[81] Dubai's economy, dependent on being a regional hub for trade and investments, was further dented by the intra-GCC crises, the scaling back of business with Iran under US maximum pressure, and the COVID-19 pandemic. Amid the twin impact of the pandemic and the oil price collapse in 2020, overall GDP growth in the UAE touched a negative record of –6.1 per cent; while falling oil revenues curtailed sectors such as real estate and construction, which still rely on public funding, sanitary restrictions heavily affected transportation, logistics, and tourism.[82] In response, the authorities provided credit lines and fiscal packages for $8.7 billion.[83] Skyrocketing energy prices after the 2022 Russian invasion of Ukraine played a significant role in absorbing the financial shock but, once again, these benefited Abu Dhabi more than Dubai, where most of the GDP is not derived from energy. In fact, Abu Dhabi had to roll over the 2009 bailout extended to Dubai twice – in 2014 and 2019 – and Dubai's political influence continued to diminish.[84] Abu Dhabi's prominence was enhanced when Mohammad bin Zayed became President of the UAE in May 2022, following the death of his brother, Khalifa bin Zayed. Mohammed bin Zayed had been the UAE's de facto ruler since his brother had suffered a stroke in 2014, but his confirmation in the UAE's highest office by the Supreme Federal Council eliminated potential bureaucratic restraints to his large-scale ambitions. This de-federalisation and hyper-centralisation also further closed space for dissenting views on regional politics, which had always existed within the UAE. In the context of the Iran–Iraq War, while the UAE officially remained neutral, Ras al-Khaimah, Ajman, Fujairah, and Abu Dhabi had already sided with Iraq, whereas Dubai, Sharjah, and Umm al-Quwain were sympathetic to Iran.[85] As mentioned earlier, Dubai maintained a pragmatic economic engagement with Iran until at least 2008, when it gradually converged on Abu Dhabi's positions.[86] Intra-Emirates divergences emerged, behind closed doors, also in the context of Islamists and the Qatar crisis: while Ras al-Khaimah refused to consider the Muslim Brotherhood threat grave enough to open a deep intra-GCC crisis, Dubai and Fujairah complained about the economic costs of the crisis.[87] Further divergences emerged on the decision to open a military front in Yemen: while the ruler of Dubai disapproved the potential negative impacts on regional stability, the rulers of the northern emirates complained that they had not been consulted by Abu Dhabi before committing troops to the war, notwithstanding the fact that their citizens filled the front lines and accounted for most of the war's casualties.[88] In this context, the defection in 2018 of a son of the ruler of Fujairah to Qatar brought to the surface the suggestion of pushback against Abu Dhabi among the northern emirates.[89]

Internal cohesion and unity of intent are treated as priorities by the Emirati regime because they are fundamental to implementing its vision for a regional order that gravitates away from pan-Arabism and pan-Islamism and towards a Westphalian network-based model.[90] The Emirati regime long worked to promote the nation-state model and nationalism through a renewed emphasis on symbolism, for instance through the large-scale exhibition of national sentiment during national holidays and the building of new national monuments, as well as through more traditional nation-building instruments such as conscription.[91] In 2014 Abu Dhabi introduced compulsory conscription, requiring men aged between eighteen and thirty to serve between nine months and two years depending on their educational level, and inaugurated women's voluntary enrolment for twelve-month terms in 2016.[92] This focus should be read against the backdrop of a heightened Emirati perception of threat vis-à-vis transnational political ideologies contesting the state-based model, or the institutions, regime, and borders of established states. These naturally include radical jihadist ideologies such as Daesh, as well as the Brotherhood, which, in the words of UAE Foreign Minister Abdullah bin Zayed, 'does not believe in the sovereignty of the state'.[93] Interestingly, this also applies, in the perceptions of the Emirati regime, to Iran's Khomeinism.[94] Abu Dhabi's ultimate aspiration is to engage with Iran at a state-to-state level, and its ultimate concern is that it sees Iran's Supreme Leader to be behaving 'not like a state leader but a representative of God who is above the nation-state order'.[95]

The UAE instead sees the networked world order with states as units as a framework for its own economic and political success, especially in a multipolar world. The Emirati leadership imagined the post-oil future of the UAE as its becoming a hub for East–West connectivity in all domains.[96] Amid US retrenchment from the Gulf and the wider MENA region, the UAE worked to diversify its regional and international partnerships, including with other global powers such as Russia and China. This strategy of extreme hedging has given the UAE the confidence to refuse to align with the USA amid the 2022 Russian invasion of Ukraine, as well as amid rising tensions with China over Taiwan. This strategy was enabled by the shrinking down of Emirati threat perceptions, which fuelled a sense of adventurism that consistently increased in the ten years following the Arab Spring.

Notes

1 Ingo Forstenlechner, Emilie Rutledge, and Rashed Salem Alnuaimi, 'The UAE, the "Arab Spring" and Different Types of Dissent', *Middle East Policy* 19:4 (2012), 54–67.

2 Courtney Freer, 'Rentier Islamism in the Absence of Elections: The Political Role of Muslim Brotherhood Affiliates in Qatar and the United Arab Emirates', *International Journal of Middle East Studies* 49:3 (2017), 379–500 (492).

3 The petition, sent via courier and posted publicly online after receiving no response for two days, is available at www.ipetitions.com/petition/uaepetitio n71/ (accessed 23 August 2022).

4 'Five Jailed UAE Activists "Receive Presidential Pardon"', BBC, 28 November 2011, www.bbc.co.uk/news/world-middle-east-15922492 (accessed 23 August 2022).

5 Simon Kerr, 'Jailing of UAE Dissenter Prompts Outcry by Rights Groups', *Financial Times*, 31 May 2012, www.ft.com/content/3a6c30b6-64e2-11e8-90c2-9563a0613e56 (accessed 23 August 2022).

6 Al-Zo'by and Birol Başkan, 'Discourse and Oppositionality'.

7 Abdullah Al-Rashid, 'The Brothers and the Emirates', *Majalla*, 14 February 2013, https://eng.majalla.com/2013/02/article55238281/the-brothers-and-the-emirates (accessed 23 August 2022).

8 'UAE Islamists Convicted for Plotting Government Coup', BBC, 2 July 2013, www.bbc.co.uk/news/world-middle-east-23142248 (accessed 23 August 2022).

9 Courtney Freer, *Rentier Islamism: The Influence of the Muslim Brotherhood in Gulf Monarchies* (Oxford: Oxford University Press, 2018), 104.

10 Simon Kerr, 'UAE Islamist Detained in Ruler's Palace', *Financial Times*, 25 April 2012, www.ft.com/content/f6aaa4cc-8e9e-11e1-ac13–00144feab49a (accessed 23 August 2022).

11 Interview by the author of an Emirati official from the Ministry of Foreign Affairs, London, 18 August 2017.

12 Ehteshami and Wright, *Reform in the Middle East Oil Monarchies*.

13 *Ibid.*

14 Sean Foley, 'The UAE: Political Issues and Security Dilemmas', *Middle East Review of International Affairs* 3:1 (1999), 25–45 (26).

15 Freer, *Rentier Islamism*.

16 Interview by the author of an Emirati diplomat, London, 3 October 2018.

17 This point is thoroughly proven by Courtney Freer in *Rentier Islamism*.

18 Interview by the author of a senior Emirati diplomatic advisor, Dubai, 27 February 2020.

19 Roberts, 'Qatar and the UAE'.

20 *Ibid.*

21 Davidson, 'The UAE, Qatar, and the Question of Political Islam'.

22 Hussein Ibish, 'The UAE's Evolving National Security Strategy', Arab Gulf States Institute in Washington, 6 April 2017, www.agsiw.org/wp-content/uploads/2017/04/UAE-Security_ONLINE.pdf (accessed 23 August 2022).

23 Interview by the author of an Emirati diplomat, London, 3 October 2018.

24 'UAE Shi'a and Their Loyalties', *Wikileaks*, 15 April 2016, https://wikileaks.org/plusd/cables/06ABUDHABI1471_a.html (accessed 23 August 2022).

25 Ahmad Khalid Majidyar, 'Is Sectarian Balance in the United Arab Emirates, Oman, and Qatar at Risk?', American Enterprise Institute, 21 October 2013, https://www.aei.org/research-products/report/is-sectarian-balance-in-the-united-arab-emirates-oman-and-qatar-at-risk/ (accessed 17 September 2022).

26 Christopher Davidson, 'Sunni–Shiite Hostility: The UAE Suggests Otherwise', *Daily Star*, 4 August 2008.

27 'Marasem-e Tasua-i Husseini dar Emaraat Bargozar Shod' (Tasua (Ninth of Muharram) Ceremonies for Hussein Were Held in Emirates), Fars News Agency, 5 December 2011, www.farsnews.com/newstext.php?nn=13900914000289 (accessed 23 August 2022).

28 Kenneth Katzman, 'The United Arab Emirates (UAE): Issues for US Policy', Congressional Research Service, Washington, DC (2016), https://sgp.fas.org/crs/mideast/RS21852.pdf (accessed 2 August 2023).

29 'UAE Shi'a and Their Loyalties'.

30 *Ibid.*

31 Dan Caldwell. 'Flashpoints in the Gulf: Abu Musa and the Tunb Islands', *Middle East Policy* 4:3 (1996), 50–57.

32 Christopher Davidson, 'The United Arab Emirates', in Davidson, *Power and Politics*, 10.

33 Caldwell, 'Flashpoints in the Gulf'.

34 'UAE Must Know that Iran's Sovereignty over Persian Gulf Islands "Non-Negotiable"', *Real Iran*, 3 December 2017, http://realiran.org/uae-must-know-that-irans-sovereignty-over-persian-gulf-islands-non-negotiable/ (accessed 23 August 2022).

35 Interview by the author of a senior professor at the National Defence College of the United Arab Emirates, Abu Dhabi, 16 April 2018.

36 Stephanie Cronin and Nur Masalha, 'The Islamic Republic of Iran and the GCC States: Revolution to Realpolitik?', Kuwait Programme on Development, Governance and Globalisation in the Gulf States, London School of Economics and Political Science, Research Paper 17 (2011), 27.

37 'Abu Dhabi Crown Prince Warns DOE DepSec Poneman about Iran', WikiLeaks, 17 December 2009, http://wikileaks.org/cable/2009/12/09ABUDHABI1151.html (accessed 23 August 2022).

38 A senior professor at the National Defence College of the United Arab Emirates, interviewed by the author in Abu Dhabi on 16 April 2018, argued: 'The UAE is in Yemen because Iran is in Yemen.'

39 Quoted in Shahram Akbarzadeh, 'Iran and the Gulf Cooperation Council Sheikhdoms', in Almezaini and Rickli, *The Small Gulf States*, 110.

40 Dazi-Héni, 'The Gulf States and Israel'.

41 Giorgio Cafiero and Joshua Hodge, 'The Saudi–Iranian Rivalry and the Gulf Littoral States', *LobeLog*, 22 June 2016, https://lobelog.com/the-saudi-iranian-rivalry-and-the-gulf-littoral-states/ (accessed 23 August 2022).

42 *Ibid.*

43 Quoted in *ibid.*

44 Karim Sadjadpour, 'The Battle of Dubai: The United Arab Emirates and the US–Iran Cold War', Carnegie Endowment for International Peace (2011), https://carnegieendowment.org/files/dubai_iran.pdf (accessed 23 July 2023).

45 Benoit Faucon, 'UAE Trade Provides Iran with Western Goods, from Perfume to Laptops', *Wall Street Journal*, 5 July 2022, www.wsj.com/articles/u-a-e-trade-provides-iran-with-western-goods-from-perfume-to-laptops-11657048 268 (accessed 11 August 2022).

46 *Ibid.*

47 Interview by the author of a senior Emirati expert at a local think tank, Abu Dhabi, 31 May 2022.

48 Interview by the author of a senior Emirati professor of political science, Dubai, 31 May 2022.

49 Kristian Ulrichsen, *The United Arab Emirates: Power, Politics and Policy-Making* (London: Routledge, 2016), 73.

50 *Ibid.*, 74.

51 See for instance Freer, *Rentier Islamism*.

52 *Ibid.*

53 Ulrichsen, *The United Arab Emirates*, 75.

54 *Ibid.*

55 Mansur al-Noqaidan, 'Al-Ikhwan al-Muslimun fi al-Imarat: Al-Tamaddad wa-l-Inhisar' (The Muslim Brotherhood in the Emirates: Expansion and Decline), in Al-Mesbar Studies and Research Centre (ed.), *Al-Ikhwan al-Muslimun fi al Khalij* (*The Muslim Brotherhood in the Gulf*) (Dubai: Al-Mesbar Studies and Research Centre, 2012), 80.

56 *Ibid.*

57 Interview with Dr Ebtesam al-Ketbi quoted in Freer, *Rentier Islamism*, 493.

58 'UAE Minimizing Influence of Islamic Extremists', Wikileaks, 10 November 2004, https://wikileaks.org/plusd/cables/04ABUDHABI4061_a.html (accessed 11 August 2022).

59 Ibish, 'The UAE's Evolving National Security Strategy'.

60 Ulrichsen, *The United Arab Emirates*, 77.

61 'UAE Minimizing Influence of Islamic Extremists'.

62 Roberts, 'Mosque and State'.

63 The argument that the internal inequalities in the balance of political and economic power in the Emirates make the poorer Emirates more vulnerable to Islamist rhetoric is convincingly made in Roberts, 'Qatar and the UAE'.

64 Al-Zo'by and Başkan, 'Discourse and Oppositionality'.

65 Yara Bayoumy, 'UAE Islamist Group Had No Desire to Topple Government: Families', Reuters, 2 July 2013, www.reuters.com/article/us-emirates-trial-islah-idUSBRE9610PT20130702 (accessed 11 August 2022).

66 Lori Plotkin Boghardt, 'The Muslim Brotherhood on Trial in the UAE', Washington Institute for Near East Policy, 12 April 2013, www.washingt oninstitute.org/policy-analysis/muslim-brotherhood-trial-uae (accessed 17 September 2022).

67 Freer, *Rentier Islamism*, 490.

68 Quoted in Ian Black, 'Emirati Nerves Rattled by Islamists' Rise', *Guardian*, 12 October 2012, www.theguardian.com/world/on-the-middle-east/2012/oct/12/uae-muslimbrotherhood-egypt-arabspring (accessed 11 August 2022).

69 Quoted in 'Dubai Police Chief Warns of Muslim Brotherhood, Iran Threat', Reuters, 26 July 2012, www.reuters.com/article/us-emirates-police-brotherh ood/dubai-police-chief-warns-of-muslim-brotherhood-iran-threat (accessed 11 August 2022).

70 Roberts, 'Qatar and the UAE'.

71 Khalil Al-Anani, 'Islamist Parties Post-Arab Spring', *Mediterranean Politics* 17:3 (2012), 466–472.

72 Vohar, 'Erdoğan's War'.

73 Burgat, 'Is the Era of Islamists Coming to an End?'.

74 Galip Dalay, 'Turkey–UAE Relations: Economic Cooperation against the Backdrop of Geopolitical Incompatibility', *SWP Comment* 1 (2022), www. swp-berlin.org/10.18449/2022C01/ (accessed 2 August 2023).

75 Jim Krane, *City of Gold: Dubai and the Dream of Capitalism* (London: Macmillan, 2009).

76 Ulrichsen, *The United Arab Emirates*.

77 *Ibid.*

78 Data quoted from Roberts, 'Qatar and the UAE', 551.

79 Shaimaa Fayed, 'Arab Unrest Puts Focus on UAE's Northern Emirates', Reuters, 6 July 2011, https://reut.rs/2fos6Dj (accessed 11 August 2022).

80 Simeon Kerr, 'UAE Offers Poorer Emirates $1.5bn', *Financial Times*, 2 March 2011, https://on.ft.com/2fpe8ky (accessed 11 August 2022); interview by the author of a senior professor at the National Defence College of the United Arab Emirates, Abu Dhabi, 16 April 2018.

81 Sadjadpour, 'The Battle of Dubai'.

82 'United Arab Emirates', MPO report, World Bank Group (2021), https:// thedocs.worldbank.org/en/doc/5bae5632e2d8425830fbf0bac721cce3-028 0012021/original/17-mpo-sm21-united-arab-emirates-kcm3.pdf (accessed 7 August 2023).

83 World Bank Group, 'COVID-19 Pandemic and the Road to Diversification'.

84 Stanley Carvalho and Davide Barbuscia, 'Exclusive: Abu Dhabi Expected to Extend Bailout Loan to Dubai, Sources Say', Reuters, www.reuters.com/article/us-dubai-debt-exclusive-idUSKCN1PU1HU (accessed 11 August 2022).

85 Christopher Davidson, *The United Arab Emirates: A Study in Survival* (Boulder, CO: Lynne Rienner, 2006), 206.

86 Sadjadpour, 'The Battle of Dubai'.
87 Interview by the author of a professor of international relations, Abu Dhabi, 17 April 2018.
88 *Ibid.*
89 David Kirkpatrick, 'Emirati Prince Flees to Qatar, Exposing Tensions in UAE', *New York Times*, 14 July 2018, www.nytimes.com/2018/07/14/world/middleeast/emirati-prince-qatar-defects.html (accessed 11 August 2022).
90 Matthew Hedges, *Reinventing the Sheikhdom: Clan, Power and Patronage in Mohammed bin Zayed's UAE* (Oxford: Oxford University Press, 2022).
91 Victor Gervais, 'Du pétrole à l'armée: Les stratégies de construction de l'état aux Emirats Arabes Unis', Ph.D. dissertation (Institut de recherche stratégique de l'Ecole militaire, Paris, 2011), 221–253.
92 *Ibid.*
93 Quoted in 'Gulf States Must Tackle Muslim Brotherhood Threat: UAE', Reuters, 8 October 2012, www.reuters.com/article/us-emirates-brotherhood/gulf-states-must-tackle-muslim-brotherhood-threat-uae-idUSBRE8970SD20121008 (accessed 11 August 2022).
94 Samuel Helfont, 'The Muslim Brotherhood and the Emerging "Shia Crescent"', *Orbis* 53:2 (2009), 284–299.
95 Interview by the author of a senior Emirati professor of political science, Dubai, 31 May 2022.
96 Mohammed Baharoon, 'The Keys to Reading the UAE's Strategic Map', Middle East Institute, 5 April 2022, www.mei.edu/publications/keys-reading-uaes-strategic-map (accessed 11 August 2022).

Part II

Kuwait and Oman: Hedging between
security and stability

6

Kuwait

The impact of the Arab Spring

There were two parallel but separate tracks to the Arab Spring in Kuwait, driven by different sociopolitical groups and motivated by different grievances. However, the most significant factor was that both protest tracks centred around the reform of Kuwaiti institutions, rather than the overthrow of the regime.

The first track was centred around the *bidoons*. Estimated to be around 120,000 in number, the bidoons – Arabic for 'without'– are residents with no citizenship and political rights and no access to public services or the generous welfare granted to Kuwaiti citizens.[1] From February 2011, bidoons started protesting this second-class status in Jahra and Sulaibiya, the impoverished northern periphery of Kuwait City, where many reside.[2] The demonstrations continued for almost a year and culminated in large-scale rallies in Jahra and Sulaibiya in January 2012.[3] The Government resorted to draconian measures: the Interior Minister Sheikh Ahmad al-Humud al-Sabah announced that the bidoons who took part in the protests might be deported, suffering the confiscation of their only form of identification and the cancellation of their applications for Kuwaiti nationality, coercing them into scaling the movement.[4] Following the adoption of these measures, the bidoons scaled back their protest movement in February 2012.[5] However, they persisted with smaller acts of protest, such as a hunger strike in 2022 that lasted for weeks.[6]

In parallel, a large and diverse coalition of Kuwaitis, involving youth groups of liberal persuasion and the Islamist parliamentary opposition, had taken to the streets to protest the elite's corruption and abuse of power in the manipulation of the parliamentary system in March 2011.[7] Protests escalated amid the eruption of a scandal in September 2011 when it was alleged that Prime Minister Nasser Mohammed al-Sabah had deposited close to $350 million (1.28 billion dirham) in public funds into the personal bank accounts of fifteen MPs in order to secure their votes on crucial issues.[8] On the night of 16 November 2011, hundreds of protesters, led by opposition lawmakers, stormed the building of the National Assembly in a brief raid.[9] This prompted the resignation of the controversial Prime Minister followed by new elections in 2012, in which the opposition, especially tribal Islamists, gained an unprecedented majority.[10] When the Constitutional Court declared those elections invalid and reinstated the previous Parliament originally elected in 2009, which included more Government supporters, people took to the streets in the largest demonstration in Kuwaiti history.[11] The authorities cracked down heavily on the protest, and Parliament was dissolved again. The first phase of this second track of the Kuwaiti Arab Spring slowly wound down.[12]

The events of 2011 uncovered several sociopolitical and socioeconomic vulnerabilities in Kuwait against which the regime filtered its own security perceptions in the ten years after the Arab Spring. First, given the prominent role of the tribal Islamist opposition, the events of 2011 aggravated a longstanding, deep fault line – and sociopolitical vulnerability – within Kuwait's national fabric: that between the *Hadhar* (urban people – those whose forefathers lived in Kuwait before the advent of the oil era in 1946) and the *Badu* (tribespeople – from among whom immigrants were naturalised between 1965 and 1981).[13] The Badu (or tribal) community – which represented the single youngest and largest group among Kuwaiti nationals and had been engaged in an escalation with the Government since the 2000s – were identified as actors in creating instability in the Government's threat perception.[14]

Secondly, the harsh crackdown on the bidoons, together with the Government's hesitant and inconclusive policy response to their grievances, exposed the magnitude of the sociopolitical and socioeconomic vulnerabilities that the community embodies.[15] The bidoons attempted to underline their nationalism and allegiance to Kuwait's Emir by 'clutching pictures of the Emir as they protested'.[16] However, from the regime's perspective, their demands were perceived as threatening. In a country of 1.2 million citizens, adding around 100,000 citizens, with all their subsidies and welfare entitlements, could take a toll on the public finance, and most importantly could alter the delicate balance of the national fabric and the political equilibrium in elected institutions. Jahra, an area populated by both bidoons and tribes, is already the largest electoral district in the country.[17]

Crucially, the Kuwaiti political system offered effective avenues to channel grievances, in a way guaranteeing its own resilience.[18] In fact, the 2011 protests cannot be singled out from a much longer tradition of political movements, meant to counterbalance the power of the royal family, that included the larger-scale Orange Movement in 2006.[19] In addition, widespread hostility towards the Prime Minister Nasser Mohammad, who survived six impeachment attempts between 2006 and 2011, should also be factored in. At least since 2009, when he had become the target of a campaign named Irhal (Leave), the Prime Minister had attracted allegations of corruption. He was also targeted by the Islamist-leaning opposition, including the political society close to the Muslim Brotherhood (Hadas), who saw him as too complacent towards Iran, and too close to the MPs representing Kuwait's Shi'a communities in the National Assembly, who were amongst the few supporting the Government in 2011.[20] Corruption suspicions were aggravated by the dissatisfaction of citizens with the pace of socioeconomic development in the country and the deterioration of public services, notwithstanding the high average standard of living.[21] In spite of a period of high oil prices from the early 2000s, the building of infrastructures, such as a new hospital, had been stalled for several years, tens of thousands of families had long been on a waiting list for housing, and power cuts in some poorer suburbs of the capital were common in the hot summer days.[22]

Overall, the Kuwaiti regime had a double perception of the Arab Spring. The domestic political turbulences were seen as evidence of serious structural vulnerabilities in the country, but were treated as internal matters that could be channelled and addressed via existing mechanisms. What triggered a more severe concern was the regional impact of the Arab Spring, which deepened the fault lines around sectarianism and Islamism and pushed regional powers into more open confrontation. For the ten years following 2011, the Kuwaiti regime remained very alert to how these fault lines could destabilise countries in the region, especially those closer to Kuwait: Iraq, Saudi Arabia, and Iran. For this reason, Kuwait focused on mediating the two intra-GCC crises of 2014 and 2017 and attempted de-escalation with Iran after 2015, deprioritising the actors identified as threats by Saudi Arabia, the UAE, and Bahrain in the Riyadh Agreements. Even under new leadership, as Emir Nawaf al-Ahmad al-Sabah succeeded his brother Sabah after the latter's death in September 2020, Kuwait continued to play a balancing act regionally. Kuwaiti efforts were crucial in facilitating the reconciliation with Qatar at the al-Ula Summit in January 2021, and Kuwait engaged in energy and environmental diplomacy with Iran in 2022. This posture is driven by the leadership's belief that, given its diverse national fabric and its history of invasion, polarisation of regional politics is the single major threat for Kuwait. This focus on regional politics, however, led the leadership to neglect its internal vulnerabilities, which resurfaced overwhelmingly in the context of the COVID-19 pandemic and the fragile leadership transition of 2020.

Kuwait and the 'Shi'a threat'

The Kuwaiti Shi'a communities, which include prominent merchant families owning large conglomerates – for example Al Kazemi International, Marafie Group, and Morad Yousuf Behbehani Group – were historically included in local politics.[23] Kuwaiti Shi'a MPs had sat in the National Assembly since the first elections in 1963 and, for the most part, built coalitions with the ruling family.[24] Shi'a MPs supported the al-Sabah family in confronting the rising influence of Arab nationalists and the IRGC's attempt to export the Islamic Revolution to Kuwait after 1979.[25] At the same time, Shi'a radical groups, such as the followers of Iraqi cleric Mohammed Mahdi al-Shirazi, the Shiraziyyun, joined that Islamic upheaval and were met with a full regime crackdown.[26] Relations between the authorities and the Shi'a communities worsened with the Iran–Iraq war, when Kuwait supported the Iraqi regime with about $15 billion in aid and the transfer of US missiles, and Iran supported transnational Shi'a groups, such as Islamic Jihad, to carry on attacks in Kuwait and make an attempt on the life of the then Emir, Jabir al-Ahmad, in 1985.[27] In the late 1980s, Iranian missiles were launched at Kuwaiti targets, including tankers and oil ports, pushing Kuwait to expel Iranian diplomats and negotiate with international powers the reflagging of its tankers.[28] Iraq's 1990 invasion of Kuwait changed the calculus again, as Iran sided with Kuwait, and Kuwaiti Shi'a actively participated in the fight against Iraqi forces.[29] After the 1990 invasion, Kuwaitis, including the Shi'a communities, united behind the al-Sabah and against an external threat.

Under the reformist presidency of Mohammad Khatami, relations between Kuwait and Iran entered a constructive phase, signposted by the 2003 security cooperation treaty on smuggling and piracy and the 2007 memorandum of understanding on cooperation in the political, economic, social, security, cultural, and scientific arenas.[30] The security landscape at the domestic level in Kuwait was stable, although the political scene remained heated, as one of the alleged masterminds of the earlier string of terrorist attacks in Kuwait, known as Abu Mahdi al-Muhandis, reappeared as the leader of Kata'eb Hezbollah. This was the main proxy of the IRGC's elite Quds Force, formed in 2004 to be the Hezbollah of post-Saddam Iraq and the Gulf.[31] Another group, al-Tahaluf al-Islami al-Watani (the Islamic National Alliance), openly identifying as followers of Ayatollah Khamenei, emerged to become the most influential Shi'a group in Kuwaiti politics.[32] In 2006, the Emir appointed Nasser Mohammed as the country's Prime Minister. A former ambassador to Iran, the PM built a coalition with Shi'a political groups to offset Sunni and tribal political groups that had increasingly become oppositional towards both the Government and the Shi'a communities.[33] This alliance with the regime was convenient for the Shi'a communities, seeking protection from growing sectarian hostility triggered off the back of the 2003 Iraq war. Indeed, Shi'a MPs did not join the mobilisation of reformist groups after 2009, supported the Prime Minister in the various grillings he faced between 2008 and 2011, and sat out the entire Arab Spring.[34] This loyalty, in turn, helped inform the perceptions of the leadership on the lack of a Shi'a threat from within the country.[35]

Following the election of moderate Hassan Rouhani as Iranian President in June 2013 and the subsequent signing of the interim nuclear deal the following year, Kuwait's Emir Sabah al-Sabah went on an official visit to Tehran in June 2014, even before the JCPOA was signed, meeting with the country's Supreme Leader, Ayatollah Ali Khamenei, and the President. It was the first visit by any Kuwaiti Emir since the 1979 Iranian revolution, and the official news agency of Kuwait published a joint statement calling the meeting 'an important turning point in the relations between the two countries'.[36] Kuwait then chose not to join Saudi Arabia and Bahrain in cutting off diplomatic relations with Iran after the assaults on the Saudi diplomatic missions in Tehran and Mashhad that took place amid the execution of Saudi Shi'a cleric Nimr al-Nimr in 2016, but downgraded its representation.[37] In 2017 Kuwait's Foreign Minister, Sabah al-Khaled al-Sabah, visId Tehran carrying a letter from Emir Sabah to President Rouhani that sought to establish the 'basis for dialogue' between the GCC and Iran.[38] To that end, Kuwait exerted efforts to negotiate between the warring parties in Yemen: althought it was part of the Saudi-led coalition in Yemen, Kuwait's role remained non-combative, and focused on negotiations.[39] Amid weak economic ties, Kuwait sought to strengthen trade in gas and fresh water with Iran.[40] This approach persisted even under a new leadership – as Emir Nawaf al-Ahmad al-Sabah succeeded his brother Sabah following the latter's death in September 2020 – and after the 2021 election of a hardliner principlist government in Iran, led by Ebrahim Raisi. In 2022, Kuwait and Iran signed a memorandum of understanding to tackle sandstorms jointly, and Kuwait invited Iran to discuss management of the offshore Dorra/Arash gas field, in case of a revival of the JCPOA.[41] That same year, Kuwait sent its ambassador back to Iran, his having previously been withdrawn after the storming of Saudi diplomatic seats in Iran in 2016.

A string of events between 2015 and 2017 shook this de-escalatory course but failed to torpedo it. In August 2015 Kuwait's security forces discovered a large cache of weapons hidden on a farm in Abdali on the Kuwait–Iraq border.[42] Twenty-five Kuwaiti Shi'a – some with ties to the Islamic National Alliance – were arrested on charges of 'spying for the Islamic Republic of Iran and Hezbollah to carry out aggressive acts against the State of Kuwait'.[43] In 2017, Kuwait's Supreme Court confirmed the involvement of Iran's IRGC and the Lebanese Hezbollah, and the Kuwaiti Government expelled fifteen

Iranian diplomats.[44] From the Government's viewpoint, the Abdali affair had 'recalled memories of the 1980s, but not eclipsed the fact that Kuwaiti Shi'a have most often been nationalistic and loyal to the ruling family'.[45] In the same year as the Abdali affair, 2015, a Daesh cell perpetrated one of the bloodiest Ittacks in the country's history, killing twenty-seven people and wounding 227, in the historic Shi'a mosque Imam Sadiq in Kuwait City.[46] In July 2016, the Interior Ministry announced that security forces had thwarted 'a number of [Daesh] plots targeting Kuwait', including a new plot against another Shi'a mosque.[47] The attacks against Shi'a targets in Kuwait were part of a specific sectarian strategy, to elicit a violent response from Shi'a violent groups and disrupt the regime's control over security and stability in the country. While the Kuwaiti regime has, at times, played a sectarian-flavoured political game of divide-and-rule, open sectarian conflict is perceived as an existential attack on the regime's stability, its diverse sectarian identity, and the functional integrity of its institutions.[48] The risk was considered so serious that thirty minutes after the attack, the Emir, Sabah al-Ahmad, visited the scene. In the following days, prayers were held in both Sunni and Shi'a mosques to commemorate the dead. The fact that, as early as 2012, Kuwait had passed laws that criminalise hate speeches, the defamation of religion, and sectarian discrimination, is testament to how crucial it is to prevent the outburst of sectarian conflict in the country.[49]

Overall, keeping in mind the history of positive interaction between Shi'a MPs and the Kuwaiti leadership, the sporadic nature of violent opposition from the fringes of the Kuwaiti Shi'a communities, and the sustained attempt by the Kuwaiti leadership to engage with the Iranian gGovernment, it seems a fair assessment that since 2011 Iran has not been perceived by the Kuwaiti regime as a full-fledged threat against its identity and stability, or the functional integrity of its borders and institutions. A Shi'a politician interviewed in Kuwait stated: 'Iranian-backed Shi'a groups are a minority in the communities and there is no indication that they are perceived as having the intent or the capacity to threaten the regime's existence. Certainly they don't have the support of the political leaders of the Shi'a communities, the MPs.'[50] The fact that Shi'a communities in Kuwait have traditionally played a significant role in the country's politics testifies to a lack of institutionalised marginalisation or, as this book calls it, sociopolitical vulnerability. While there is some sectarianism at the social level, there is very little at a government level, and Shi'a Kuwaitis have held very high-level positions in the country. In fact, Ali al-Mu'min went from being the military's Chief of Staff to being nominated the Kuwaiti ambassador to Iraq. Mohammed Abul-Hassan, the former Minister of Information, was known to be one of the closest advisors to Emir Sabah. At the same time, the issues of clandestine cells, such as the Abdali cell, as well as past instances of sympathies for insurgency, cannot be eclipsed, given how the Shi'a communities represent a consistent and largely politicised group. These elements underpin the Kuwaiti regime's perceptions of Iran and the 'Shi'a threat' in the period 2011–2021 as an acute intermestic risk.

Kuwait and the 'Islamist threat'

In Kuwait, branches of the Muslim Brotherhood have existed since individual members of the Egyptian organisation escaped prosecution by Egyptian President Gamal Abd al-Nasser.[51] As elsewhere, the Brotherhood first established a social arm, Islah (or the Social Reform Association), in 1951. The Muslim Brotherhood enjoyed political support and even financial assistance from the Government in the period between the 1960s and the 1980s, since it was seen as a bulwark against Arab nationalism.[52] A political branch, the Islamic Constitutional Movement (ICM, or Hadas, as it is known in Arabic), was created in 1991. In the aftermath of the 1990 Iraqi invasion, the Kuwait Brotherhood underwent a period of significant change, formally breaking organisational ties with the international Muslim Brotherhood over Islamist support for Saddam Hussein, as the movement wanted to avoid being perceived as more loyal to the transnational Brotherhood than to the Emir.[53] Following the 1992 elections, the organisation became integrated into parliamentary politics and focused on conservative social policies.[54] The 2000s marked a significant change in Government–Hadas relations. In 2006, for the first time, Hadas supported more vocal, extra-parliamentary opposition, namely the Orange Movement, and Islamist groups – Hadas, but also Salafi organisations such as Hizb al-Ummah – started to acknowledge a convergence of interests with tribal communities.[55]

Residing in the outer districts of Kuwait, for decades tribes such as the al-Rashaida, al-Awaem, and al-Ajman were viewed by the ruling family as providing a counterweight to the more politically sophisticated and demanding urban population, in exchange for economic benefits and incentives.[56] However, over time, tribes developed a wider political awareness and increasingly saw Islamist movements, very active in their outer districts through social programmes, as palatable allies.[57] A new generation of tribal youth found in these movements a vehicle for upward mobility into politics, while the support of tribes guaranteed a considerable pool of votes to Islamist movements. As a reaction to the increasingly vocal nature of tribal Islamist opposition, the Government banned the practice of tribal primaries, which were an effective system to rally tribal votes for fewer candidates in national elections, and yet, in the new elections called in 2008, the tribal Islamist coalition gained new seats.[58] The leadership of Musallam al-Barrak, who in the

2006 elections won a record number of votes, started to emerge.[59] A member of the large and influential al-Mutayr tribe, al-Barrak was continuously re-elected from 1999 to 2012.[60] During this time he was active on different fronts as an opposition politician, including in the Orange Movement, and 'he slowly became the most vocal politician against the corruption of the regime, especially of Prime Minister Nasser Mohammed'.[61]

Tribal Islamist MPs joined the 2011 protests early on and, in June, grilled the Prime Minister on issues ranging from alleged misuse of public funds to harming national security and relations with Arab countries by favouring ties with Iran.[62] When the Constitutional Court dissolved the post-Arab Spring Parliament, where al-Barrak again broke voting records to reinstate a pro-regime 2009 National Assembly on the Emir's orders, he gave a fiery speech including the famous sentence 'We will not allow you, your highness.'[63] This earned him a sentence of two years' imprisonment for criticising the Emir, in breach of Article 54 of the Kuwaiti Constitution, which declares the Emir 'immune and inviolable'.[64] Hadas and other opposition blocs boycotted the following two parliamentary elections in 2012 and 2013, but subsequently returned to politics.[65] This signalled that Hadas's opposition continued to play by the rulebook of Kuwait's political system: by being embedded into the institutional mechanism, 'the movement wanted to avoid being labelled subversive'.[66]

Another contentious moment in relations between the regime and Hadas came in the summer of 2013, when Kuwait's Government backed the Egyptian military ousting of the Brotherhood's Mohammed Morsi from the presidency. Hadas members were very vocal in their condemnation of Egypt's military and their criticism of the Sabah rulers for their anti-Morsi line.[67] Such a reaction prompted opponents of the party to accuse Hadas of being subservient to the Brotherhood in Egypt, and scheming against the Kuwaiti Government through infiltration into government institutions to undermine the State from within.[68] This was the traditional accusation levelled against the Brotherhood in the GCC and most commonly in the United Arab Emirates, the most hostile government to political Islam. Indeed the UAE even linked some prominent Kuwaitis to the individuals arrested in Abu Dhabi on a charge of being Brotherhood members.[69] However, the Kuwaiti Government, while arresting and deporting Egyptians accused Brotherhood membership, did not take offensive actions against Kuwaiti members of the group.[70] On the other hand, when, in January 2015, former Hadas MP Mubarak al-Duwailah appeared on television accusing Abu Dhabi Crown Prince Shaykh Mohammed bin Zayed al-Nahyan of being 'against Sunni Islam', he was arrested on charges of endangering ties with an ally and sentenced to two years in prison.[71] Despite higher tensions, Hadas continued to organise and take part in smaller protests throughout 2015 against judicial corruption, the Government's policy of stripping citizenship, and the detention of political prisoners.[72] The group's members were still allowed to compete in the 2016 general elections in Kuwait, when they performed relatively well.[73] They fared even better in the 2020 elections, when most incumbents lost their seats, while Islamists gained roughly 20 per cent of the votes and the number of tribal MPs increased to twenty-nine out of fifty seats in total.[74] The following year, Musallam al-Barrak was pardoned by the Emir and returned to Kuwait after two years in prison and three years of self-imposed exile in Turkey, giving symbolic closure to the post-Arab Spring Islamist question in Kuwait.[75]

The trajectory of Hadas's and tribal Islamists' parliamentary life is illustrative of the peculiar history of the Muslim Brotherhood in Kuwait, where the institutional reality constrains the perimeter of activities. Although Islamists become undeniably more vocal in the 2010s, the regime has developed a system to handle their activism through a careful mix of co-optation and coercion and, therefore, doesn't see them as an existential political threat. This explains why Kuwait repeatedly refused to join the UAE, Saudi Arabia, and Bahrain in designating the Muslim Brotherhood a terrorist organisation. Instead, the Government focused on making sure that the local Muslim Brotherhood would not threaten relations with Saudi Arabia or the UAE, and therefore cracked down on individuals who attracted their neighbours' hostility, such as al-Duwailah, who, however, was released in 2020. Similarly, in 2019 Kuwait arrested and extradited eight Egyptian nationals, members of the Muslim Brotherhood, on behalf of the Egyptian Government.[76] The Government did not escalate actions against the Brotherhood even as Mishaal al-Ahmad al-Sabah, former head of the National Guard and notoriously hostile to Islamists, became the country's Crown Prince in 2020 and caretaker leader amid the Emir's illness in 2021.

The Kuwaiti Government also clearly focused on maintaining a separation between parliamentary and extra-parliamentary Islamist forces, and between the Muslim Brotherhood and jihadist movements. In some specific cases, Daesh and other jihadi groups received financial resources via fundraising campaigns from within Kuwait, even organised by Islamist politicians or prominent clerics, under the cover of humanitarian aid, between 2013 and 2018.[77] The three blacklists issued by Saudi Arabia, the UAE, and Bahrain during the Qatar crisis included the names of several Kuwaitis accused of funding jihadist organisations. One of those names was that of Hamid Hamad al-Ali, who allegedly travelled to Syria to mediate a reconciliation among the leaders of Jabhat al-Nusra (Syrian al Qa'ida), Abu Mohammed al-Jawlani, and Daesh leader Abu Bakr al-Baghdadi.[78] Another name was that of Hajjaj bin Fahad Hajjaj Mohammed al-Ajmi, a Kuwaiti-born Salafi cleric who allegedly channelled funds to Jabhat al-Nusra, coming from a prominent Kuwaiti tribe that included Kuwait's former Minister of Islamic Affairs.[79] In August 2013, the Kuwaiti Government cancelled the television show of religious scholar Shafi al-Ajmi and banned him from giving sermons after he voiced support for jihadist fighters in Syria. Both al-Ajmi clerics were designated as terrorist supporters by the USA and were briefly detained.[80] Then, in June 2015, a Daesh cell perpetrated an attack on the historic Shi'ite Imam Sadiq mosque in Kuwait City, one of the bloodiest attacks in the country's history.[81] Asked about the bidoon community's involvement with Kuwait-based jihadi groups and this specific attack, in which the attackers' ringleader, Abdulrahman Sabah Saud, was a bidoon, a Daesh member said: 'People who are very frustrated about the life they are living, like the *bidoons* in Kuwait, they believe that the Islamic State will give them their rights ... there were some *hadhar* but the majority around 90 per cent were *bidoons*.'[82]

With regard to Islamism, the Kuwaiti Government remained alert to two security risks: first, the potential for individual Islamists to turn towards extremism or to create partnerships with jihadi groups as a tool to acquire influence at the expense of the regime's stability. At the political level, on the other hand, the focus was on Islamist political forces' tendency to form cross-ideological coalitions with extra-parliamentary forces and, especially, tribes, against the Government. The local Muslim Brotherhood was never treated as a full-fledged threat by the Kuwaiti regime, which restrained its punitive and coercive actions. However, policy-makers remained alert to these two risks, and their potential political and security dimensions.[83]

Kuwait's security priorities after 2011

Kuwait's position in the context of the 2014 and 2017 intra-GCC crises, serving as the principal mediator between the parties, is telling of the regime's perceptions of threat. In 2017 Kuwait's Emir Sabah declared of the crisis: 'Any escalation will bring with it an outright call for regional and international intervention, which will destroy the security of the Gulf.'[84] This position was linked to Kuwait's historical background and collective memory, its geopolitical identity, and sociopolitical features.

Kuwait is a small country with a diverse national fabric, including a large Shi'a community representing roughly 28 per cent of the population.[85] The country borders two of the largest players in the Gulf, Iraq and Saudi Arabia, and is very close to Iran. In its history, Kuwait has suffered repercussions from confrontations between these larger players, or their ambitions, and has consistently built its security perceptions around them.[86] The most pressing security trauma suffered by the country, embedded in its collective memory, is the invasion by Saddam Hussein's Iraq in 1990.[87] Emir Sabah was then Foreign Minister, a capacity in which he served between 1963 and 2003, until he became the country's leader in 2006. In 1981 he had played a key role in the very founding of the GCC, and always saw GCC unity and regional diplomacy as key in confronting common challenges.[88] The 1990 invasion pushed Kuwaiti leaders to embrace a balancing policy that serves external as well as internal equilibrium: with a diverse national fabric, and citizens hailing originally from all around the region, Kuwait has traditionally been impacted by regional events. The impact of the Iran–Iraq war was, indeed, formidable, as in the 1980s 'it wasn't rare to see the Shi'a houses with pictures of Ayatollah Khomeini on the wall, and the Sunnis' with pictures of Saddam Hussein'.[89]

The importance of internal balance is also enshrined in Kuwait's foundational myth, featuring the country's origins as a merchant port, founded by tribes from the Najd, and attracting merchant families from Iran, Bahrain, eastern Saudi Arabia, and Iraq, who jointly selected their leadership, built the institutions of the country, and protected the emirate from invasion.[90] While certainly simplistic, this myth is still routinely employed in local political narratives.[91] A possible explanation is that the radicalisation of one specific community, supporting an external challenger, would fatally weaken the country. In this scenario, external threats could morph into intermestic ones. Hence, a confrontation between Iran and the GCC states could, in theory, radicalise part of Kuwait's Shi'a communities. Given the diversity of the Sunni camp in Kuwait, polarisation within the GCC could also have a dangerous divisive effect.

Kuwait is also concerned about becoming a direct target again. Indeed, one reason that Kuwait made efforts to normalise relations and provide much-needed support to Iraq's rebuilding after the 2003 US invasion was to discourage Baghdad from potential predatory intent.[92] The regime also viewed the intra-GCC crisis with concern at the possibility of becoming engulfed by it, as the increasingly muscular axis between the UAE and Saudi Arabia pressured Kuwait to scale back relations with Iran, Qatar, and Turkey, all perceived as rival actors by Riyadh and Abu Dhabi.[93]

This acute perception of external threats and geopolitical vulnerabilities is exemplified by the surge in defence and security agreements signed since 2016 by Kuwait. In January 2016 NATO inaugurated the NATO–Kuwait Istanbul Cooperation Initiative Regional Center.[94] In 2018 Kuwait announced that construction was almost complete on the largest US military airport in the Middle East.[95] In the same year, the UK negotiated the stationing of a small but permanent group of armed forces in Kuwait.[96] A few months later news surfaced that Kuwait had signed a protocol to boost defence industry cooperation with China, and an agreement to strengthen military cooperation with Turkey.[97]

On the other hand, while regional polarisation was prioritised, the internal vulnerabilities clearly emerging in 2011 were quasi-neglected, and were magnified by COVID-19. When the pandemic struck, Kuwait applied lengthy lockdowns but lagged behind other GCC monarchies in its vaccination campaign. With Kuwait the most oil-dependent among GCC monarchies, the 2020 oil price shock was particularly acute in Kuwait, resulting in a 9.9 per cent GDP drop and causing the state deficit to skyrocket by 175 per cent in 2020.[98] This went hand in hand with a far-reaching political crisis. Parliamentary opposition prevented the Government borrowing from the international market or accessing funds from the Future Generations Fund, accusing it of corruption.[99] The new Emir, Nawaf al-Ahmad al-Sabah, succeeding his brother Sabah in 2020 after serving as Crown Prince since 2006, was unable to rein in the clash between Government and opposition. The confrontation resulted in a stagnation of reforms, including those linked to post-oil diversification, part of Kuwait Vision 2035.[100] For years, Kuwait has been the GCC monarchy attracting the smallest FDI inflows, with job creation remaining flat.[101]

Despite having been a major flashpoint for political mobilisation, corruption remained rampant and Kuwait's score on Transparency International's Corruption Perception Index even deteriorated between 2015 and 2021.[102] There was no major change in the sociopolitical and socioeconomic marginalisation lamented by the bidoons, despite the fact that as a marginalised, disenfranchised community the bidoons harbour serious sociopolitical and socioeconomic grievances that make them susceptible to the influence of Islamist extremism.[103] The frequent cycles of elections, with Parliament dissolved seven times between 2011 and 2022, have started eroding the citizens' confidence in the Kuwaiti political system, thus depriving the State itself of a key source of resilience.[104] Finally, the leadership transition in 2020 empowered two brothers of Emir Sabah – Emir Nawaf and Crown Prince Mishal – postponing the contentious question of transitioning the leadership to the next generation, and placing the two octogenarian leaders, both suffering from chronic illnesses, in charge of a country in stalemate.

Notes

1 For a comprehensive look at the condition of the bidoons in Kuwait, see Claire Beaugrand, *Stateless in the Gulf: Migration, Nationality and Society in Kuwait* (London: IB Tauris, 2017).

2 *Ibid.*

3 *Ibid.*

4 'Kuwait to Deport Stateless Protesters: Report', Al Arabiya, 17 January 2012, www.alarabiya.net/articles/2012/01/17/188847.html (accessed 17 September 2022).

5 'Kuwait Says Stateless Protesters Carried Out Criminal Acts', Reuters, 2 May 2012, www.reuters.com/article/us-kuwait-protest-idUSBRE84111E20120502; (accessed 17 September 2022).

6 'Stateless Bidoon Activists in Kuwait Enter Third Week of Hunger Strike', *The New Arab*, 12 April 2022, https://english.alaraby.co.uk/news/bidoon-activists-kuwait-enter-third-week-hunger-strike; (17 September 2022).

7 Alnoud Alsharekh, 'Youth, Protest and the New Elite', in Kristian Ulrichsen (ed.), *The Changing Security Dynamics of the Persian Gulf* (Oxford: Oxford University Press, 2018).

8 Mary Ann Tétreault, 'Bottom-Up Democratization in Kuwait', in Mary Ann Tétreault, Gwenn Okruhlik, and Andrzej Kapiszewski (eds), *Political Change in the Arab Gulf States: Stuck in Transition* (Boulder, CO: Lynne Rienner, 2011).

9 Kristin Smith Diwan, 'Kuwait's Constitutional Showdown', *Foreign Policy*, 17 November 2011, http://foreignpolicy.com/2011/11/17/kuwaits-constitutional-showdown/ (17 September 2022).

10 'Kuwait Orders Tight Security after Parliament Stormed', Reuters, 17 November 2011, www.reuters.com/article/us-kuwait-protest-idUSTRE7AF2RL20111117 (17 September 2022).

11 Kristian Ulrichsen, 'Kuwait: Political Crisis at Critical Juncture', BBC, 23 October 2012, www.bbc.com/news/world-middle-east-20026581 (17 September 2022).

12 *Ibid*.

13 Anh Nga Longva, 'Nationalism in Pre-Modern Guise: The Discourse on Hadhar and Badu in Kuwait', *International Journal of Middle East Studies* 38:2 (2006), 171–187.

14 Interview by the author of a Kuwaiti Government official, Kuwait City, 11 December 2018.

15 Jane Kinninmont, 'Citizenship in the Gulf', in Ana Echagüe (ed.), *The Gulf States and the Arab Uprisings* (Madrid: Fundación para las Relaciones Internacionales y el Diálogo Exterior, 2013), 57.

16 Simon Atkinson, 'Kuwait's Stateless Bidun Demand Greater Rights', BBC, 19 July 2011, www.bbc.co.uk/news/mobile/business-14185365 (accessed 17 September 2022). In an interview with the author on Skype on 21 January 2019, a young Kuwaiti activist stated that: 'I have been talking to the leaders of the bidoon community: their utmost concern is not the regime's legitimacy but their basic rights. They didn't even join the opposition because they didn't want to give the Government any excuse to be harsher on them.'

17 Interview by the author of a Kuwaiti political economist, Kuwait City, 11 December 2018.

18 Interview by the author of a Kuwaiti diplomat, London, 13 November 2018; interview by the author of a Kuwaiti researcher at the Center for Gulf and Arabian Peninsula Studies, Kuwait City, 13 December 2018; interview by the author of a Kuwaiti Shi'a politician, Kuwait City, 12 December 2018; interview by the author of a young Kuwaiti activist, Skype, 21 January 2019.

19 Mary Ann Tétreault, *Stories of Democracy: Politics and Society in Contemporary Kuwait* (New York: Columbia University Press, 2000).

20 Alsharekh, 'Youth, Protest and the New Elite'.

21 A Kuwaiti political economist interviewed by the author in Kuwait City on 11 December 2018 stated: 'Kuwait has a high GDP but the costs of living soared, so purchasing power has declined and young people perceive themselves as poorer than their parents. It is a consequence of the unsustainable rentier political economy.'

22 Fahad Al-Zumai, 'Kuwait's Political Impasse and Rent-Seeking Behaviour: A Call for Institutional Reform', research paper, London School of Economics Kuwait Programme (2013), http://eprints.lse.ac.uk/55014/1/__Libfile_reposi tory_Content_Kuwait%20Programme_AL-Zumai_2013.pdf (accessed 4 August 2023).

23 Rivka Azoulay, 'The Politics of Shi'i Merchants in Kuwait', in Steffen Hertog, Giacomo Luciani, and Marc Valeri (eds), *Business Politics in the Middle East* (London: Hurst, 2013).

24 *Ibid.*

25 *Ibid.*

26 *Ibid.*

27 Hamad Albloshi, 'Iran and Kuwait', in Bahgat, Ehteshami, and Quilliam (eds), *Security and Bilateral Issues*, 135.

28 Efraim Karsh, *The Iran–Iraq War 1980–1988* (Oxford: Osprey, 2002), 9–12.

29 Rivka Azoulay and Claire Beaugrand, 'Limits of Political Clientelism: Elites in Kuwait Fragmenting Politics', *Arabian Humanities* 4 (2015), 1–20.

30 Khaled Abdulaziz Alsalloum and Mohamed Salman Tayie, 'The Present and Future of Kuwaiti–Iranian Relations and Their Influence on the Security of the Arabian Gulf', *Asian Social Science* 14:1 (2017), 102–111 (102).

31 Wehrey, *Sectarian Politics in the Gulf*.

32 *Ibid.*

33 *Ibid.*

34 Hamad Albloshi, 'Sectarianism and the Arab Spring: The Case of the Kuwaiti Shi'a', *The Muslim World* 106:1 (2016), 109–126 (120).

35 Interview by the author of a Kuwaiti diplomat, London, 13 November 2018; interview by the author of an expert on Kuwaiti politics, London, 17 January 2019.

36 'Kuwait, Iran Vow Joint Work to Develop Ties', press release, Kuwait News Agency (KUNA), 2 June 2014, www.kuna.net.kw/ArticlePrintPage.aspx?id= 2380502&language=en (accessed 7 September 2022).

37 Albloshi, 'Iran and Kuwait', 138.

38 Diwan, 'Kuwait'.

39 Interview by the author of a Kuwaiti diplomat, London, 13 November 2018.

40 According to Hussein Amery, 'Water Security for Kuwait: Assessing the Feasibility of Water Imports from Iran', *International Journal of Hydrology Science and Technology* 2:3 (2012), 292–305, the desalination process for Kuwait is 20 per cent more costly than importing fresh water from Iran would

be, and Iran stands to gain at least $75 million annually. 'Kuwait Seeks Gas from Iran', Economist Intelligence Unit, 4 June 2014, https://country.eiu.com/article.aspx?articleid=161878600&Country=Iran&topic=Economy&subtopic=Forec_6 (accessed 4 August 2023).

41 'Kuwait, Iran Sign Agreement to Combat Sandstorms', *Kuwait Times*, www.kuwaittimes.com/kuwait-iran-sign-agreement-to-combat-sand-storms/ (accessed 14 September 2022); 'Iran Ready to Resume Talks with Kuwait over al-Durra Field', *Asharq al-Awsat*, 2 May 2022, https://english.aawsat.com/home/article/3623971/iran-ready-resume-talks-kuwait-over-al-durra-field (accessed 14 September 2022).

42 Sylvia Westall, 'Terror Case Opens Up Kuwait's Sectarian Divisions', Reuters, 2 June 2016, www.reuters.com/article/us-kuwait-security-iran-insight/terror-case-opens-up-kuwaits-sectarian-divisions-idUSKCN0YO0VH (accessed 14 September 2022).

43 'Kuwait Charges 24 "linked to Iran" with plotting attacks', *Khaleej Times*, 1 September 2015, www.khaleejtimes.com/region/mena/kuwait-charges-24-linked-to-iran-with-plotting-attacks (accessed 14 September 2022).

44 Kristian Ulrichsen, 'Walking the Tightrope: Kuwaiti–Iranian Relations in the Aftermath of the Abdali Affair', *IndraStra Global* 8 (2017), www.ssoar.info/ssoar/handle/document/53497 (accessed 23 July 2023).

45 Interview by the author of a Kuwaiti Government official, Kuwait City, 11 December 2018.

46 'Daesh Claims Responsibility for Mosque Explosion in Kuwait', Gulf News, 27 June 2015, https://gulfnews.com/world/gulf/kuwait/daesh-claims-responsibility-for-mosque-explosion-in-kuwait-1.154108 (accessed 17 September 2022).

47 'Kuwait Says It Thwarted 3 Planned ISIS Attacks', *New York Times*, 3 July 2016, www.nytimes.com/2016/07/04/world/middleeast/kuwait-isis-shiite-muslims (accessed 17 September 2022).

48 Interview by the author of a Kuwaiti academic researching sectarianism in Kuwait, Kuwait City, 11 December 2018. Very similar points were also raised by Shi'a MP Hamid Dashti, interviewed by Hamad Albloshi; see Albloshi, 'Sectarianism and the Arab Spring', 123.

49 Abdulrahman al-Rashed, 'Criminalization of Sectarian Speech', Arab News, 6 August 2012, www.arabnews.com/criminalization-sectarian-speech (accessed 17 September 2022).

50 Interview by the author of a Kuwaiti Shi'a politician, Kuwait City, 12 December 2018.

51 Freer, *Rentier Islamism*, 15–16.

52 *Ibid.*

53 *Ibid.*, 109.

54 *Ibid.*, 85.

55 Fatiha Dazi-Héni, 'The Arab Spring Impact on Kuwaiti "Exceptionalism"', *Arabian Humanities* 4 (2015), https://doi.org/10.4000/cy.2868 (accessed 4 August 2023).

56 *Ibid.*

57 *Ibid.*

58 Nathan Brown, 'Kuwait's 2008 Parliamentary Elections: A Setback for Democratic Islamism?' (Washington, DC: Carnegie Endowment for International Peace, 2008), Universitäts-und Landesbibliothek Sachsen-Anhalt, https://menadoc.bibliothek.uni-halle.de/menalib/content/pageview/1605846 (accessed 19 July 2023).

59 Shafeeq Ghabra, 'Kuwait at the Crossroads of Change or Political Stagnation', Middle East Institute, 20 May 2014, https://www.mei.edu/publications/kuwait-crossroads-change-or-political-stagnation (accessed 17 September 2022).

60 *Ibid.*

61 Interview by the author of a young Kuwaiti activist, Skype, 21 January 2019.

62 Azoulay and Beaugrand, 'Limits of Political Clientelism: Elites' Struggles in Kuwait Fragmenting Politics', *Arabian Humanities* 4 (2015), 1–20.

63 Ahmed Hagagy, 'Kuwaiti Politician Jailed for Insulting Emir', Reuters, 15 April 2013, www.reuters.com/article/us-kuwait-sentence-idUSBRE93E11120130415 (accessed 17 September 2022).

64 Hamad Albloshi and Michael Herb, 'Karamet Watan: An Unsuccessful Nonviolent Movement', *Middle East Journal* 72:3 (2018), 408–430 (411).

65 Freer, *Rentier Islamism*, 123.

66 Interview by the author of an expert on Kuwaiti politics, London, 17 January 2019.

67 Scott Williamson and Nathan Brown, 'Kuwait's Muslim Brotherhood under pressure', *Foreign Policy*, 20 November 2013, http://foreignpolicy.com/2013/11/20/kuwaits-muslim-brotherhood-under-pressure/ (accessed 17 September 2022).

68 Freer, *Rentier Islamism*, 109.

69 Interview by the author of an Emirati diplomat, London, 3 October 2018.

70 Williamson and Brown, 'Kuwait's Muslim Brotherhood'.

71 Habib Toumi, 'Kuwait Former MP Sentenced for Insulting UAE', Gulf News, 13 April 2016, http://gulfnews.com/news/gulf/kuwait/kuwait-former-mp-sentenced-for-insulting-uae-1.1710578 (accessed 17 September 2022).

72 Linah Alsaafin, 'Kuwait Security Forces Violently Disperse Anti-Government Protest', *Middle East Eye*, 23 March 2015, www.middleeasteye.net/news/kuwaiti-security-forces-violently-disperse-anti-government-protest-1878869579. (accessed 17 September 2022).

73 'Kuwait Poll: Opposition Wins Nearly Half of Parliament', Al Jazeera, 27 November 2016, www.aljazeera.com/news/2016/11/kuwait-poll-opposition-wins-parliament-161127060822207.html (accessed 17 September 2022).

74 Daniel Tavana and Abdullah al-Khonaini, 'Kuwait Voted This Weekend. Who Won?', *Washington Post*, 8 December 2020, www.washingtonpost.com/politics/2020/12/08/kuwait-voted-this-weekend-who-won/ (accessed 17 September 2022).

75 Isabel Debre and Malak Harb, 'Kuwait's Pardoned Dissidents Return to a Country in Crisis', Associated Press, 2 March 2022, https://apnews.com/article/business-middle-east-persian-gulf-tensions-kuwait-kuwait-city-5ae042cd17dbce4b1c9aac6ab999413b (accessed 17 September 2022).

76 'Kuwaiti Authorities Arrest Militant Cell Linked to Muslim Brotherhood', Arab News, 13 July 2019, www.arabnews.com/node/1524706/middle-east (accessed 17 September 2022).

77 Elizabeth Dickinson, 'Playing with Fire: Why Private Gulf Financing for Syria's Extremist Rebels Risks Igniting Sectarian Conflict at Home', Brookings Institution, 6 December 2013, www.brookings.edu/research/playing-with-fire-why-private-gulf-financing-for-syrias-extremist-rebels-risks-igniting-sectarian-conflict-at-home/ (accessed 17 September 2022).

78 *Ibid.*

79 *Ibid.*

80 'Kuwait Releases Detained Cleric Suspected of Financing Militants', Reuters, 21 August 2014, www.reuters.com/article/us-syria-crisis-kuwait-cleric/kuwait-releases-detained-cleric-suspected-of-financing-militants-idUSKBN0GL1X12 0140821 (accessed 17 September 2022).

81 'Daesh Claims Responsibility for Mosque Explosion'.

82 Quote by participant no. 4, a member of ISIS, in Nicholas Scull, Othman Alkhader, and Salman Alwadi, 'Why People Join Terrorist Groups in Kuwait', presentation for the American Psychology Association Annual Convention, 3 August 2017, Washington, DC, https://doi.org/10.1111/pops.12622 (accessed 4 August 2023).

83 Interview by the author of a senior Kuwaiti diplomat, Brussels, 13 June 2022.

84 'Kuwait Emir Warns of GCC Collapse and Crisis Escalation', Al Jazeera, 24 October 2017, www.aljazeera.com/news/2017/10/kuwait-emir-warns-gcc-colla pse-crisis-escalation-171024122229727.html (accessed 17 September 2022).

85 In 2018 Kuwait's Central Statistical Bureau estimated the country's total population to be 4,226,920, with immigrants accounting for more than 69.5 per cent. Official website of the Central Statistical Bureau, www.csb.gov.kw/Def ault_EN.aspx (accessed 17 September 2022).

86 Anthony Cordesman, *Kuwait: Recovery and Security after the Gulf War* (New York: Routledge, 1997).

87 Michael Casey, *The History of Kuwait* (London: Greenwood, 2007).

88 *Ibid.*

89 Interview by the author of a Kuwaiti academic researching sectarianism in Kuwait, Kuwait City, 11 December 2018.

90 For a more academic view of the narratives that structure Kuwaiti politics, see Tétreault, *Stories of Democracy*.

91 *Ibid.*

92 Interview by the author of a senior Kuwaiti diplomat, Brussels, 13 June 2022.

93 Neil Partrick, 'Kuwait: The Permanent Struggle for Security', 14 August 2018, www.neilpartrick.com/blog/kuwait-the-permanent-struggle-for-security (accessed 17 September 2022).

94 'Activities at NATO–Kuwait ICI Regional Center Start', NATO official website, 17 September 2017, www.nato.int/cps/ra/natohq/news_147010.htm (accessed 17 September 2022).

95 Ramadan Al Sherbini, 'Key US Military Air Hub to Open in Kuwait', Gulf News, 13 July 2018, https://gulfnews.com/world/gulf/kuwait/key-us-military-air-hub-to-open-in-kuwait-1.2250807 (accessed 17 September 2022).

96 George Allison, 'UK Is Considering a "Permanent Military Presence" in Kuwait', *UK Defence Journal*, 19 February 2018, https://ukdefencejournal.org.uk/uk-considering-permanent-military-presence-kuwait/ (accessed 17 September 2022).

97 Sinem Cengiz, 'Kuwait Looks to Turkish and Chinese Military Power', Arab News, 19 October 2018, www.arabnews.com/node/1390646 (accessed 17 September 2022).

98 Ghaida Ghantous and Yousef Saba, 'Kuwait's Economy Contracted by 9.9% in 2020 – State News Agency', Reuters, 13 June 2020, www.reuters.com/world/middle-east/kuwaits-economy-contracted-by-99-2020-state-news-agency-2021-06-13/ (accessed 17 September 2022).

99 Ahmed Hagagy, 'Kuwait Parliament Approves 2021–2022 Budget – Speaker', Zawya, 22 February 2021, www.zawya.com/mena/en/economy/story/Kuwait_parliament_approves_20212022_budget__speaker-TR20210622nC6N2O2037X2/ (accessed 17 September 2022).

100 Sophie Olver-Ellis, 'Building the New Kuwait: Vision 2035 and the Challenges of Diversification', Kuwait Programme, London School of Economics and Political Science (2020), http://eprints.lse.ac.uk/103198/1/Olver_Ellis_building_the_new_Kuwait_published.pdf (accessed 20 July 2023).

101 *Ibid.*

102 'Kuwait', Corruption Perception Index 2021, Transparency International, www.transparency.org/en/cpi/2021/index/kwt (accessed 4 August 2023).

103 Claire Beaugrand, 'Biduns in the Face of Radicalization in Kuwait', Arab Gulf States Institute in Washington, 18 August 2015, https://agsiw.org/biduns-in-the-face-of-radicalization-in-kuwait/ (accessed 17 September 2022).

104 Mohammad Alwuhaib, 'Kuwait: The Crisis and Its Future', Brief 63, Arab Reform Initiative, 12 November 2012, https://www.arab-reform.net/publication/kuwait-the-crisis-and-its-future/ (accessed 17 September 2022).

7

Oman

The impact of the Arab Spring

The trajectory of Oman's security calculus in the ten years after the Arab Spring has reaffirmed that status of exceptionalism within deep regional ties that traditionally defined the sultanate. Oman's experiences with the Arab Spring and the impact of the changing geopolitics of the Gulf and wider MENA region were similar to that of its neighbours, and yet different.

In February 2011, young Omanis started to organise rallies through the internet, while a couple of hundred citizens started to protest Government corruption and the rising prices of basic goods, asking for larger allowances for water, electricity, and housing, as well as higher wages.[1] While the Arab Spring worked as a catalyst, these demands had already featured in online forums and small-scale protests for over ten years.[2] The protesters gathered their grievances in a petition addressed to the Sultan himself, as a way to show loyalty to him, and to ensure a distinction between Sultan Qaboos and Government ministers, who were seen as corrupt.[3] Gradually, protests and sit-ins grew in numbers, gathering tens of thousands of citizens, and spread across the country: to Dhofar in the south; Sur; and Sohar, site of highest industry concentration in Oman, in the north. The Government started taking measures to sooth protesters early on, such as raising the minimum salary; monthly stipends for students, military, and security staff; higher pensions; creating 50,000 new public sector jobs, mostly in the security forces; and replacing long-serving ministers widely perceived as embodying corruption – such as 'Ali al Ma'amari, the Minister for the Royal Office; Ahmed Makki, the Minister for National Economy; and Maqbool al-Sultan, the Minister for Commerce and Industry – with elected members of the Omani Parliament, the Majlis as-Shura.[4] In less than a month, the Sultan issued more than forty decrees at a pace unprecedented in his four decades of rule, although some of them – such as the creation of a National Audit Committee tackling corruption, and the concession of some legislative and regulatory powers to the Majlis as-Shura – remained unimplemented.[5] The Government also attempted to engage in consultations with the protesters via intermediaries. In the restive Dhofari region, dozens of protesters were received by a prominent tribal figure, Mustahail bin Ahmed al-Maashani, belonging to one of the largest local tribes, and a blood relative of the royal family.[6] In the meantime, the Government launched violent crackdowns in both Sohar and Salalah in March and April, issuing arrest warrants for some protesters and deploying the army.[7] This response drove protests into limbo: while small rallies and strikes would persist for the entire decade that followed, the main chapter of the Omani Arab Spring could be considered closed.

After the initial reaction, the regime conceptualised the events of 2011 not as an existential threat to the regime, but rather as a stress test. The protesters' overall hesitation, with a few exceptions, to question the legitimacy of Sultan Qaboos or call for the overthrow of the regime was a key driver for these restrained perceptions. In March, protesters in Sohar issued a public statement regretting the violence and publicly apologising to the Sultan, while stating 'We have confidence in the Sultan that he will respond to our demands.'[8] As Marc Valeri highlighted, 'The now famous "The people want the fall of the regime" [al-sha'ab yurid isqat al-nizam] … was appropriated in Oman in 2011, where it was converted to "The people want the reform (islah) of the regime" and "The people want the fall of corruption" (isqat al-fasad).'[9] The fact that Omanis openly acknowledged the legitimacy of the Sultan in addressing their grievances remains one of the distinctive features of the Omani Spring's inception.[10] Another key element in explaining why the regime's perception of the potential threat posed by the protesters remained low was the lack of organisational skills or political leadership in a very diverse movement, which included public sector employees, industrial workers, students, and teachers: a coalition with no common trait, which could not resemble the cohesive disgruntled community that protested in Bahrain, and lacked the coordination of the Kuwaiti dissidents.[11] Two elements momentarily triggered the regime's red lines. First, one of the largest protests – allegedly gathering up to 10,000 people – took place in the southern centre of Salahah, the epicentre of a long-lasting leftist insurgency, followed by the Dhofar war.[12] In Salalah, some protesters made explicit references to the Dhofar Liberation Front, a youth group inspired by Marxist-Leninist ideology, which led a years-long armed rebellion driven by political and ideological rejection of the Sultanate as a regime.[13] The second element was a solid belief that the UAE was lending financial support to protesters – especially in Sohar, where several cars carrying Emirati plates were allegedly spotted during the protests.[14]

Despite these two red flags, the dominant perception among decision-makers in Oman was that the 2011 protest movement was a fully domestic phenomenon centred around socioeconomic grievances and, especially, unemployment, one of the country's key economic vulnerabilities.[15] The sultanate in fact shares with Bahrain the highest jobless rate among the six GCC states: in 2011 unemployment was approximately 15 per cent, and youth unemployment was running at around a whopping 39 per cent.[16] Like other countries in the region, Oman had been facing a youth bulge and was unable to create sufficient jobs to absorb these new entrants to the workforce in the bloated public sector or in the private sector, dominated by foreigners.[17] In this sense, even the most political demands – the firing of National Economy Minister Ahmad bin Abdul Makki and other officials, the establishment of an independent anti-corruption authority within the Majlis as-Shura – were focused on quintessentially economic matters, centred on the misappropriation of public funds and corruption that generated inequality between elites and ordinary people.[18] The focus of the Omani regime over the following ten years would be to contain the political ramifications of this dissent, domestically and regionally. At both levels, the regime prioritised stability and economic development, and saw uncertainty and unsteadiness as major threats.

From this viewpoint, the Omani Government saw the decision by Saudi Arabia and the UAE to extend a political boycott and economic embargo against Qatar as 'impossible to agree with'.[19] Oman officially declared a neutral stance in the crisis, keeping dialogue open with all parties. However, interestingly, Sultan Qaboos sent his State Minister Responsible for Foreign Affairs, Yusuf bin 'Alawi bin 'Abdullah, to visit the Qatari Emir in Doha on the same day that the crisis erupted.[20] Oman also stepped forward as a vital economic partner for Qatar. Following the decision of the UAE to deny entry to its ports of Jebel Ali and Fujairah, the regional refuelling and bunkering hub, Oman opened up the use of its ports, especially Salalah and Sohar, to exporters selling goods to Qatar and to Qatari ships exporting LNG.[21] Transiting through Iranian and Omani waters was essential for Qatar to avoid the quartet's territorial waters.[22] Oman's national carrier, Oman Air, launched additional flights to Qatar, as direct flights between Qatar and the four countries involved in the boycott were suspended, turning Muscat Airport into a regional hub for Qataris. According to Oman's Chamber of Commerce and Industry, from June to September 2017, 'the exchange of products between Oman and Qatar has more than tripled while transactions between the two countries soared by 2,000 per cent, reflecting hundreds of millions of dollars in trade'.[23] The increased trade volume also included the sale of Oman-produced goods, however – including food, consumer goods, and construction materials – another significant element for a country needing to increase the percentage of non-oil related activities' contribution to its GDP, as well as creating non-oil related jobs.[24]

Unquestionably, the economic and financial motives of Oman's posi-tion in the 2017 spat were paramount, given how the Sultanate's economy was severely weakened by the 2014 collapse of oil prices.[25] However, the political motives are also worth highlighting. Facilitating de-escalation between Qatar and its opponents would be in accordance with declared foreign policy objectives under Sultan Qaboos, and with the traditional prioritisation of regional stability, a behaviour often ascribed to small states by international relations literature.[26] Additionally, standing by Qatar, even if not openly, might also be a way to safeguard Muscat's own right to an independent foreign policy. Oman has rarely prioritised GCC unity in its foreign policy, as Muscat has rarely seen eye to eye with the security priorities of other GCC countries.[27] In fact, balancing among different neighbours and international partners to achieve security and autonomy has long been Oman's approach, and it was so in the ten years after the Arab Spring.

The most salient challenge in the post-2011 decade was certainly pursu-ing this delicate balancing policy amid the ongoing leadership transition from Sultan Qaboos bin Said al-Sa'id, who had ruled Oman since 1970, to his cousin Sultan Haitham bin Tariq al-Sa'id. Sultan Qaboos was seventy-one years old and terminally ill when the Arab Spring came to Oman, which limited his ability and inclination to embrace the public call for reforms. He had no direct heir, refused to name a successor, and stood at the centre of the sultanate's centralised system: he served as Prime Minister, Defence Minister, and Foreign Minister, and oversaw all aspects of the country's finance. Moreover, he had long deployed a strategy of becoming the embod-iment of the very national identity of the sultanate. For instance, Oman's National Day was traditionally celebrated on the Sultan's birthday, an extremely powerful symbolism. This pervasiveness of the Sultan's persona had generated deep-seated uncertainties over the sultanate's fate after his death. For most of the decade, this was the country's main sociopolitical vulnerability.[28]

While the leadership transition itself was remarkably and surprisingly smooth, the death of Sultan Qaboos in 2020 marked the beginning of a new phase for the Omani regime, which impacted significantly its security think-ing and alerted threat perceptions. Between 2011 and 2020, the Omani regime did not see significant political threats coming from Iran, the Muslim Brotherhood, or other regional and international actors, and prioritised the de-escalation of regional instability, even over its own economic challenges. After 2020, the Omani regime redefined its threat perceptions vis-à-vis its neighbours, with an increased sense of their interests in leveraging Oman's socioeconomic vulnerabilities to affect Oman's regional positioning and gain influence over and within the sultanate.

Oman and the 'Shi'a threat'

Oman's perceptions of Iran are affected by a number of factors – including the sultanate's sociopolitical, sociocultural, and socioeconomic features and the leadership's ideology – and are grounded in the history of bilateral relations between Muscat and Iran.

Iran was the first neighbouring power to sign a border agreement with Muscat in 1972, and the Shah's assistance – including logistics, weaponry, and at least 3,000 troops – proved to be instrumental in turning the tide to the advantage of the Sultan against the Dhofar Liberation Front.[29] Therefore, in diametrical opposition to the experience inscribed in the collective memory of other GCC countries, Iran represented for the Sultan a force supporting its stability rather than aiming at destabilisation.

The 1979 Islamic revolution did not disrupt Omani–Iranian relations, as Ayatollah Khomeini, who was threatening other GCC regimes, reassured Oman that all existing agreements would be honoured.[30] In 1984 Sultan Qaboos warned other GCC leaders that 'here in Muscat we do not believe it to be in the interest of security in the Gulf that Iran feels we intend to establish an Arab military pact that will always be hostile to it, or we are about to form a joint force, whose main task is to fight Iran'.[31] While the other Gulf monarchs wanted to establish the GCC to balance against Iran, Sultan Qaboos vociferously opposed any plan for military action against Iran, deeming the fallout from such action to be profoundly destabilising and, therefore, a tremendous risk to regional security.[32]

For one, Oman shares with Iran control over the strategic Strait of Hormuz, through which 17 billion barrels of oil – 20 per cent of global volume – are transported every day.[33] To keep the Strait safe and open for navigation, Oman has to cooperate with Iran, and has done so since 1995, with several agreements signed regarding smuggling, border intelligence sharing, and joint exercises.[34] Iran is also an important energy partner for Oman, as both countries share some major oil and natural gas fields, such as the off-shore Hengham oilfield or the Henjam/Bukha gas field, jointly developed since 2006.[35] Off the back of the JCPOA, in 2014, Oman and Iran also tentatively agreed on the construction of a pipeline providing Oman with convenient Iranian gas to cover its energy needs and, potentially, to re-export to India.[36] This deal was one of a series in which Muscat tried to position itself to benefit from the potential reintegration of Iran into the international community after the signing of a nuclear deal. Oman aspired to a become a re-export hub for Iran and to benefit from joint investments in manufacturing, pharmaceutical, and other sectors, as a reward for its role as facilitator of the nuclear talks between the USA and Iran. These moves were consistent with Oman's plans for economic diversification, creating employment opportunities and stimulating the private sectors, and turned Iran into a potential source of stability for the vulnerable economic development of the sultanate, where the real risk to stability was perceived to be in 2011.[37] In fact, when the USA pulled out of the deal under the administration of Donald Trump in 2018, this resulted in an increaced threat perception for the Omani regime. The promising potential to use the JCPOA as a platform for economic development evaporated. Higher tensions between the USA and Iran resulted in greater regional instability, with a kinetic tit-for-tat in the UAE, Saudi Arabia, and Iraq, long seen as a major threat in Oman. Finally, the Trump administration's anti-Iranian attitude caused Washington to ostracise Muscat for four years, and the Omani regime lost confidence in its major international security partner.

Under Trump, the USA was particularly suspicious of Oman's unique attitude towards Iran's regional and international postures, which was in fact rooted in the longstanding belief that constructive relations with Iran were necessary to guarantee Oman's security from Iranian aggression, but also to ensure Oman's ability to hedge against pressures from Saudi Arabia and, later, the UAE. Oman flourished its neutrality and its ability to facilitate diplomacy with Iran in order to carve autonomy and attract regional and international good will. In the 1990s, Oman had helped to facilitate dialogue between Iran and Saudi Arabia, who had cut bilateral relations in 1988, and passed messages to Iranian President Mohammad Khatami on behalf of the US President, Bill Clinton.[38] Since then, the Omani leadership has facilitated communication repeatedly between the USA and Iran, including, notably, to reach the JCPOA, kept secret from other GCC partners. While the Saudi, Emirati, and Bahraini leaders were of the opinion that such a deal would provide Iran with new financial resources for what they perceived as Tehran's destabilising regional policy, Omani leaders, as Foreign Minister Yusuf bin 'Alawi stated in 2013, were reluctant to admit that a nuclear-armed Iran would destabilise the region.[39] Muscat chose to stay neutral in the post-2011 Syrian conflict – where Saudi Arabia and Qatar were involved in supporting the opposition to the regime – and never broke diplomatic relations with the Assad regime, hosting both regime and opposition representatives, but then supported the 2018 airstrikes by the USA, France, and the UK as retribution for the regime's use of chemical weapons.[40] Despite political pressure from Saudi Arabia and the UAE, and accusations of failing to obstruct the smuggling of Iranian weapons to Yemen's Shi'a-aligned Houthi rebels, Oman also refused to join the Saudi-led military campaign started in 2015, exerting efforts for informal negotiations among all Yemeni actors, and hosting parts of the Houthi leadership.[41]

A major factor explaining Oman's perception of Iran is the lack of socio-political vulnerabilities that make other GCC countries prone to perceive an Iran-backed 'Shi'a threat'. The Omani Shi'a communities' interaction with wider Omani society and the leadership has historically been non-confrontational: Shi'a citizens identify themselves as Omanis and are integrated into the sultanate's religious, political, and economic life.[42] Shi'a merchants and intellectuals were actively co-opted into the Sultan's early nation-building efforts, aimed at creating stable political authority out of sociopolitical fragmentation.[43] There are no known official estimates of the number of Shi'a in Oman, but academic studies argued that Shi'a citizens represent approximately 5 per cent of the Omani population and are divided into three main groups: the Lawatiyya, the Baharna, and the 'Ajam.[44] Originally from the Indian subcontinent, the Lawatiyya, the main Shi'a community, run big commercial conglomerates, such as W. J. Towell Group, and hold sizable shares in top economic bodies such as the National Bank of Oman and Petroleum Development Oman.[45] Members of the family have held senior positions in the Government, including posts as cabinet ministers and in the Diwan of the Royal Court.[46] Some of the Baharna families – who are instead originally from Bahrain, Iraq, and eastern Saudi Arabia – also have significant influence. Prominent Baharna include Asim al-Jamali, who was the country's first Minister of Health and later served as Prime Minister, and Ahmed bin Abdul Nabi Makki, the powerful and controversial Minister of Economy.[47] The third Shi'a group, the 'Ajam, trace their origins to ancient Persia and, despite being well assimilated into Omani society, are less prominent within it.[48]

As a result of the small size of the community and its relative integration, transnational Shi'a movements with a strong presence in the wider Gulf, such as Hezbollah or the Shiraziyyun, have failed to elicit substantial support in Oman.[49] While Omani internal security services still monitor the community's activities, as well as foreign Shi'a leaders travelling to Oman, the regime's susceptibility to the perceived threat of Iranian meddling is very limited.[50] As mentioned earlier, the regime never accused Iran of stoking protests in 2011, which neither centred on grievances specific to Oman's Shi'a communities, nor included a Shi'a-specific movement.[51] This was a very visible difference vis-à-vis, for instance, protests in Bahrain and Saudi Arabia, which showed a deep fault line and sociopolitical vulnerability in their respective nation-states.

Oman's history of engagement with Iran and Iranian regional policy, their shared political and economic interests, and the absence of a deep sectarian fault line in the country are sufficient elements to argue that Oman does not perceive Iran as a threat: i.e. a force willing and able to pose an existential danger to the regime's stability and identity, or to the functional integrity of the country's boundaries and its institutions. Ultimately, Iran never showed an intent to challenge the fundamental structures of sovereignty in the sultanate, and never posed a threat to Oman's internal stability or undermine its national unity.[52] On the contrary, Oman sees regional confrontation with Iran as a direct threat to the internal stability and security of the country.[53]

And yet, the death of Sultan Qaboos in 2020 did result in a slight repositioning vis-à-vis Iran. While Muscat was as careful as always in not alienating Tehran, the proximity decreased. Sultan Qaboos's personal relationship with Iranian leaders, including Ayatollah Khamenei, was a pivot for Omani–Iranian relations. Shortly after Sultan Qaboos's death, another figure who had longstanding personal relations with key interlocutors of the Iranian regimes, the Minister Responsible for Foreign Affairs Yusuf bin 'Alawi, retired. The new Sultan of Oman, Haitham bin Tariq al-Sa'id, did not enjoy similar ties to Iran and did not empower Omani officials who had these special connections. When the Biden administration restarted negotiations to revive the JCPOA in 2021, Oman let Qatar be the main facilitator. Muscat was concerned it might be ostracised again for being perceived to support Iran, as had happened during the Trump administration. Amid lack of confidence in the prospects for success and the economic boost of a revived JCPOA, with individual Omani traders targeted by US sanctions for trading Iranian oil in 2021, Muscat prioritised relations with players who could more credibly intervene to assuage its socioeconomic vulnerabilities, such as Saudi Arabia. So, departing from a decades-long tradition, when Iranian President Ebrahim Raisi embarked on his first official Gulf trip in 2022, his first stop was Doha, not Muscat. Iran was still not viewed as a threat by the Omani regime, but started to be viewed as a risk, especially to its regional and international relations.

Oman and the 'Islamist threat'

The influence and presence of Sunni Islamist organisations such as the Muslim Brotherhood are often described as more limited in Oman than in other GCC countries.[54] This may be because Sunnis are not a majority in Oman, as well as because of two Government crackdowns since the 1990s.[55] In 1994, Omani authorities arrested over 300 people and tried about 130 for joining a 'subversive group, conspiring to damage the Sultanate's national unity and misusing the Islamic faith'.[56] The regime was particularly alarmed by two factors: that members of said organisations occupied positions within the State's bureaucracy – such as State undersecretaries – and that the group seemed to have a cohesive, semi-institutionalised internal structure resembling a branch of the Muslim Brotherhood, connected organisationally and financially with the 'global mother organisation in Egypt and similar groups in other countries, mostly Saudi Arabia'.[57] Most of the defendants were given long prison sentences, while two received death sentences, and yet, to general astonishment, Sultan Qaboos signed a general amnesty freeing all those involved in November 1995.[58]

Later, Omani authorities arrested around 100 people in 2005 for involvement in 'an attempt to form an organisation to tamper with national security'.[59] Among those arrested were military officers and civil servants, Islamic scholars, preachers, and university professors, both Sunni and Ibadi.[60] Allegedly, the group was plotting terrorist attacks against the Muscat cultural festival, and authorities also found a cache of weapons and explosives linked to the plot.[61] This alerted the Government as, in the early 2000s, there had been a few attacks, especially against westerners residing in Oman, and an alleged al-Qa'ida cell had been broken up.[62] After the investigation, thirty-one people were sentenced for involvement in an Ibadi Islamist militia called the al-Bashaer group, which, according to the authorities, was 'plotting to take over the country's energy fields and overthrowing the government'.[63] The accused confessed to some of the charges, while denying their intent to overthrow the Government, and all were pardoned by Sultan Qaboos a month later, but encouraged to go into self-exile.[64] The dominant sentiment among members of the regime was that one of this organisation's main goals was to topple the regime and restore the rule of the imamate in Oman.[65] Crucially, most of the accused were from the region around Nizwa, the imamate's historical capital located in the country's conservative interior, and the epicentre of the conflict between the sultanate and the imamate in the 1950s.

The imamate was a millenary institution that had ruled over the Omani interior since 750 CE, led by Ibadi imams.[66] Between the 1850s and the 1950s, the imamate coexisted with the sultanate. In 1954, open conflict erupted between Imam Ghalib bin Ali al-Hinai and Sultan Said bin Taimur al-Said – Sultan Qaboos's father – over the right to the energy revenues from oilfields in contested territory.[67] As the imamate forces were initially defeated by the sultanate, with the support of British-led paramilitary groups, Imam Ghalib's brother, Talib bin Ali al-Hinai, retreated to Saudi Arabia. He then formed the Oman Liberation Army with financial and training support from Saudi Arabia and Egypt, and waged a new phase of the guerrilla in 1957, surrendering two years later.[68] The Sultan declared the imamate over and officially extended his control over the country's interior. However, Imam Talib and a few other leaders from the Oman Liberation Army fled once again to Saudi Arabia, where they continued ntermittently to plot small-scale operations to destabilise the regime.[69]

While the imamate's ideology was that of a fundamentalist Islamic semi-theocracy, Sultan Said bin Taimur never aimed to compete with the imamate on the grounds of religious legitimacy. Neither did Sultan Qaboos, who built his legitimacy on the socioeconomic development of Oman and worked to reshape the religious ingredient of the national identity mix, attempting to enshrine ideas of tolerance and moderation as structural features of the domestic and international discourse of Omani Ibadi Islam.[70] By promoting ideas of moderation through public education, religious indoctrination, media discourse and political rhetoric, Sultan Qaboos 'tried to make religious moderation and tolerance key elements of the country's national identity'.[71] These efforts were instrumental in the Sultan's nation-building efforts at the beginning of his reign in the 1970s.[72] At that time, Oman had been through two civil conflicts – the imamate's insurgency and the Dhofari rebellion – and had been attracting immigrants of Omani descent from Africa and Asia with the prospect of oil-derived economic development. It was an ethnically, linguistically, religiously, and culturally diverse and potentially conflictual society, which had to be turned into a nation. The values of moderation and tolerance also worked well to 'make sure that Islamist groups would have less traction in the country and, therefore, their capabilities to become a serious threat to the regime would be limited'.[73] Sultan Qaboos's approach largely succeeded. The number of Omanis supporting or partaking in jihadi activities remained very low, even after the rise of Daesh.[74] Non-violent or Ibadi Islamists were largely co-opted. Those arrested in 1995 and 2005 were all pardoned months later. Former dissidents – Omanis from imamate stronghold Nizwa and descendants of former Imams – were given positions of prestige and State responsibility in ministries and the security forces.[75] A nephew of Imam Muhammad al-Khalili even became Oman's first Minister of Education.[76]

Islamists have not been perceived as an existential threat by the Omani leadership since 2011 either. Individuals that could be identified as Islamists did take part, in small numbers, in the 2011 protests, both in Sohar and in Salalah, and the influence of Muslim Brotherhood cells was 'visible but underground', given that membership of the Brotherhood in Oman is a criminal offence that may result in being blacklisted from holding public office.[77] However, generally speaking, the Islamists' demands seconded the socioeconomic grievances of the wider population, adding a call for more conservatism in societal customs.[78] At a regional level, when, in 2013, Saudi Arabia, the UAE, and Kuwait supported the military coup by Abdel Fattah al-Sisi against the Brotherhood-led Government of Mohammad Morsi in Egypt, Oman did not take a distinct side but criticised the post-coup crackdown on Brotherhood supporters in the country, fearing that repression would radicalise non-violent Egyptian Islamists.[79]

This eclectic approach by the Omani regime indicated that the potential political danger posed by Islamism, be it Sunni or Ibadi, had been conceptualised as a risk rather than a threat in Oman. Given their limited capabilities, the prospects for Islamist groups to become dominant actors in the sultanate's political, social, and religious landscapes are relatively small. Still, Islamism theoretically has the historical legacy and the ideological charge to be perceived as a threat with a potential political dimension and, given Oman's high degree of sociopolitical diversity, a societal dimension. This perhaps also explains why, while the Omani regime did not join the Saudi–Emirati post-2011 policies against the Brotherhood, it also never subscribed to Qatar's engagement policies, either under Sultan Qaboos or under Sultan Haitham after 2020. Moreover, Sultan Haitham feared that Omani tolerance of the Brotherhood might provoke Saudi and Emirati hostility towards the sultanate. In fact, in response to Saudi–Emirati accusations that the sultanate was supporting Hamoud Saeed al-Makhlafi, a leading figure from Yemen's Muslim Brotherhood, Sultan Haitham ejected a number of Yemeni Islamist politicians and media representatives from the sultanate in October 2020. As with other questions, the leadership transition had heightened the self-consciousness of the Omani regime vis-à-vis its vulnerabilities and, therefore, its perception of looming threats against its stability and identity, or the functional integrity of the country's boundaries and institutions.

Oman's security priorities after 2011

The security calculus of the sultanate in the ten years after the Arab Spring can be divided into two phases: before and after the death of Sultan Qaboos in 2020. Between 2011 and 2020, the Omani regime acknowledged the country's socioeconomic vulnerabilities, but its threat perceptions focused on the impact of regional instability on the sultanate, and Muscat was more actively involved in pursuing de-escalation. After 2020, the regime reshuffled its security priorities, focusing on its socioeconomic vulnerabilities as an access point for exogenous and intermestic threats, and diverted its political energy from regional de-escalation towards securing the identity and stability of the new fragile leadership. Haitham bin Tariq al-Sa'id became Sultan just as the COVID-19 pandemic hit, and was soon faced with protests based on socioeconomic grievances across the sultanate in May 2021. Throughout the decade, Muscat's perceptions of Iran and Islamists, as well as of fellow GCC monarchies, remained unique compared to the other GCC states.

If maintaining regional balance has traditionally been a major foreign policy priority for Oman, this became even more relevant after the Arab Spring, as regional politics became polarised and fault lines around Iran and Islamism deepened.[80] After 2011, Saudi Arabia and Iran had become involved in proxy confrontations on several fronts, from Lebanese and Iraqi politics to the battlefield of Syria and Yemen. From 2015 onwards, the Yemen war in particular represented the most significant security concern for Oman: first, because it brought the Iranian–Saudi confrontation directly to the sultanate's southern borders, with potential spill-overs of violence into the sultanate; then, because the Omani leadership did see the assertive course followed by the Saudi Crown Prince Mohammad bin Salman and Emirati Crown Prince Mohammad bin Zayed as a threat.[81] For example, the Omani leadership grew increasingly convinced that the true aim of the draconian measures taken by Riyadh and Abu Dhabi against Qatar was to coerce Doha into aligning fully with the quartet's regional politics, renouncing its independent stance.[82] As a GCC member that has consistently made foreign policy choices diverging from those of Saudi Arabia, and as the Gulf monarchy closest to Iran, Oman feared it might become a future target of the same pressure strategy, particularly from the UAE.[83]

The historical background for this lingering hostility between Oman and the UAE is substantial. The two countries had decades-long open disputes and occasional small-scale armed confrontations until as late as 2000.[84] Oman did not open an Embassy in the UAE until 1987, and did not send an Ambassador until 1992.[85] Amid this historical context, after Mohammad bin Zayed became Crown Prince of Abu Dhabi in 2004 there was deterioration in bilateral relations.[86] At the end of 2010, Oman's State news agency reported that its 'security services uncovered a spying network belonging to the state security apparatus of the United Arab Emirates, targeting Oman', and that an undisclosed number of Omani nationals had been arrested, including some who worked for the Government.[87] Omani authorities then claimed that the UAE had deployed other operatives to support the Sohar protests in 2011.[88] Again, in 2019 Oman's Criminal Court sentenced five Emiratis and one Omani for spying on behalf of the UAE.[89] The UAE's growing influence in the southern Yemeni region of al-Mahra, which borders Dhofar, as a consequence of its participation in the Saudi-led war in Yemen, was also considered as deeply problematic.[90] The Omani leadership was concerned that Abu Dhabi would dislodge Omani influence in al-Mahra, upsetting local stability and using the region as a platform for an infiltration strategy, similar to what they believe was orchestrated in Sohar, into the politically sensitive region of Dhofar.[91]

The Yemen war also threatened Oman's ability to remain neutral, given the importance of the dossier for Tehran on one hand, and Riyadh and Abu Dhabi on the other.[92] In general, rising tensions with Iran resulted in unprecedented pressure on Muscat. The election of a Republican administration led by Donald Trump and featuring anti-Iran hawks – such as State Secretary Mike Pompeo and National Security Advisor John Bolton

– resulted in the 2018 US withdrawal from the JCPOA and a full-fledged ostracism of Oman. Rising tensions led to Iranian attacks on Emirati tankers in Emirati territorial waters, as well as on Saudi energy infra-structures, in 2019. It also led to a tit-for-tat between Iran and the USA, with attacks on American forces in Iraq, Tehran downing a US drone, and ultimately the assassination of IRGC General and Commander of the Quds Force, Qasem Suleimani, in January 2020. The Omani leadership viewed this gradual but relentless escalation as the most severe threat. It was an external threat damaging the sultanate's international political interests, such as maintaining the regional balance, as well as its inter-national economic and security interest: free and safe circulation in the Strait of Hormuz.

In comparison, at least before the COVID-19 pandemic, the leadership seemed to underestimate the countries economic imbalances and socioeco-nomic vulnerabilities that had emerged in 2011 and persisted more or less unresolved ten years later.[93] In 2011, the Government published its highest budget ever, by a margin of 29 per cent, to cover emergency measures, such as the raising of subsidies and pensions, to soothe protesters.[94] With the oil and gas sector still accounting for more than 70 per cent of Government revenues, the drastic fall of energy prices in 2014 then pushed the budget deficit to 15.95 per cent of the GDP in 2015, 21.3 per cent in 2016, and 12.8 per cent in 2017.[95] These numbers, in turn, plunged Oman's interna-tional credit agencies' ratings to 'junk' level in 2017.[96] International bod-ies, including the International Monetary Fund, have consistently asked the Omani Government to cut back public spending, including by drastically reducing subsidies.[97] While some benefits have since been eliminated and new fees introduced, the Government avoided sensitive spending cuts in welfare (which constitutes around 40 per cent of the budget), and contin-ued to create public sector jobs, with further public debt, to address rising youth unemployment.[98] After hiring 50,000 young people in 2011, mainly in the bloated security forces, in 2017 the Government promoted new plans to hire 25,000 more young Omanis.[99] In 2019 the World Bank estimated Omani youth unemployment still to be 49 per cent. The Government has also extended in scope its 'Omanisation' policies: i.e. labour policies aimed at pushing private sector companies to hire at least a minimum quota of Omani nationals in their workforce.[100] The sultanate's economic diversifica-tion strategy,, Oman 2040, and the country's Five-Year Development Plan (2016–2020) has struggled to attract foreign investments and to create jobs and prosperity in the non-oil sector. In this context, the impact of the 'dou-ble shock' linked to the COVID-19 pandemic was very significant.[101] As a consequence of the collapse in energy prices and the prolonged lockdown on economic activities, Oman's GDP contracted by 6.4 per cent in 2020;

the fiscal deficit rose to 17.3 per cent of GDP; and central government debt increased to 81 per cent of GDP, up from 60 per cent in 2019.

With no significant improvement to the economic outlook, small-scale rallies by unemployed Omani youth restarted in Muscat, Salalah, and Sur in 2018. The Government again responded with an arrest campaign – especially in Dhofar – as well as with the promise to create 25,000 jobs for Omani nationals in the public sector, and to introduce restrictions on the employment of foreign nationals.[102] Yet, contained unrest and strikes continued in 2019 and significantly escalated in 2021, as a result of the economic shocks created by the COVID-19 pandemic. Originating in the northern coastal city of Sohar on 23 May 2021, turmoil rapidly spread to several towns and cities across the country. The protesters demanded better job opportunities, the eradication of corruption, and the enhancement of their living conditions, and lamented the introduction of a 5 per cent VAT a month before. Although the demonstrations were brought under control by June, there is no doubt that the 2021 wave of unrest had echoes of the Arab Spring, posing a substantial challenge to Sultan Haitham, only four months after his enthronement.[103]

Under Sultan Qaboos, the strategy of involving exponents of the different sociopolitical and tribal groups of the sultanate in the management of economic power, thus giving them a stake into the regime's stability, worked as an antidote to the transformation of threats from external to intermestic. While this strategy has prevented the emergence of sociopolitical vulnerabilities, it has left socioeconomic vulnerabilities to fester. Under the new leadership of Sultan Haitham, these vulnerabilities have come to be viewed as potential pressure points to be leveraged by other regional players in order to accrue influence in the sultanate at the expense of the regime's stability and identity, and the functional integrity of the country's boundaries and its institutions. Ten years after the Arab Spring, Oman felt less safe than ever.

Notes

1 A participant at these rallies (the Green Marches) wrote a comprehensive account of the Omani Spring in Said al-Hashimi, *Al-Rabi al-Umani: Qaraa fi al-Siyaqat wa-l-Dalalat (The Omani Spring: A Reading of Its Context and Implications)* (Beirut: Dar al-Farabi, 2013).

2 Marc Valeri, 'Simmering Unrest and Succession Challenges in Oman', Carnegie Endowment for International Peace (2015), https://carnegieendowment.org/2015/01/28/simmering-unrest-and-succession-challenges-in-oman-pub-58843 (accessed 17 September 2022).

3 *Ibid.*

4 *Ibid.*

5 Said Sultan al-Hashimi, 'The Omani Spring: Towards the Break of a New Dawn', Brief 52, Arab Reform Initiative, 27 November 2011, www.arab-ref orm.net/publication/the-omani-spring-towards-the-break-of-a-new-dawn/ (accessed 17 September 2022).

6 Interview by the author of a Government official and member of the royal family, Muscat, 24 April 2018.

7 Al-Hashimi, 'The Omani Spring'.

8 Valeri, 'Simmering Unrest'.

9 *Ibid.*, 9

10 Basma Mubarak Said, 'The Future of Reform in Oman', *Contemporary Arab Affairs* 9:1 (2016), 46–67 (61).

11 Interview by the author of an Omani Government official, Muscat, 24 April 2018; interview by the author of a former Middle East advisor at the UK's Ministry of Defence, London, 1 April 2019.

12 A full account of the Dhofar war can be found in Abdel Razzaq Takriti, *Monsoon Revolution: Republicans, Sultans, and Empires in Oman, 1965–1976* (Oxford: Oxford University Press, 2013).

13 See *ibid.* After the war, several former dissidents associated with the Dhofar Liberation Front were by-and-large co-opted, the main example in this regard being Yusuf bin 'Alawi bin 'Abdullah, Minister Responsible for Foreign Affairs since 1982.

14 Interview by the author of an Omani Government official, Muscat, 24 April 2018.

15 J. Romano and Lee Seeger, 'Rentierism and Reform: Youth Unemployment and Economic Policy in Oman', Institute for Middle East Studies, IMES Paper Capstone Series (May 2014), https://cpb-us-e1.wpmucdn.com/blogs.gwu.edu/ dist/6/1613/files/2018/11/Romano-Seeger-Capstone-Final-xlu6ps.pdf (accessed 20 July 2023).

16 *Ibid.*, 43.

17 Sasha Hodgson and Darren Hanson, 'Enforcing Nationalisation in the GCC: Private Sector Progress, Strategy, and Policy for Sustainable Nationalization', *Middle East Journal of Business* 9:2 (2014), 17–24 (21).

18 *Ibid.*

19 Interview by the author of an Omani diplomat, Rome, 14 December 2017.

20 Cafiero and Karasik, 'Kuwait, Oman, and the Qatar Crisis'.

21 *Ibid.*

22 *Ibid.*

23 'Qatar–Oman Trade Volume Increases', *The Peninsula*, 10 September 2017, www.thepeninsulaqatar.com/article/10/09/2017/Qatar-Oman-trade-volume-increases (accessed 17 September 2022).

24 Ahmed Nawaz Hakro and Abdallah Mohammed Omezzine, 'Oil Prices and Macroeconomic Dynamics of the Oman Economy', *Journal of Developing Areas* 5:1 (2016), 1–27.

25 *Ibid.*

26 See for instance a classic work on the topic by Robert Keohane, 'Lilliputians' Dilemmas: Small States in International Politics', *International Organization* 23:2 (1969), 291–310.

27 Ana Echagüe, 'Oman: The Outlier', Fundación para las Relaciones Internacionales y el Diálogo Exterior, 27 November 2015, http://fride.org/publ ication/1279/oman:-the-outlier. (accessed 17 September 2022).

28 The challenges triggered by the Sultan's illness as well as by the uncertainty over the succession are explored in detail in Said, 'The Future of Reform in Oman'.

29 Takriti, *Monsoon Revolution*.

30 Jones and Ridout, *A History of Modern Oman*, 166.

31 Quoted in Joseph Kechichian, *Oman and the World* (Washington, DC: RAND, 1995), 104.

32 Basma Mubarak Said, 'Oman, Iranian Rapprochement and a GCC Union', Al Jazeera Centre for Studies, 21 January 2014, https://studies.aljazeera.net/en/reports/2014/01/20141218365065800.html (accessed 17 September 2022).

33 Marc Valeri, 'Iran–Oman Relations since the 1970s: A Mutually Beneficial Modus Vivendi', in Bahgat, Ehteshami, and Quilliam, *Security and Bilateral Issues*.

34 *Ibid.*

35 *Ibid.*

36 *Ibid.*

37 *Ibid.*

38 Jeffrey Lefebvre, 'Oman's Foreign Policy in the Twenty-First Century', *Middle East Policy Council* 12:1 (2010), 99–114.

39 Kenneth Katzman, 'Oman: Reform, Security and Foreign Policy', Congressional Research Service, 27 December 2013, www.fas.org/sgp/crs/mideast/RS21534.pdf, 14 (accessed 17 September 2022).

40 Telephone interview by the author of an Omani journalist, 23 April 2018.

41 Echagüe, 'Oman'.

42 Marc Valeri, 'High Visibility Low Profile: The Shi'a in Oman under Sultan Qaboos', *International Journal of Middle East Studies* 42:2 (2010), 251–268.

43 Calvin Allen and W. Lynn Rigsbee, *Oman under Qaboos: From Coup to Constitution, 1970–1996* (London and Portland: Frank Cass, 2000).

44 *Ibid.*

45 Khalid Al-Azri, *Social and Gender Inequality in Oman: The Power of Religious and Political Tradition* (London: Routledge, 2012), 50–51.

46 Valeri, 'High Visibility Low Profile'.

47 Zaynab Motaqizada, 'Shia'yan Oman' (Oman's Shi'ites), in *Joghra ya- e Siasi Shi'yan Manteqa Khalij Fars (Political Geography of Shi'ites in the Persian Gulf)* (Qom: Shia Shenasi, 2005), 129.

48 Valeri, 'High Visibility Low Profile', 254.

49 Louër, *Transnational Shiite Politics*, 146–149.

50 Interview by the author of an Omani Government official, Muscat, 24 April 2018; interview by the author of a senior advisor to Oman's Ministry of Foreign Affairs, London, 8 April 2019.

51 Said, 'The Future of Reform in Oman'.

52 Interview by the author of an Omani Government official, Muscat, 24 April 2018; interview by the author of a senior advisor to Oman's Ministry of Foreign Affairs, London, 8 April 2019.

53 Said, 'Oman, Iranian Rapprochement and a GCC Union'.

54 See for example Courtney Freer, 'The Changing Islamist Landscape of the Gulf Arab States', Issue Paper 9, Arab Gulf States Institute in Washington (2016), https://issuu.com/agsiw/docs/freer_print_issuu (accessed 4 August 2023); Hedges and Cafiero, 'The GCC and the Muslim Brotherhood'.

55 Telephone interview by the author of an Omani journalist, 23 April 2018; interview by the author of an Omani professor of political science, Muscat, 25 April 2018.

56 Quoted in Hedges and Cafiero, 'The GCC and the Muslim Brotherhood'.

57 Abdullah Baabood, 'Islamism in the Gulf Region', in Khaled Hroub (ed.), *Political Islam: Context versus Ideology* (London: Saqi, 2010), 68.

58 *Ibid.*

59 Quoted in Hedges and Cafiero, ' The GCC and the Muslim Brotherhood'.

60 Valeri, 'Simmering Unrest', 8.

61 *Ibid.*

62 J. E. Peterson, 'Oman: Three and a Half Decades of Change and Development', *Middle East Policy* 11:2 (2004), 125–137.

63 *Ibid.*

64 Baabood, 'Islamism in the Gulf Region', 69.

65 Interview by the author of a Government official and member of the royal family, Muscat, 24 April 2018.

66 John Craven Wilkinson, *The Imamate Tradition of Oman* (Cambridge: Cambridge University Press, 1987), 169–176.

67 *Ibid.*, 182.

68 J. E. Peterson, 'Britain and the Oman War: An Arabian Entanglement', *Asian Affairs* 7:3 (1976), 285–298.

69 *Ibid.*

70 Dale Eickelman, 'From Theocracy to Monarchy: Authority and Legitimacy in Inner Oman, 1935–1957', *International Journal of Middle East Studies* 17:1 (1985), 3–24 (12); Judith Miller, 'Creating Modern Oman: An Interview with Sultan Qabus', *Foreign Affairs* 76:3 (1997), 13–18.

71 Interview by the author of a senior advisor to Oman's Ministry of Foreign Affairs, London, 8 April 2019.

72 *Ibid.*

73 Interview by the author of an Omani diplomat, Rome, 14 December 2017.

74 In 2015 it was even suggested in a report titled 'Who Inspires the Syrian Foreign Fighters' by the UK-based International Centre for the Study of Radicalisation and Political Violence (ICSR) that no Omanis had joined the group at all. See Fahad Al Mukrashi, 'No Omanis Have Joined Daesh, Monitoring Group Says', Gulf News, 1 July 2015, https://gulfnews.com/world/gulf/oman/no-omanis-have-joined-daesh-monitoring-group-says-1.1544007 (accessed 17 September 2022).

While this seems an overly optimistic assumption, several sources have agreed that a very low number of Omani recruits joined Daesh; see Efraim Benmelech and Esteban Klor, 'What Explains the Flow of Foreign Fighters to ISIS?', National Bureau of Economic Research, Working Paper 22190 (2016), https:// www.nber.org/system/files/working_papers/w22190/w22190.pdf (accessed 4 August 2023).

75 Marc Valeri, 'The Ṣuḥār Paradox: Social and Political Mobilisations in the Sultanate of Oman since 2011', *Arabian Humanities* 4 (2015), https://doi.org/ 10.4000/cy.2828 (accessed 23 July 2023).

76 Allen and Rigsbee, *Oman under Qaboos.*

77 Valeri, 'The Ṣuḥār Paradox'.

78 *Ibid.*

79 Interview by the author of an Omani diplomat, Rome, 14 December 2017.

80 Gause, 'Beyond Sectarianism'.

81 Comments by a senior official within Oman's Ministry of Foreign Affairs at a closed-doors roundtable, Muscat, 25 February 2020.

82 Joe Gill, 'Saudi–UAE Pact's Aggressive Policies Could Break Up GCC: Oman Source', *Middle East Eye*, 19 December 2017, www.middleeasteye.net/ news/saudi-uae-reckless-policies-could-break-gcc-oman-source-435138828 (accessed 17 September 2022).

83 Comments by a senior official within Oman's Ministry of Foreign Affairs at a closed-doors roundtable, Muscat, 25 February 2020.

84 Fatma Al-Sayegh, 'The UAE and Oman: Opportunities and Challenges in the Twenty-First Century', *Middle East Policy* 9:3 (2002), 124–137.

85 *Ibid.*

86 Comments by a senior official within Oman's Ministry of Foreign Affairs at a closed-doors roundtable, Muscat, 25 February 2020.

87 'Oman Says Uncovers UAE Spy Ring', Reuters, 30 January 2011, www.reuters. com/article/uk-oman-emirates-spying-idUKTRE70T13720110130 (accessed 17 September 2022).

88 *Ibid.*

89 'Oman Jails Members of UAE Spy Cell', Economist Intelligence Unit, 23 April 2019, http://country.eiu.com/article.aspx?articleid=647916448 (accessed 17 September 2022).

90 Eleonora Ardemagni, 'Strategic Borderlands: The UAE–Oman Rivalry Benefits Tehran', Istituto Studi di Politica Internazionale, 21 June 2019, www.ispionl ine.it/it/pubblicazione/strategic-borderlands-uae-oman-rivalry-benefits-tehran-23347 (accessed 17 September 2022).

91 Interview by the author of an official at Oman's National Defence College, Muscat, 25 February 2020.

92 Mehran Kamrava, *Troubled Waters: Insecurity in the Persian Gulf.* (New York: Cornell University Press, 2018), 165.

93 Interview by the author of an Omani economist, Berlin, 15 September 2022.

94 Weshah Razzak, 'Examining the Performance of Oman's Economy', Research Paper 103379, University of Munich, 2020, 11.

95   *Ibid.*, 12.

96   Robert Mogielnicki, 'Oman's VAT Implementation Is Necessary and Not Enough', Arab Gulf States Institute in Washington, 8 April 2021, https://agsiw. org/omans-economic-reforms-struggle-to-keep-pace-with-mounting-challen ges/ (accessed 18 September 2022).

97   *Ibid.*

98   Interview by the author of an Omani economist, Berlin, 15 September 2022.

99   Razzak, 'Examining the Performance of Oman's Economy', 12.

100 *Ibid.*, 13.

101 Robert Mogielnicki, 'Oman's Economic Reforms Struggle to Keep Pace with Mounting Challenges', Arab Gulf States Institute in Washington, 22 October 2020, https://agsiw.org/omans-economic-reforms-struggle-to-keep-pace-with-mounting-challenges/ (accessed 18 September 2022).

102 *Ibid.*

103 Rafiah al-Talei, 'Oman's Protesters Seek Jobs and Reform', Arab Gulf States Institute in Washington, 11 June 2021, https://agsiw.org/omans-protesters-seek-jobs-and-reform/ (accessed 9 September 2022).

Part III

The centrifugal nature of Qatar's security

8

Qatar

The impact of the Arab Spring

When looking at threat perceptions in the Arab monarchies of the Gulf in the 2010s, Qatar stands out as a unique case. These divergences are particularly evident in the different experience lived by Qatar during the 2011 Arab Spring. For starters, the Qatari regime did not witness meaningful street protests in 2011 or perceive an actual challenge to its identity, sovereignty, or stability.

In Qatar the demographics don't really allow for dissent: in a population of 2.6 million, there are only 300,000 Qataris, '10 per cent of whom is made by the royal family and related clans and 30 per cent of whom is constituted by supporting tribes'.[1] Qatari citizens enjoy the highest GDP per capita worldwide, are entitled to a cradle-to-grave generous welfare system including free healthcare and education, and have the assurance of getting a well-paid job in the public sector as well as several subsidies and grants.[2] Unlike in neighbouring Bahrain, the resources at the disposal of the State for these provisions are so significant that all Qatari citizens, irrespective of their ethnic origin or sectarian affiliation, have been the recipients of some of this largesse.[3] As a result, no significant economic inequality or active economic marginalisation – i.e. socioeconomic vulnerabilities – appears evident in relation to wealth distribution among Qatari citizens. Qataris simply have too much at stake in their system: something that often turns into political apathy and a lack of democratic aspiration.[4]

And yet, encouraged by events in Egypt and Tunisia, a small reformist group named Qataris for Reform emerged in March 2011.[5] Around sixty Qataris, led by academic Ali Khalifa al-Kuwari, started discussing economic and political reform. Al-Kuwari gathered their ideas in a 2012 book titled *Al Sha'hab Yurid Islah fi Qatar... Aidan (The People Want Reform in Qatar... Too)*, which was quickly banned in Qatar.[6] The author did not call for the overthrow of the regime but complained about the lack of freedom of expression, the lack of transparency in the management of the public finances, and the lack of popular participation in all domains of decision-making.[7] This comprehensive criticism of the State and the related calls for reform weren't embraced by the wider public outside small elite groups, however. There were other instances of individual dissidents, such as poet Muhammad al-Ajami and blogger Sultan al-Khulaifi, who were detained for posting a poem 'inciting the overthrow of the regime and insulting Emir Hamad', and for writing on censorship in Qatar, respectively.[8]

The Qatari Government had confidence that the leadership was not going to be destabilised by the Arab Spring.[9] Doha thus did not embrace the process of hyper-securitisation that characterised post-2011 policy-making in the GCC vis-à-vis the actors that emerged empowered from the Arab Spring, such as Iran and the Muslim Brotherhood.[10] In fact, where the other GCC regimes saw a threat to their stability, Doha's leaders saw an opportunity. Qatari officials reacted to popular protests in the wider MENA region with enthusiasm, declaring support for the opposition movements and for 'institutions that guarantee … participation', 'comprehensive reform', and the dissemination of 'democratic awareness'.[11] The Government supported groups linked to the Muslim Brotherhood, as they seemed well placed to emerge victorious after the regime changes regionally. Al Jazeera, particularly in its Arabic version, rode the wave of popular mobilisation in Egypt, Libya, Yemen, and Syria, providing a platform to anti-regime activists.[12] The coverage of protests in Bahrain was markedly milder, featuring only a documentary on Al Jazeera English (*Shouting in the Dark*) that was withdrawn after protests by Saudi Arabia and Bahrain, prompting accusations of Doha for inconsistency and hypocrisy.[13] Even there, the Qatari leadership, while supporting the Peninsula Shield intervention in Bahrain with two advisors, was actively involved in negotiations between the Manama Government and the main Shi'a opposition bloc, al-Wefaq, an initiative that would later be denounced by the quartet as an attempt to destabilise Bahrain.[14]

Domestically, the Qatari regime did not even feel the need to introduce reforms or enticements to secure the population's allegiance. Interestingly, the young Emir Tamim instead opened a new season of reforms as a consequence of the 2017 intra-GCC crisis.[15] Pushing limited liberalisation was deemed valuable in attracting international support as well as reinforcing the Emir's domestic legitimacy, challenged by the quartet's initiative against Doha. For example, in November 2017, Emir Tamim announced that in 2019 Qatar would hold long-promised elections for two-thirds of the Majilis as-Shura (Consultative Assembly) for the first time in the country's history. Elections were then postponed to October 2021, when thirty elected members joined fifteen royally appointed others on the Shura Council.[16]

If, given the absence of strong socioeconomic and sociopolitical vulnerabilities and fault lines, the Arab Spring did not pose a threat to its rulers, the hostile actions of Qatar's neighbours were instead perceived as challenging the legitimacy of the regime and, hence, its stability. The 2014 and 2017 intra-GCC crises saw the risks posed by Saudi Arabia – and its revamped alliance with the UAE – becoming acute external threats, potentially turning into intermestic ones, with multiple dimensions. The threat had a clear economic dimension, as, for example, the closure of Emirati territorial waters to vessels flying the Qatari flag or coming from and going to Qatar on 5 June 2017 risked crippling LNG export, cutting off the main source of revenues for the State.[17] Similarly, the closure of the land border between Qatar and Saudi Arabia presented a severe socioeconomic threat, as, for example, approximately 80 per cent of Qatar's food needed to be transported across that border.[18] The threat had a political dimension too, as both the UAE and Saudi Arabia supported alternative, more accommodating, figures within Qatar's al-Thani royal family – such as Saud bin Nasser al-Thani, Sultan bin Suhaim al-Thani, and Abdullah bin Ali al-Thani – as more legitimate Qatari leaders. Finally, this threat had a societal dimension, in terms of the attempt to target tribal unity. In particular, a red flag was raised after a meeting in the summer of 2017 of the leaders of the al-Murrah tribe, the same clan involved in the 1996 attempted coup, and Saudi Crown Prince Mohammed bin Salman in Jeddah, causing tribal leader Sheikh Taleb bin Lahom bin Shuraim subsequently to declare that the Qatari authorities had turned Qatar into a 'haven for terrorists and their sponsors'.[19] Consequently, in September 2017, fifty-five members of the al-Murrah tribe were stripped of Qatari citizenship, highlighting the regime's sensitivity to the instrumentalisation of cross-border tribes.[20] This particular risk then re-emerged during the 2021 Shura elections, once again highlighting the centrifugal nature of Qatar's security perceptions.

At the same time, the fact that the Qatari regime was resilient to this multi-dimensional threat in 2017 ultimately bolstered its sense of security, solidified with the resolution of the intra-GCC crisis at the al-Ula Summit of January 2021. Having consolidated domestically, Qatar recalibrated its regional and international activism, remaining highly alert to its neighbours' red lines and threatening potential.

Qatar and the 'Shi'a threat'

Post-2011 perceptions of the Qatari leadership vis-à-vis Iran are largely centred around the danger Iran may pose to Qatar's regional interests – rather than to the stability, identity, and sovereignty of the Qatari regime – and are outweighed by Iran's ability to counterbalance other external threats. Iran is thus mostly perceived in Doha as posing an acute external risk, not an existential, political threat. For both Qatar and Iran 'the benefits of mutual accommodation have outweighed the costs of confrontation'.[21] Iran has been a key factor in Qatar's hedging strategy, which is to say that Doha employed relations with Tehran as a counterweight to Riyadh, while attempting not to antagonise either.[22] Iran and Qatar also share sovereignty of the largest gas field in the world, South Pars/North Dome, the source of most of Qatar's wealth, which has given Doha the resources to punch above its weight in international politics.[23] Following to the first deal related to the gas field in 1990, Doha and Tehran consistently maintained some level of cooperation, and in 2008 they even co-founded, with Russia, the Gas Exporting Countries Forum.[24] Another key factor to consider is that in Doha Iran is not perceived as having the intent and capability to pose the threat perceived by other GCC countries: using the local Shi'a population as a leverage against the regime.[25] Qatari Shi'a are estimated to constitute only between 5 and 10 per cent of its citizenry, and they enjoy the same State largesse and generous welfare as other citizens.[26] Generally speaking, it is often noted that, unlike in other GCC countries, Shi'a in Qatar are virtually indistinguishable from their Sunni co-citizens in appearance and behaviour.[27] Like the rest of Qatari society, Shi'a are not particularly active politically, as generally their political and economic status does not elicit specific demands or grievance.[28] Religious discrimination seems uncommon, while many Qatari Shi'a belong to merchant families and are present in most Government departments, albeit that few reach the most senior positions.[29] Sectarian relations have been, at times, under stress, but mostly at moments of intense sectarian violence in the region.

Indeed, throughout history, maintaining working relations with Iran has had a strategic value for Qatar. The Islamic revolution did not have a destabilising echo in Qatar, but Doha remained suspicious of the new Iranian regime and, for instance, sided unequivocally with the UAE on the issue of the islands occupied by Tehran, perhaps fearing that Iran might be harbouring territorial ambitions against Doha too.[30] The reformist presidency of Ali Akbar Hashemi Rafsanjani was well received by Emir Hamad bin Khalifa al-Thani, who, seeking to disenfranchise Qatar from the Saudi shadow, accelerated the hedging strategy towards Iran.[31] The Emir even invited Iranian President Mahmoud Ahmadinejad to attend a GCC meeting in Doha in December 2007, to the annoyance of other GCC leaders.[32]

Emir Hamad's strategy to turn Qatar into a small power with far-reaching capabilities in regional diplomacy, while shielding it from its larger neighbours, encouraged the Qatari leadership even to open channels of communication with Iran-backed non-State actors involved in regional conflicts. In 2008, Qatar negotiated a peace agreement between Saudi Arabia and Iran-backed Houthi rebels in Yemen, whereby Doha pledged over $300 million in reconstruction assistance for the northern Yemeni province of Saada, where the Houthis reside.[33] Qatar joined the military intervention against the Houthis – who had taken over Sana'a in 2014 – only after Saudi pressures and in the aftermath of the 2014 intra-GCC crisis, to debunk accusations of collusion with Iran.[34] Yet in December 2017, the UAE Minister Responsible for Foreign Affairs argued that 'Qatari mediation to save the Houthi sectarian militia is well documented', and between 2017 and 2018 two Qatari intelligence officers – Mohammad al-Otaibi and Mohsen al-Karbi – were arrested while crossing into Yemen and accused of wanting to mediate on behalf of the Houthis.[35] Another controversial case was related to Qatar's engagement with Lebanese Hezbollah. Amid an escalation of political violence in the country, in 2008 Qatar managed to convince Hezbollah to sign the Doha Agreement, which called for a national-unity government and granted the Hezbollah-led opposition voting power in the Lebanese Government.[36] Both the political empowerment and the large funds – totalling around $300 million – pledged by Doha as diplomatic leverage, sparked outrage in Riyadh. Fast-forwarding to 2011, Qatar and Hezbollah found themselves on opposite trenches in the Syrian civil war, during which Qatar supported the Sunni opposition, while Hezbollah intensely fought the regime of Bashar al-Assad.[37] Yet, Qatar was back into a – forced – dialogue with Hezbollah as a consequence of the 2015 kidnapping of a group of Qatari royals in the Iraqi desert by Kata'eb Hezbollah, an Iraqi Shi'a faction funded and supervised by Iran's Quds Force.[38] The hostages became valuable assets for Iran's Quds Forces leader, Qasem Suleimani, who sent a Hezbollah intermediary to Doha offering their release in exchange for Qatar pressuring some rebel groups it sponsored in Syria into a local compromise with Hezbollah.[39] In addition to agreeing to facilitate such a deal, Qatar also had to pay around $700 million to secure the release of the hostages in April 2017: these millions ended up in the coffers of Shi'a militias and were again used by Qatar's GCC neighbours as evidence of Doha's complicity in dealing with groups accused of destabilising the region.[40]

Qatar downgraded its engagement with regional actors considered controversial by other GCC states after the 2014 diplomatic crisis and the ascension of Emir Tamim bin Hamad, who was also less prone than his father to regional adventurism.[41] Emir Tamim rejected the invitation by Iranian President Hassan Rouhani to a 2015 summit in Tehran and downgraded diplomatic relations with the Islamic Republic when the Saudi embassy in Tehran was attacked in January 2016.[42] However, Doha did not sever relations with Iran. Crucially, the posture adopted by Qatar towards the JCPOA was conciliatory: Khalid al-Attiyah, then Qatar's Foreign Minister, was one of the first officials in the region to welcome the nuclear agreement, stating that the deal would make the region safer.[43] A few weeks after the agreement Qatar even spoke in favour of launching a dialogue between Tehran and its Arab neighbours.[44] Qatar also stepped forward in speeding up economic engagement with Iran, and in 2014 the two sides established three joint free trade zones, in Bushehr, Doha, and al-Ruwais.[45] In 2017, this pragmatic attitude paid off in the context of the GCC crisis, when Iran opened its territorial waters to Qatar, allowing it to keep energy export lines active.[46] By attempting to block Qatar's exports and imports, the quartet countries intended to create an economic cost to Qatar's politics, thus potentially tarnishing the leadership's legitimacy. Iran's support was thus a factor in the regime's stability, its identity, and the State's functional integrity: as a result there were no grounds to perceive it as a threat in arguably the most vulnerable moment for the Qatari regime after 2011.

Qatari royals have maintained an effective working relationship with foreign Shi'a leaders, including Iran's Supreme Leader, and revamped those relations after 2017.[47] Qatar leveraged those direct ties by deploying its Foreign Minister Mohammad bin Abdulrahman al-Thani to Tehran to lower tensions after a US strike killed IRGC General Qasem Soleimani in Iraq in January 2020, and to avert a potential Iranian retaliation on the Qatar-located US military base of al-Udeid. Moreover, Qatar replaced Oman as the regional go-between amid the Biden administration's efforts to revive the JCPOA after 2021, trying to entice Iran with the prospect of further Qatari investments in the shared gas field.

Qatar and the 'Islamist threat'

As Qatar's Foreign Minister, Mohammed bin Abdulrahman, often declared, there was no compelling reason to undertake any drastic measure against the Brotherhood, as 'the organization represents no threat to Qatar's security'.[48]

Starting from the 1960s, the Qatari leadership stipulated the import of human resources to build schools and State bureaucracies and, subsequently, the first Egyptian Brotherhood members arrived in Qatar.[49] Galvanised by the retreat of pan-Arab nationalism in the early 1970s, Brotherhood intellectuals saw their influence increase, and finally decided to establish an official branch in Doha in 1975.[50] The Qatari Brotherhood was 'an informal organisation focused primarily on *da'wa* (proselytisation), intense study of *shari'a*, organisation of sporting and social activities'.[51] In 1999, the organisation was dissolved by its members, who were fullu co-opted by the State and continued to staff Qatar's administrative offices.[52]

Yet, instead of ideologically influencing Qatari politics, the Muslim Brotherhood focused mostly on pushing conservative social provisions, such as restricting alcohol sales.[53] The organisation's lack of influence over policy-making is linked to its meagre political penetration among Qatari citizens, and to the small space to perform the welfare functions that the group undertakes elsewhere in the region, which are 'largely satisfied by the state in Doha's archetypal rentier system'.[54]

Rather, the Brotherhood was long seen as a tool by the Qatari regime.[55] The Brotherhood could, for example, be useful as a counterweight to Wahhabism, officially embraced by Qatari leaders, limiting the level of influence that Saudi scholars and jurists – and, therefore, rulers – would exercise on Qatari schools and institutions. Muslim Brotherhood chief ideologue Yousef al-Qaradawi was given a prominent platform and his own show on Al Jazeera 'because he could then work to counterbalance Saudi religious authority, often used to strong-arm Qatar politically'.[56] Similarly, in 2011 Qatar's Emir, perceiving no threat to his political stability, looked at the ousting of old regimes and the rise of Brotherhood-linked political actors as an opportunity to expand his network and influence. Benefiting from consolidated relations with the group, the Qatari Government reached out directly to personalities connected to the Muslim Brotherhood in Egypt, Libya, and Tunisia, channelling support; engaging in dialogue; and building convergences with those who, elected into government between late 2011 and 2012, seemed in the position to shape the region's future.[57] The Qatari leadership had, for instance, longstanding personal connections to Rashid Ghannouchi, leader of Tunisia's Brotherhood-linked Ennahda Party, winning the 2011 elections for the constituent assembly and coming second in the 2014 parliamentary elections.[58] Ghannouchi's son-in-law, Rafik Abdessalem, who spent years in Doha as the head of research at the Al Jazeera Center for Studies, became the country's Foreign Minister from 2011 to 2013.[59] Qatar pledged loans of $1 billion and additional billions in investments to the new Government, becoming the main supporter of post-revolutionary Tunisia.[60] Likewise, in Libya, Qatar channelled substantial support through the exiled cleric Ali al-Sallabi, a long-term resident of Doha and the son of a founding member of the Muslim Brotherhood branch in Benghazi.[61] However, the main case of Qatari support for Brotherhood-affiliated movements emerging after the Arab Spring was in Egypt. There, Doha supported the Muslim Brotherhood's candidate Mohamed Morsi, elected President in June 2012, granting free shipments of LNG, promising tens of billions of dollars in investment, and extending loans of similar magnitude to the Central Bank of Egypt to prop up the economy.[62] Moreover, Qatar strongly supported the new Government on the political front by setting up a new Al Jazeera channel covering Egyptian politics around the clock in a way that was favourable to the Morsi Government, known as Mubasher Misr.[63] Qatar also nurtured links with the local branch of the Muslim Brotherhood and its associates in Syria. To those groups Qatar devolved the lion's share of the billions spent arming Syrian opposition groups between 2011 and 2013.[64] Doha also supported Brotherhood-affiliated candidates politically, such as Ghassan Hitto, who was briefly provisional Prime Minister of the Syrian Government-in-exile.[65] This strategy was underpinned by Qatar's progressive vicinity to Turkey, led by Recep Tayyip Erdoğan and his party Adalet ve Kalkınma Partisi, also sympathetic to Islamism domestically and regionally.

Ankara and Doha coordinated their attempted but unsuccessful response to the 2013 setback that broke the short-lived Brotherhood's momentum. In July 2013 large-scale rallies triggered a coup d'état by the Supreme Council of the Armed Forces in Egypt that put General Abdel Fattah al-Sisi in charge of the country.[66] Al-Sisi, who was supported by Saudi Arabia, the UAE, and Kuwait, subsequently initiated a crackdown against the Brotherhood in Egypt, crushing the group. From 2014, al-Sisi offered decisive support to the UAE militarily and politically to fight the Brotherhood-sympathising Government of Libya, officially recognised by the United Nations, via their allied militias led by General Khalifa Haftar.[67] As Libya subsequently plunged into a stagnating status of cyclical conflict, the UN-recognised Government maintained control over a portion of territory in the western region of the country around the capital, Tripoli. In Syria, Russia's intervention in the war – coupled with US inertia – turned into a string of military victories for the Assad regime and its backers, and a debacle for the Sunni opposition, in particular that linked to the Muslim Brotherhood.[68] Only in Tunisia did the Ennahda Party continue to hold its place in the country's parliamentary democracy. However, in 2016 Ennahda formally declared a division between religion and politics and the desire to go beyond the Muslim Brotherhood model of political Islam.[69]

Perceiving Islamism as a severe threat, the UAE led Saudi Arabia into putting Doha's relations with the Muslim Brotherhood at the centre of the intra-GCC crises of 2014 and 2017. By 2014, Bahrain, Saudi Arabia, and the UAE had designated the Brotherhood a terrorist organisation, conflating the organisation with jihadist others. Based on this, they accused Qatar of supporting terrorism, generating a media storm against Doha.[70] This narrative posed a significant risk to Qatar: it threatened to damage the 'Qatar brand' and to disrupt its strategic interest in being seen as an international business hub.[71]

At the same time, Emir Tamim showed a discontinuous approach to Qatar's engagement with the Brotherhood, cautiously scaling back Doha's involvement in regional conflicts, especially when this involved instrumental interaction with controversial groups, as in Syria.[72] After 2014, Emir Tamim expelled a number of Brotherhood figures – including top foreign affairs official and former minister Amr Darrag; fiery cleric Wagdi Ghoneim; and the Brotherhood's secretary general, Mahmoud Hussein – shut down Al

Jazeera Mubasher Misr, and significantly downsized Doha's relations with Brotherhood affiliates in the region, as stipulated in the Riyadh Agreements.[73] Still, Doha did not fully cut relations with the Brotherhood, as the organisation was still perceived as a political actor legitimated by its vast popularity across the region, and the view that such organisations are 'hard-line Islamists only until they get power, pragmatists after'.[74] Moreover, Qatar became even closer to Turkey, which opened a military base in the emirate in 2016. The Turkish military presence in Qatar was largely perceived as 'the most significant deterrent to a military escalation by the quartet in 2017'.[75] In turn, Qatar significantly boosted the stability and capabilities of inflation-ridden Turkey with direct financial aid, currency swap deals for $15 billion, and investments worth another $15 billion. Ankara and Doha also continued to coordinate in bolstering their regional allies: in late 2019 and early 2020 Turkey intervened militarily in Libya in support of the Tripoli-based Government, and the limited Turkish victory led to a flurry of tripartite deals on political, military, and economic cooperation among Tripoli, Ankara, and Doha that summer.

And yet the priority for Qatar remained to resolve the intra-GCC crisis, perceived as posing a full-fledged threat to the regime. For this reason, at the 2021 al-Ula Summit, Qatar committed fully to reining back support for the Brotherhood regionally.[76] Al Jazeera, both in English and Arabic, toned down criticism of Saudi Arabia and the UAE with regard to human rights violations as well as foreign and domestic policies at large.[77] Al Jazeera and the entire media network funded by Qatar abroad started avoiding *tout court* topics related to the Muslim Brotherhood, removed content critical of the Egyptian Government, and carried out limited and dry reporting on the tenth anniversary of the Arab Spring. Doha preserved its relations with Ankara, but let Turkish President Erdoğan return empty-handed from a trip to Qatar in December 2021, despite a historic financial crisis crippling Turkey.[78] Ankara proceeded to solidify its own rapprochement with the UAE and Saudi Arabia in 2021.[79] That same year, Brotherhood-affiliated parties suffered a crushing electoral defeat in Morocco and were ostracised from political life during a soft coup by Tunisian President Kais Saied, supported by Riyadh and Abu Dhabi.[80] Qatar did not lend support to the Moroccan Justice and Development Party or to Tunisian Ennahda: Doha had pivoted to seek security in its immediate neighbourhood.[81]

Qatar's security priorities after 2011

The 2014 and 2017 intra-GCC crises were perceived as the most significant security threats in the decade between 2011 and 2021. These 'reminded the leaders of the main challenge for Qatar's security: that it is a small country, surrounded by big neighbours with an expansionist, hegemonic policy'.[82]

Open competition among the GCC states, and a related sense of animosity, escalated in the aftermath of the Arab Spring before erupting into the 2014 intra-GCC crisis. Within eight months of young Emir Tamim taking over, in February 2014, Saudi Arabia, Bahrain, and the UAE withdrew their ambassadors from Doha. They believed that Father Emir Hamad and former Prime Minister Hamad bin Jassim bin Jabr al-Thani, the architects of Doha's interventionist Arab Spring policies, were still leading the country from behind the scenes.[83] President Obama's Deputy National Security Advisor for Strategic Communications and Speechwriting, Ben Rhodes, would later declare that only pressures from the USA prevented a military escalation.[84] Although Doha didn't cut relations with the Brotherhood, the leadership believed it had made all the necessary compromises to repair relations with its neighbours.[85] When, three years later, a new and much graver crisis erupted, the perception in Doha was that its GCC neighbours had taken advantage of an opportunity provided by a different White House administration, that of Donald Trump, to pursue a much more hostile scheme.[86] In 2018, Qatar's Defence Minister, Khalid bin Mohammad al-Attiyah, declared that the UAE and Saudi Arabia had had intentions to intervene militarily against Qatar in June 2017.[87] He stated: 'They have tried everything. They tried to provoke the tribes. They used mosques against us. Then they tried to get some puppets to bring in and replace our leaders.'[88] These few sentences sum up the dominant perspective in Doha, that the main goal of the crisis was replacing the incumbent Emir with a more docile candidate, who would throw Doha's financial and political capital behind the regional policies of Riyadh and Abu Dhabi.

Saudi Arabia had long struggled with Qatar's yearning for an autonomous regional policy, embodied by former Emir Hamas. As Crown Prince, Hamad bin Khalifa had been working to diversify Qatar's relations in order to create space for a more independent foreign policy, while his father, Khalifa bin Hamad al-Thani, had ruled in full alignment with Riyadh.[89] In 1992, Qatar signed a defence cooperation agreement with the United States that paved the way for the transfer of US military personnel from Saudi Arabia to Al Udeid air base, not far from the royal palace in Doha, in 2003.[90] That same year, border skirmishes between Saudi Arabia and Qatar broke out in Khafus.[91] In 1995, Hamad took over from his father in a bloodless coup. Saudi Arabia and Bahrain were adamant that Sheikh Khalifa be returned to his position, and allegedly supported at least one counter-coup, enlisting dozens of members from the al-Ghufran branch of the al-Murrah tribe – the largest tribe in Qatar and one that has both Qatari and Saudi connections – to overthrow the new Emir. Once the counter-coup was foiled, Emir Hamad consolidated his position and doubled down on trying to free Qatar from Riyadh's shadow. The establishment in 1996 of the global satellite network Al Jazeera was a milestone. While Al Jazeera was founded primarily to boost the State's soft power, it was also a vehicle to undermine Saudi Arabia's regional leadership: the channel started hosting Saudi dissidents and calling into question Saudi policies to the point that in 2002 Riyadh withdreI its ambassador from Doha for six years. Additionally, Emir Hamad developed Qatar's LNG industry to become a major energy source for the world's most powerful states.[92] Doha could then rely on huge revenues, boosted by the price boom of the early 2000s, to invest in strategic assets around the world. Financial resources were also a key instrument in a diplomatic offensive, dubbed *riyalpolitik*, that allowed Qatar to broker high-profile deals in the first decade of the twenty-first century, as well as play out its post-Arab Spring strategy. It is in this context that decision-makers in Doha see the 2017 decision to close all land and sea borders between Qatar and its neighbours as trying to cut LNG export lines and, therefore, to flatten Qatar's resources.

When, on 5 June 2017, vessels flying the Qatari flag, coming from or going to Qatar, were not allowed to transit through the UAE's territorial waters or call at Emirati ports – which serve as regional bunkering or refuelling hubs – Qatar's energy industry risked being crippled. Only Iran's willingness to allow transit through its territorial waters and Oman's willingness to welcome vessels into its ports allowed Qatar to preserve its fundamental energy trade. This was also possible because of the political position of the big Asian and European powers depending on Qatari gas, including China, Japan, and the United Kingdom, keen on avoiding disruptions to their supplies.[93] However, the rerouting of energy trade came with costs that had to be sustained by the Qatari State. Similarly, rearranging imports away from the land border with Saudi Arabia was a challenge. As mentioned earlier, approximately 80 per cent of Qatar's food needs to cross that border, and the Qatari Government needed quickly to arrange the air-lifting of food, as well as other goods, from Turkey and Iran, with a significant increase in expenditure.[94] The financial sector was also impacted, as banks from the quartet began removing term deposits held in Qatar. Three months after the crisis, rating agency Moody's stated that Qatar had injected more than $40 billion of its state reserves into supporting its economy and financial system, and Qatar's Sovereign Wealth Fund, the Qatar Investment Authority, had liquidated foreign assets for more than $20 billion in order to inject them into the domestic banking system.[95] Although, a year later, economic data showed the resilience of Qatar's financial system as well as its domestic economy, with the GDP growing by approximately 2 per cent, there is no denying that such resilience necessitated the diversion of financial resources inwards.[96]

By draining the surplus in Qatari resources invested in its regional *riyal-politik*, the quartet aimed at downsizing, if not neutralising, Qatar's role in regional politics.[97] In addition, creating economic and financial damage was perceived in Qatar as a way to induce members of the al-Thani royal family, heavily invested in international business, to support an alternative contender for the throne or to pressure Emir Tamim to comply with the quartet's demands.

Both the UAE and Saudi Arabia have pushed and supported alternative, more accommodating, figures within Qatar's al-Thani royal family as challengers to the throne. In June 2017, Abu Dhabi's *The National* was already promoting a little-known descendant of Emir Sheikh Ahmed bin Ali, deposed in 1972 – Sheikh Saud bin Nasser al-Thani – as 'Qatar's leading opposition figure'.[98] As months went by, other royal dissidents, including Sultan bin Suhaim al-Thani and Sheikh Abdullah bin Ali al-Thani, were presented as legitimate heirs.[99] The al-Thani royal family – long the most fractious in the GCC – did initially split, with some members advocating a capitulation to the Saudi–Emirati demands and others suggesting a reliance on Iranian protection.[100] However, the family ultimately stood behind Emir Tamim, also encouraged by the strong popular support shown towards the Emir, as the crisis triggered an outpouring of 'rally-round-the-flag' nationalism.[101]

While the population was mostly cohesive in its loyalty to the incumbent rulers, the leadership in Doha did perceive a societal dimension in the threat posed by the intra-GCC crisis, in terms of the attempt to target tribal unity. In particular, a red flag was raised after a meeting between leaders of the al-Murrah tribe, the same clan involved in the 1996 attempted coup, and Saudi Crown Prince Mohammed bin Salman in Jeddah in the summer of 2017.[102] Tribal leader Sheikh Taleb bin Lahom bin Shuraim, who was among those meeting the Saudi Crown Prince, later stated in an interview with Dubai-based, Saudi-owned outlet Al-Arabiya that the Qatari authorities had turned Qatar into a 'haven for terrorists and their sponsors'.[103] While the State has largely co-opted Qatari tribes over the decades, tribes 'were looked upon with suspicion, if they had Saudi origins or maintained relations with the kingdom'.[104] Consequently, in September 2017, fifty-five members of the al-Murrah tribe were stripped of Qatari citizenship, highlighting how the instrumentalisation of cross-border tribes employed as sociopolitical ammunition was perceived as a source of serious intermestic risk for the leadership in Qatar.[105] The tribal question heated up again significantly ahead of the country's first ever Shura Council elections in 2021. The Council consists of thirty elected members and fifteen appointed by the Emir. The Council has no legislative but only advisory powers, and is asked for an opinion on rather than approval of the budget and ministers, with particularly limited influence over portfolios such as defence and foreign affairs.

A sharp controversy erupted on Qatari social media after the country's new electoral law indirectly blocked members of the al-Murrah tribe from running for office. The protest also move offline, lasting for over a month and resulting in fifteen arrests. Law no. 6 regulating elections of the Shura Council divided Qatari citizens into descendants of Qataris who were citizens in 1930 – who are entitled both to run for office and to vote, naturalised Qataris born in Qatar and whose grandfathers were Qatari – who have the right to vote but are not entitled to run for office, and Qataris naturalised after 1930 – who are neither eligible to run for office nor to vote.[106] The al-Murrah tribe fell into the second category, and members of the tribe claimed the law was 'specifically designed to exclude them'.[107] Certainly, Qatar set up its elections with tribes as the central political unit, as instead of creating electoral districts comprising various tribal groups the legislation asked candidates to stand in districts closely linked to the origins of their tribe, harking back to 1930s data. Under this system, several former Government officials and prominent businessmen were elected, and a broadly equitable tribal balance was achieved. But the regime's sensitivity to the issue persisted, with Emir Tamim focusing his opening speech at the first session of the Shura Council on 'negative manifestations' of tribalism in the country, which, he said, could jeopardise national unity.[108]

While the sociopolitical dimension of the intra-GCC crises left some sort of trace for years, the economic impact was neutralised so effectively that Qatar weathered the COVID-19 pandemic much more easily than any of its neighbours. While the number of cases was relatively high, the death rate stayed low thanks to effective legislation and a good healthcare system.[109] Moreover, the macroeconomic shock was limited compared to the other Gulf monarchies, with the GDP falling negative by 3.7 per cent and the deficit never exceeding 2 per cent of the GDP.[110] That was possible because the Qatar hydrocarbon industry relies on LNG, the price of which – unlike that of oil – remained stable throughout 2020.[111] Nonetheless, travel bans and lockdowns damaged the tourism, entertainment, and trade sectors, causing around two-thirds of the overall GDP loss. In response, Doha implemented a series of macroeconomic stimulus measures worth around 14 per cent of GDP.[112]

In early 2021, the non-energy sector was already showing signs of recovery, and the Government doubled down on infrastructural projects, especially those related to the 2022 FIFA World Cup. The World Cup became the major focus of the Qatari Government as a catalyst for international prestige and soft power. Positive relations with its neighbours and as many international actors as possible would underpin the success of this conspicuous investment.[113]

Indeed, by 2021, Qatar had gone back to the future and embraced the centripetal nature of its security by balancing its position in the immediate neighbourhood, the Gulf, and internationally.[114] While struggling to reconcile fully with Bahrain and the UAE, who led the political boycott and economic embargo against Doha, Qatari leaders focused on repairing ties with Riyadh, and reverted to a hedging policy between Saudi Arabia and Iran, with the addition of Turkey. Internationally, Qatar doubled down on solidifying its decades-long security partnership with the USA. Shocked at the White House's support for the Saudi–Emirati hostilities in 2017 under the Trump administration, Doha found new ways to solidify the US–Qatar partnership. Qatar worked to become a useful regional pivot for Washington, seeking to retrench from the wider MENA region, by fully supporting – politically and financially – US interests in complex challenges, such as the withdrawal from Afghanistan in August 2020.[115] In turn, the new and more orthodox US administration, led by Democratic President Joe Biden, rewarded Qatar with major non-NATO ally status in March 2022. Finally, Qatar emerged as a key interlocutor for European countries seeking to diversify away from dependence on Russian gas after Moscow's invasion of Ukraine in early 2022.[116] This was a departure from the approach of other Gulf monarchies, such as the UAE and Saudi Arabia, who focused on diversifying their international partnerships away from western countries.

Feeling more or less secure in the absence of significant socioeconomic and sociopolitical vulnerabilities, Qatar had rebuilt its regional and international support systems along traditional lines, by embracing a nonconfrontational approach and focusing on soft power. At the same time, the 2014 and 2017 experiences had an impact on the regime's security perceptions, which remained alert to the threatening potential of its neighbours, its stability identity, and its functional integrity.

Notes

1 Interview by the author of a Qatari academic at Qatar University, Doha, 14 April 2019.
2 Jocelyn Sage Mitchell, 'Beyond Allocation: The Politics of Legitimacy in Qatar', Ph.D. thesis, Georgetown University, 2013.
3 Jill Crystal, *Oil and Politics in the Gulf: Rulers and Merchants in Kuwait and Qatar* (Cambridge: Cambridge University Press, 1990), 156–157.
4 This was validated, for instance, by the results of two separate public opinion polls conducted by Qatar University's Social and Economic Survey Research Institute revealing that, between December 2010 and June 2011, the proportion of Qataris who rated living in a democratic country as 'very important' dropped from 74 per cent to 65 per cent, with a relative decrease of 12 per cent. Justin Gengler, 'Qatar's Ambivalent Democratization', *Foreign Policy*,

1 November 2011, https://foreignpolicy.com/2011/11/01/qatars-ambivalent-democratization/ (accessed 17 September 2022).

5 'Interview with Dr Ali Khalifa Al Kuwari, Author of "The People Want Reform … in Qatar, Too" – Statehood & Participation', *Heinrich-Böll-Stiftung*, 3 March 2014, https://lb.boell.org/en/2014/03/03/interview-dr-ali-khalifa-al-kuwari-author-people-want-reform-qatar-too-statehood (accessed 17 September 2022).

6 'Democracy? That's for Other Arabs', *Economist*, 8 June 2013, www.economist.com/middle-east-and-africa/2013/06/08/democracy-thats-for-other-arabs (accessed 17 September 2022).

7 'Ali Khalifa al-Kuwari, *Al Sha'hab Yurid Islah fi Qatar … Aidan (The People Want Reform in Qatar … Too)* (Beirut: Al Maaref Forum, 2012).

8 Freer, *Rentier Islamism*, 119.

9 Interview by the author of a senior advisor to Qatar's Ministry of Foreign Affairs, Doha, 14 April 2019.

10 Almezaini and Rickli, *The Small Gulf States*.

11 Quotes are extracted from 'Doha Forum 2013 – the Speech by His Highness Hamad bin Khalifa al-Thani, Emir of the State of Qatar', Doha, 20 May 2013, https://dohaforum2014.qatarconferences.org/includes/data/2013/speeches/Emir_speech.pdf (accessed 7 August 2023).

12 Kristian Ulrichsen, *Qatar and the Arab Spring* (Oxford: Oxford University Press, 2014).

13 Elias Groll, 'Hypocrisy Alert: Qatari Leader Throws Weight behind Pluralism and Inclusiveness', *Foreign Policy*, 24 February 2014, https://foreignpolicy.com/2015/02/24/hypocrisy_alert_qatari_leader_throws_weight_behind_pluralism_and_inclusiveness_obama_thani/ (accessed 18 September 2022).

14 'Bahrain Accuses Opposition Leaders of Spying for Qatar', Reuters, 1 November 2017, www.reuters.com/article/us-bahrain-security-arrests-idUSKBN1D14YX (accessed 18 September 2022).

15 Interview by the author of a senior Qatari diplomat, Brussels, 13 June 2022.

16 Dania Thafer, 'Qatar's First Elected Parliament May Have More Power than Other Persian Gulf Legislatures. Here's Why', *Washington Post*, 14 October 2021, https://tinyurl.com/mr3mc26c (accessed 18 September 2021).

17 Ulrichsen, *Qatar and the Gulf Crisis*.

18 *Ibid*.

19 Maryam Al-Kuwari, 'State–Tribe Relations and Political Legitimacy in Qatar and Kuwait: A Comparative Study', Ph.D. dissertation (University of Exeter, 2021).

20 *Ibid*.

21 Mehran Kamrava 'Iran–Qatar Relations', in Bahgat, Ehteshami, and Quilliam, *Security and Bilateral Issues*, 167.

22 *Ibid*.

23 Mehran Kamrava, *Qatar: Small State, Big Politics* (New York: Cornell University Press, 2015).

24 *Ibid*.

25 'Iran has supported Shi'a opposition in several GCC countries, but never in Qatar', argued an advisor to Qatar's Ministry of Defence in an interview with the author, Doha, 15 April 2019.

26 'Shia in Qatar Quiet on Political Issues, Bothered by Qaradawi', *Wikileaks*, 7 February 2007, https://wikileaks.org/plusd/cables/07DOHA137_a.html (accessed 18 September 2022).

27 Interview by the author of a Qatari academic at Qatar University, Doha, 14 April 2019.

28 Interview by the author of a Doha-based professor of international relations, Doha, 15 April 2019.

29 Majidyar, 'Is Sectarian Balance in the United Arab Emirates, Oman, and Qatar at Risk?'.

30 Rouhullah Ramazani, 'Iran's Islamic Revolution and the Persian Gulf', *Current History* 84:498 (1985), 5–8 (7).

31 Kamrava, 'Iran–Qatar Relations'.

32 *Ibid.*

33 Abdullah Baabood and Ahmed Baabood, 'Omani and Qatari Roles in the Yemen Crisis', in Stephen W. Day and Noel Brehony (eds), *Global, Regional, and Local Dynamics in the Yemen Crisis*. (Cham: Palgrave Macmillan, 2020).

34 *Ibid.*

35 'Qatar Intelligence Officer Arrested over Al Houthi Links', Gulf News, 3 May 2018, https://gulfnews.com/news/gulf/qatar/qatar-intelligence-officer-arrested-over-al-houthi-links-1.2215773 (accessed 18 September 2022); 'UAE: Qatar Tried to Mediate in Yemen to Save Houthis', Al Arabiya, 20 December 2017, https://english.alarabiya.net/en/News/gulf/2017/12/02/UAE-Qatar-tried-to-mediate-in-Yemen-to-save-Houthis.html (accessed 18 September 2022).

36 Kamrava, *Qatar*.

37 *Ibid.*

38 Robert Worth, 'Kidnapped Royalty Become Pawns in Iran's Deadly Plot', *New York Times*, 14 March 2018, www.nytimes.com/2018/03/14/magazine/how-a-ransom-for-royal-falconers-reshaped-the-middle-east.html (accessed 18 September 2022).

39 *Ibid.*

40 Mohammed Alyahya, 'The Rift with Qatar as Seen in Riyadh', Atlantic Council, 13 June 2017, www.atlanticcouncil.org/blogs/menasource/the-rift-with-qatar-as-seen-in-riyadh/ (accessed 18 September 2022).

41 Interview by the author of an advisor to Qatar's Ministry of Defence, Doha, 15 April 2019.

42 Kamrava, 'Iran–Qatar Relations', 178.

43 Quoted in Ali Mamouri, 'Is Qatar Iran's Door to the Gulf?, *Al-Monitor*, 4 November 2015, www.al-monitor.com/pulse/originals/2015/11/iran-qatar-rapprochement-middle-east.html (accessed 18 September 2022).

44 *Ibid.*

45 'Tehran, Doha Will Establish Free Trade Zones', *Iran Daily*, 6 July 2014.

46 Boussois, 'Iran and Qatar'.

47 'Leader Meets with Emir of Qatar', official website of Ayatollah Khamenei, 20 December 2010, http://english.khamenei.ir/news/1396/Leader-Meets-with-Emir-of-Qatar (accessed 18 September 2022).

48 Mohammed al-Sulaimi, ' "We Don't, Won't and Didn't Support the Muslim Brotherhood"', Qatar FM Tells Arab News', *Arab News*, 17 May 2017, www.arabnews.com/node/1100781/middle-east (accessed 5 August 2023).

49 See Rosemarie Said Zahlan, *The Creation of Qatar* (London: Croom Helm, 1979), 96.

50 Abd Allah al-Nafisi, 'Al-Hala al-Islamiyya fi Qatar' (The Status of Islam in Qatar), *IslamToday*, 12 March 2007, www.islamtoday.net/bohooth/artshow-19-8828.htm (accessed 14 July 2018).

51 Freer. 'Rentier Islamism', 486.

52 *Ibid.*, 488.

53 *Ibid.*

54 *Ibid.*, 488.

55 David Roberts, 'Qatar and the Brotherhood', *Survival* 56:4 (2014), 23–32.

56 Interview by the author of a senior Qatari diplomat, Skype, 3 October 2017.

57 A Doha-based senior professor of international relations and Gulf studies, interviewed by the author in Doha on 15 April 2019, argued that: 'After the Arab Spring, Doha saw the Islamists as being in the strongest position to obtain power, because of their large social traction across the region. The Emir and Prime Minister of Qatar thought they could position themselves well by leveraging their longstanding personal connections with Brotherhood-associated figures.'

58 Ulrichsen, *Qatar and the Arab Spring.*

59 Roberts, 'Qatar and the Muslim Brotherhood', 90.

60 *Ibid.*

61 *Ibid.*

62 Ulrichsen, *Qatar and the Arab Spring.*

63 *Ibid.*

64 Kamrava, *Qatar.*

65 *Ibid.*

66 David Butter, 'Egypt and the Gulf: Allies and Rivals', Research Paper 20, Chatham House (2020), www.chathamhouse.org/sites/default/files/CHHJ8 102-Egypt-and-Gulf-RP-WEB_0.pdf (accessed 5 August 2023).

67 *Ibid.*

68 Phillips, *The Battle for Syria.*

69 Anne Wolf, *Political Islam in Tunisia: The History of Ennahda* (Oxford: Oxford University Press, 2017).

70 'Qatar Must Stop Supporting Terror, Jubeir Tells UN', *Saudi Gazette*, 24 September 2017, http://saudigazette.com.sa/article/517879/SAUDI-ARABIA/Qatar (accessed 18 September 2022).

71 Kamrava, *Qatar.*

72 Kamrava, *Troubled Waters*, 52.

73 *Ibid.*, 134.

74 Interview by the author of a senior Qatari diplomat, Skype, 3 October 2017.
75 Interview by the author of a Doha-based senior advisor to Qatar's Ministry of Defence, Doha, 15 April 2019.
76 Kabalan, 'The Al-Ula GCC Summit'.
77 *Ibid.*
78 Interview by the author of an official from Qatar's Ministry of Foreign Affairs, Doha, 28 March 2022.
79 Vohar, 'Erdoğan's War'.
80 Burgat, 'Is the Era of Islamists Coming to an End?'.
81 Interview by the author of an official from Qatar's Ministry of Foreign Affairs, Doha, 28 March 2022.
82 Interview by the author of a Qatari academic at Qatar University, Doha, 14 April 2019.
83 Alyahya, 'The Rift with Qatar'.
84 Susan Glasser, 'The Full Transcript: Ben Rhodes and Samantha Power', podcast, *The Global Politico*, 15 January 2018, www.politico.com/magazine/story/2018/01/15/the-full-transcript-ben-rhodes-and-samantha-power-216322 (accessed 8 August 2022).
85 Interview by the author of an official from Qatar's Ministry of Foreign Affairs, Doha, 28 March 2022.
86 *Ibid.*
87 Lally Weymouth, 'Qatar to Saudi Arabia: Quit Trying to Overthrow Our Government', *Washington Post*, 2 February 2018, www.washingtonpost.com/outlook/qatar-to-saudi-arabia-quit-trying-to-overthrow-our-government/2018/02/02 (accessed 8 August 2022).
88 *Ibid.*
89 David Roberts, *Qatar: Securing the Global Ambitions of a City State* (London: Hurst, 2017), 18–22.
90 Brahim Saidy, 'Qatari–US Military Relations: Context, Evolution and Prospects', *Contemporary Arab Affairs* 10:2 (2017), 286–299.
91 Roberts, *Qatar*.
92 Kamrava, *Qatar*.
93 Ulrichsen, *Qatar and the Gulf Crisis*.
94 *Ibid.*
95 *Ibid.*
96 *Ibid.*
97 Interview by the author of an official from Qatar's Ministry of Foreign Affairs, Doha, 28 March 2022.
98 'Qatar Should Stop Funding Terrorism, Says Leading Opposition Figure', *The National*, 3 June 2017, www.thenational.ae/world/qatar-should-stop-funding-terrorism-says-leading-opposition-figure-1.52119 (accessed 18 September 2022).
99 David Roberts, 'Qatar's Domestic Stability and the Gulf Crisis', Policy Watch 2847, Washington Institute for Near East Policy, 18 August 2017, www.washingtoninstitute.org/policy-analysis/qatars-domestic-stability-and-gulf-crisis (accessed 17 September 2022).

100 'Qatar: Al-Thanis Divided over Future Direction', *Gulf States News* 1039, 22 June 2017.

101 Roberts, 'Qatar's Domestic Stability'.

102 Al-Kuwari, 'State–Tribe Relations'.

103 *Ibid.*

104 Interview by the author of a researcher specialising in political sociology in Qatar, London, 5 February 2019.

105 Al-Kuwari, 'State–Tribe Relations'.

106 Nadda Osman, 'Qatar's "Discriminatory" Laws Exclude Thousands from Voting or Running in Elections', *Middle East Eye*, 10 September 2021, www.middleeasteye.net/news/qatar-discriminatory-laws-exclude-thousands-voting-elections (accessed 17 September 2022).

107 Interview by the author of a researcher specialising in political sociology in Qatar, Doha, 28 March 2022.

108 'Emir of Qatar Wary Tribal Tensions Could Spill over into Shura Council Much as in Kuwait', *The Arab Weekly*, 27 October 2021, https://thearabweekly.com/emir-qatar-wary-tribal-tensions-could-spill-over-shura-council-much-kuwait (accessed 17 September 2022).

109 Amit Varma, Ismail Gergaa, Maysaa Ashkanani, Sarah Musa, and Miaaz Zidan, 'Analysis of Qatar's Successful Public Health Policy in Dealing with the COVID-19 Pandemic', *International Journal of Medical Reviews and Case Reports* 5:2 (2021), 6–11.

110 Manal Shehabi, 'Quantifying Long-Term Impacts of COVID-19 and Oil Price Shocks in a Gulf Oil Economy', Oxford Institute for Energy Studies (2021), www.oxfordenergy.org/wpcms/wp-content/uploads/2021/06/Quantifying-Long-Term-Impacts-of-COVID-19-and-Oil-price-Shocks-in-a-Gulf-Oil-Economy-MEP25.pdf (accessed 23 July 2023).

111 *Ibid.*

112 *Ibid.*

113 Interview by the author of a senior Qatari diplomat, Brussels, 13 June 2022.

114 *Ibid.*

115 Cooper, 'As Qatar Becomes a Non-NATO Ally, Greater Responsibility Conveys with the Status'.

116 Hubbard, 'The War in Ukraine'.

9

Conclusions

The security agenda in the GCC monarchies after 2011

The Arab Spring represented the trigger for a transformative process for the interpretation of the notions of threat and security in the GCC monarchies. This transformation also had substantial repercussions for the monarchies' domestic and foreign policies, which remain, as they traditionally were, structurally linked to their security needs and perceptions. Post-Arab Spring dynamics defied conventional wisdom and disproved long-held assumptions, such as the presence of a common perception and prioritisation of threats among the six monarchies, rarely questioned before 2011. In fact, even in 2011 most of the literature highlighted that, while at the regional level the GCC countries' response to the events of 2011 were markedly divergent, the Council's members closed ranks in a display of shared security priorities to push back against change when protests reached their own backyard.[1] In fact, while efforts towards cooperation and even integration accelerated immediately after the Arab Spring reached the shores of the GCC, between 2011 and 2012, these were tactical and short-lived, rather than strategic. This lack of alignment broke a pattern of GCC member states closing ranks around one another when confronted by threatening external events, a pattern that had surfaced during the wave in the 1960s and 1970s of pan-Arab nationalism and socialism, then with the Iranian revolution and its aftermath in the 1980s, and in the 1990 Iraqi invasion of Kuwait.

In fact, perceptions of the Arab Spring itself were significantly different in the GCC capitals. As the one GCC country perceiving virtually no domestic repercussions from the 2011 uprisings, Qatar showed no intention of adopting the hyper-securitised positions of the other GCC monarchies in the years that followed. Oman and Kuwait, perceiving predominantly causes for dissent rather than insurgency, focused their response on containing identified root causes for the protests at the domestic level. Saudi Arabia, Bahrain, and the UAE instead perceived the protests of 2011 as the result of an overlapping of domestic and international forces, whereby hostile external actors were at work to leverage the grievances of 'otherised' domestic communities.[2] These different perspectives soon shaped policies, resulting in the two intra-GCC crises of 2014 and 2017.

In-depth analysis of the drivers and consequences of the intra-GCC crises has shown that the sub-regional level of study is no longer sufficient to decode security perceptions in the GCC, and the domestic level is necessary. The steps taken in the past decades at the GCC level towards increased integration are counterbalanced by the setbacks in the same process, and all of these trends align in the inability to treat the GCC as a fully coherent body or referent object of security. Moreover, the many domestic specificities of individual countries, including differences in the macroeconomic or socioeconomic indicators, sociopolitical cultures, and systems need to be appreciated, as they all work as inputs into the security thinking of GCC leaders.

Over the years, these national specificities have been increasingly diverging rather than converging.[3] The national chapters of the Arab Spring brought to the surface the different sociopolitical and socioeconomic vulnerabilities of the individual countries that, interpreted by the political culture and filtered by the governing systems, accelerated the polarisation of their security calculus, setting the monarchies on a collision course. Against the backdrop of the longstanding issue of preserving sovereignty from neighbours, state-centric considerations became predominant, even in the face of external threats. At the same time, the security interdependencies deepened both among the six GCC countries within the Gulf, plus Iraq, Iran, and Yemen, as a security sub-complex, and the larger security complex of the MENA region. It is hard to dispute that the Gulf states are part of the larger MENA system, tied to it though the transnational identity of Islam, longstanding relations at the political level, centuries-long trade relations, and a history of cultural exchanges and migrations.[4] The security and political trends defining the post-2011 environment in the GCC have emerged, in the analysis, as strictly interdependent with the same trends taking hold in the wider MENA region. When, as traditional key regional players from North Africa and the Levant were weakened and destabilised by the uprisings and subsequent volatility, the GCC monarchies stepped up their regional postures to an unprecedented level of proactivity – with the additional aim of filling the vacuum created by the perceived retrenchment of the United States – they became further embroiled in regional security trends. As a result, unpacking the security calculus of the GCC monarchies also enables us better to understand the increasingly complex political security environment in the wider region.

As a matter of fact, in the ten years after the Arab Spring, the entire MENA region witnessed both polarisation and fragmentation, on several levels.[5]

Beyond the upsurge of sectarianism, fuelled by a power fight between Saudi Arabia and Iran, fault lines within the Sunni communities have become deeper, through competition between a pro-Islamist and an anti-Islamist camp. These trends, locking regional actors in a zero-sum game, manifested themselves in the context of all other challenges – including civil wars, the empowerment of non-State actors, and economic volatility – that rose in the aftermath of 2011. In fact, given the multitude of challenges simultaneously emerging at a regional and domestic level, the years after the Arab Spring have proved apt to examine how leaderships' security perceptions vary when exogenous and endogenous issues interact and overlap with the background of hyper-securitisation. This hyper-securitisation and polarisation only partially subsided in 2021, allowing for the start of the strategic pause. By that point, GCC regimes generally felt they had weathered the strategic chaos ushered in by the Arab Spring and that the regional order was not going to be upheld by either Iran and its allies or Sunni Islamists affiliated to the Muslim Brotherhood, who were significantly weakened.

Rethinking threat analysis

The objects at the centre of this study, threat perceptions, can be elusive. It remains a major challenge to differentiate between the actual perceptions of the State leadership and State-orchestrated narratives on security threats created via the securitisation of non-threatening issues, instrumentally employed for political reasons.[6] By exaggerating threat levels and emphasising their ability to guarantee security, GCC regimes reinforce domestic backing and guarantee political quiescence.[7] For instance, the 'Iran threat' is often magnified in the public discourse of certain GCC countries, especially Saudi Arabia and Bahrain. At the same time, this is not entirely manufactured, in the sense that it genuinely features in the security calculus at leadership level as an existential and multi-dimensional threat. This is similar to the perception in the UAE of the Muslim Brotherhood and related Islamist movements, which were indeed seen as an existential intermestic threat between 2011 and 2014, and as a severe external political risk between 2014 and 2020. Two considerations apply to the analysis of these idiosyncrasies: first, that the narratives themselves, even when inflated, inevitably influence perceptions, and second, that regimes' perceptions of their stability are routinely equated with national security in the cognition of local leaders so that, therefore, these are not necessarily dependent on objective considerations, i.e. the threatening actors' capabilities or intent. This strategy of exaggerating threat levels, while useful in the short term, is problematic in the longer term. Although heightening security concerns amongst the population, or rallying it against a common enemy, have long been considered effective political tactics to guarantee quiescence, in the long term the magnification of sectarian threats and the hyper-securitisation of political dissent deepen the sociopolitical cleavages that constitute the main sociopolitical vulnerability of the GCC countries and increase their exposure to threats.

The analysis of threat perceptions in this volume started by rethinking the definition of key concepts, as relevant to the context studied. Security – as perceived by the GCC leaders – has hereby been defined to be about the ability of regimes to maintain their independent identity, functional integrity, and sovereignty against forces of change, which they see as hostile. It is a definition that assumes the basic primacy of political variables in determining the degree of security that states and regimes enjoy. This research has confirmed, among other things, the conflation of regime security with national security in the perspective of regional policy-makers, as long established by the area literature.

Moreover, building on Barry Buzan's ideas about the comprehensiveness of the concept of security, and his approach of mixing, loosely, neorealism and constructivism, this volume has embraced the idea of security as a matter of degree, and theorised a differentiation between threats and risks. The term 'threat' has thus been employed specifically to define risks that become acute enough to take on overtly political dimensions, i.e. dangers perceived as having intent and capability to hinder State boundaries, State institutions, regime stability, or sovereignty. This distinction has proved particularly appropriate and useful in the hyper-securitised GCC region. In rejecting the uncritical and too frequent use of the term 'threat' to indicate dangers of various intensity, this threat/risk distinction has allowed for a more nuanced description of how dangers are perceived in the different countries of the GCC region, and it has shown how dangers perceived as full-fledged threats in certain countries are viewed merely as risks by the leaders of others.

Strictly related to the work on definitions has been the development of paradigms to systematise security thinking, by categorising pre-existing and emerging threats as they are perceived by policy-makers in the GCC. This system, categorising perceived threats by dimension and type, has helped to build a nuanced and comprehensive analysis of threat perceptions, paving the way for further findings on the process of prioritisation, including as a crucial element to analyse and, to a certain extent, anticipate, policy actions. The five dimensions employed in this study are inspired by those that Buzan indicated in the 1990s: political, military, economic, societal, ecological.[8] In addition, in order to take into account the increasing multi-dimensionality of threats and their intersections, this system has gone beyond the distinction between external and internal threats offered by the existing literature, speaking of three types of threats: external threats, originating from external sources that affect the international interests of the country; internal threats, which have endogenous roots and affect the internal stability of the country; and intermestic threats, having a mixed external and internal nature, such as those moved by exogenous motives but spreading internally and having domestic implications and, vice versa, those that have endogenous stimuli but repercussions in the international sphere.

This intermestic category has featured prominently in all six empirical chapters, as findings show how every GCC regime is concerned with intermestic risks or intermestic threats. This is a validation of the conclusions reached in the area studies literature with regard to the porosity of borders in the MENA region, where trans-border political identities are strong and transnational links have historically been able to mobilise people across borders.[9] However, the perceived threats are more often considered to originate in the Gulf itself rather than in the wider MENA region, as was the case between the 1960s and the 1990s. In fact, intermestic threats have emerged in this volume as the most salient in the perceptions of GCC leaders, and ot is these that are given priority. Certainly, all potential dangers of domestic destabilisation are treated as more serious and immediate than the classic power capabilities of external menace. However, the research also showed that intermestic threats can proliferate chiefly by leveraging pre-existing socioeconomic and sociopolitical internal vulnerabilities, and these are not at all times acknowledged by the regimes, so they don't necessarily inform their perceptions as key factors. At times GCC leaders ignore or exploit said vulnerabilities to perpetuate a status quo that preserves their hegemonic position in the short term, despite weakening State stability in the long term. Defined as conditions thought to determine the incapacity of the State to contain, cope with, adapt to, and recover from a damaging phenomenon, vulnerabilities have been divided into the sociopolitical and the socioeconomic, the former described as an institutionalised low level of sociopolitical cohesiveness determining a deficit of ruling legitimacy, and the latter as large inequalities, imbalances, or idiosyncrasies in the national economy. While socioeconomic vulnerabilities are far more frequently leveraged in the narratives and discourses, sociopolitical vulnerabilities are not, and yet feature more prominently in leaderships' perceptions. This emerged especially in the chapter dedicated to Saudi Arabia: while, since 2014, socioeconomic challenges have featured prominently in the State narratives, the country's much less talked-about sociopolitical vulnerabilities – in terms of lack of cohesion, contested legitimacy, and fragile social contract – occupy a markedly stronger position in informing the leadership's perceptions on security. In addition, other vulnerabilities, such as the GCC countries' location in a geopolitically volatile and unstable context – especially given the fact that five out of the six are small states – and the fragmented and underskilled status of their armed and security forces, feature strongly in the regimes' perceptions of external threats. However, the fact that these shortcomings in their armed forces are a known consequence of the conscious policy of 'coup-proofing' highlights how external threats, in most cases, have not retained priority status. [10]

Vulnerabilities are often overshadowed by other factors that inform the shaping of security perceptions more prominently.[11] Systemic or historical sociocultural factors, including the countries' sociopolitical identities as Arab-Islamic monarchies and tribal societies, maintain a crucial role. Contingent factors such as events and actors, both the senders and the receivers of threatening signals, are also relevant.[12] Senders – i.e. the sources of potential threats – can represent the embodiment and personification of a threat, and can be neutralised much more easily than the actual danger. Receivers – i.e. the threatened – are even more central, down to the analysis of their individual cognition and even emotions.[13] These 'human factors', including personality, political cognition, and socialisation, have emerged as crucial in the GCC context, where all states are autocratic, and leaders, who are seen as the final representatives of the national interest, face little to no constraint in acting according to their own perceptions in foreign and security policies.[14] This mechanism has surfaced prominently in all cases explored, with the partial exception of Kuwait, where the National Assembly has been able to influence the leadership's threat perceptions, as well as foreign and security policies. In the other cases, with varying degrees of intensity, human factors remain predominant, and it becomes key to identify who are the most influential securitising individuals in each regime. It then falls upon them to acknowledge or ignore the role of structural vulnerabilities when operationalising threat images.

The polarisation of security agendas

In the decade following the Arab Spring, the actors emerging as catalysts of the GCC countries' security calculus were Iran – and its allied regional groups – and the diverse constellation of Islamist groups coalescing around the Muslim Brotherhood. These were the actors at the centre of the Riyadh Agreements and the intra-GCC crises. Yet, while there is general agreement on the fact that these actors can represent potential risk to regimes' stability, each leadership in the GCC views them differently with regard to their own stability and security.

This also applies to the signatories of the Riyadh Agreements – Saudi Arabia, the UAE, and Bahrain – whose security thinking has shown divergences in this research. While the Muslim Brotherhood and Iran-supported Shi'a groups were presented as absolute priority threats in the Riyadh Agreements and the subsequent public discourse from senior leaders in Riyadh, Manama, and Abu Dhabi, the actual perceptions are much more nuanced. The strongest convergence found has been between Saudi Arabia and Bahrain, where Iran and its proxies are perceived and treated as priority threats, with a strong intermestic dimension. Iran is also perceived as a crucial danger in the UAE, especially since 2018, where, however, the threat is perceived as an exogenous and external one. As a very small state, Bahrain has mitigated the domestic component of the Iranian threat through repression, especially following the disbanding of the Shi'a opposition party known as al-Wefaq in 2016, while the external dimension has gained more prominence since. Indeed, after 2014 Bahrain focused on strengthening relations with its external backers, especially Saudi Arabia and the UAE, including at the risk of needing unconvincingly to re-examine relations with Islamist groups such as the Muslim Brotherhood, perceived in Manama simply as a risk and part and parcel of its – shrinking – domestic loyalist base. Saudi Arabia underwent a similar re-examination process from 2015, following the ascension to Riyadh's royal palace of Mohammad bin Salman, who started treating Islamism as an intermestic threat. In fact, since 2015 Saudi Arabia has exhibited the most hyper-securitised approach among all cases studied, with a totalitarian attitude towards any potential political challenge to the royal family, including, for instance, tribalism. This speaks of strong underlying vulnerabilities weakening the State from within and creating enabling conditions for exogenous dangers to develop an internal presence – or, in other words, of Saudi Arabia's ontological insecurity, i.e. the vulnerability of the Saudi State's identity.[15] Matters of ontological insecurity and developing State–society relations not based on totalitarian tactics remain the most crucial questions for long-term stability in both Saudi Arabia and Bahrain. Similarly, the insufficient coherence and strIngth of the ideational foundations underpinning the nation-state are also central in the security thinking of the UAE. The internal coherence of the UAE's federal system, weakened by institutionalised intra-Emirates differences and divergences, remains at the centre of the UAE's security calculus.

Divergences on the substance of the intra-GCC crises are undoubtedly more substantial in Kuwait and Oman. In neither country have Iran-backed Shi'a groups and the Muslim Brotherhood been perceived by the regime as having the intent and capabilities to undermine their identity, stability, and sovereignty, or the functional integrity of the country's borders or institutions. To Kuwait and Oman these actors are better described as risks. In both countries, the local chapters of the Arab Spring have represented watershed moments in their security calculus. However, these have been regarded as endogenous phenomena, highlighting socioeconomic vulnerabilities with sociopolitical implications, such as the perceived high level of corruption in Kuwait and the rampant economic stagnation in Oman. The unique semi-democratic political system in Kuwait, in particular, seems to have had a role in mitigating the Kuwaiti leadership's security perceptions with regard to endogenous political risks. For both countries, the security priorities instead revolve around the possible escalation of regional instability. As two small states in one of the world's most volatile regions, both Kuwait and Oman have always treated regional balance as a major foreign policy priority. However, in the post-Arab Spring era this matter grew in urgency as the likelihood of regional conflicts increased. The difference between the two is that for Kuwaiti policy-makers, still affected by the memories of Iraq's 1990s invasion, active regional balancing also serves needs of internal equilibrium: with a diverse national fabric, and citizens hailing originally from all around the region, Kuwait has traditionally been exposed to the reverberations of regional events, and related deepening of internal rifts and fault lines. In other words, the potential for external issues to morph into intermestic ones is regarded as substantial, with marginalised communities such as the bidoons being kept under strict observation. In Oman, on the other hand, Sultan Qaboos's strategy of giving stakes in the regime's stability to the exponents of the different sociopolitical and tribal groups of the Sultanate was long considered an antidote to the consolidation of an internal dimension to exogenous dangers. This induced Sultan Qaboos to underestimate the potential threat of socioeconomic vulnerabilities, prioritising political instability in the neighbourhood and potential spill-overs form the Yemen war. For both Kuwait and Oman the 2020 leadership successions, following the deaths of Sultan Qaboos and Emir Sabah, were a flashpoint that shook the foundations of their resilience. For both – but especially for the latter – the focus of security perceptions moved to the risk that regional powers would exploit royal factionalism to influence the leadership contest, or leverage the temporary weakness of the countries, and their vulnerabilities, to extend their own influence.

Indeed, one of the main findings of this research is that GCC countries increasingly started to look at one another as potential sources of threats to stability. Kuwait and Oman worried about how their sovereignty might be impinged in the tense regional environment. But it was in Qatar that other GCC players emerged as the priority threat in the leadership's perceptions. In fact, the initiatives pursued by the quartet countries have been perceived in Doha as a substantial external threat, intended to become an intermestic one. The quartet countries, from Doha's perspective, targeted the regime's stability and identity, through an international campaign to delegitimise the Qatari regime by proposing alternative contenders for the throne, as well as endangering the functional integrity of the country's boundaries and its institutions by sealing all land, sea, and air borders with Qatar, and cutting all economic and financial relations. The fact that the Qatari population seemed to remain receptive to the leadership's message of unity at this most vulnerable moment in politics was evidence that, similarly to what happened during the 2011 Arab uprisings, threats do not easily propagate from the regional to the domestic level in Qatar, where socioeconomic and sociopolitical vulnerabilities are, largely speaking, contained. For the same reason, Islamist movements such as the Muslim Brotherhood and Iran and its proxies are not perceived as existential or intermestic threats in Qatar. Iran does feature in the security calculus of the Qatari leadership, but as an external risk rather than a threat, and one mitigated after the 2017 intra-GCC crisis, when Tehran extended some assistance to Doha.

Overall, this volume's findings confirmed that GCC security is not a one-dimensional phenomenon but is instead a complex matrix of domestic and regional factors, each playing a distinctive role in formulating the definition, categorisation, perception, and prioritisation of threats. In light of these factors, further studies should once and for all overcome the idea of the GCC region as a security community. Given the growing interdependence of security in the Gulf, the theoretical paradigm of the regional security complex might be more useful. In fact, future studies and research on Gulf security could further unpack the fragmentation of the security calculus by comparing and contrasting perceptions of the different countries, including the GCC monarchies, but also Iraq and Iran. Applying the theoretical framework for analysis developed in this volume to the security calculus of Iran and Iraq would prepare the ground for a scholarly comparative analysis. Finally, even keeping a more traditional focus – on the impact of changing security perceptions on the international relations of the Gulf – would provide for original descriptive and analytical works, given that two core elements have substantially changed since 2011: security perceptions, as demonstrated in this volume, and the global geopolitical order, which after the Arab Spring has definitively moved to competitive multi-polarity, with considerable implications for policy-making.

Multi-polarity in the Gulf: thoughts and inputs on policy

The GCC monarchies' expanded role in the wider MENA region – and, increasingly, beyond – is a long-term trend, for several reasons. One is the largesse accumulated in GCC capitals with the post-2022 energy prices boom, which is being deployed – in the MENA region, Europe, Africa, and central Asia – in the form of strategic investments, to shore up soft power and influence.[16] Such largesse is set to last, given the stronger position of GCC producers in the global energy market amid the enduring weakness of Russia's post-sanctions standing. The GCC countries are set to be increasingly in demand as energy partners, especially considering that they kick-started production and policy efforts to add green energy and renewables – chiefly hydrogen – to their portfolio, and thus could remain leading global exporters even in the post-hydrocarbons era.[17] This is particularly true for Europe, in need of replacing sanctioned Russian energy, which covered 40 per cent of its needs before the invasion of Ukraine.[18] It is equally true for Japan and South Korea, whose pre-existing reliance on GCC energy has deepened since 2022.[19]

Moreover, the strategic value of the GCC's geographic location is also growing, as rising political tensions between China and the USA result in both seeking to deepen rather than weaken ties in the other's geographic space. For instance, between January 2020 and December 2021, EU imports from China increased by 55.2 per cent, and EU exports to China increased by 9.9 per cent, more than double the growth of trade volumes with other non-EU countries.[20] Similarly, US trade with the Association of South East Asian Nations (ASEAN) increased by over 22 per cent between 2020 and 2021.[21] These trade flows – via both sea and air – often transit via hubs located in the Arabian Peninsula. Indeed for China, the GCC countries are not only the most important oil and gas providers, but also strategic partners for the Belt and Road Initiative. For the USA, despite ongoing retrenchment, maintaining a strategic foothold in the GCC is still indispensable both to contain regional antagonists, such as Iran, and to project towards the new central theatre – the Indo-Pacific – of which the Arabian Peninsula represents the western flank.[22]

This strategic relevance for global actors will make the Gulf region a hotspot of the new competitive multi-polar world order. In some areas, such as energy or freedom of navigation, this relevance gives global players stakes in the stability of the Gulf region, pushing them to insulate the GCC from the disruptions linked to multi-polar competition. Rival global actors may find in the GCC a space to keep interaction and contact with one another. In other areas, such as digital infrastructures or defence, heightened competition between great powers will further polarise the region – pushing GCC governments either to choose sides or to play these powers off against one another, embracing strategic hedging. In this sense, the GCC and MENA regions should be factored into the larger conversations among global players on the rules of engagement in their competition. The GCC monarchies' reluctance to join the sanctions against Russia is a clear indication that they oppose the idea of multi-polar competition playing out in trade wars. Given the entrenchment of their economies with both the USA and China, the

GCC countries will work to prevent a US–China trade war, from which they would lose out the most. At the same time, the monarchies will continue to hedge between the multiple poles in this multi-polar world, including by inviting China to play a more geopolitical role in the region. In fact, on 11 March 2023, China pushed a deal between Iran and Saudi Arabia over the finish line, launching a roadmap to re-establish diplomatic relations after seven years. The deal, including guarantees of non-interference and respect for sovereignty, was negotiated bilaterally in on-and-off secret talks hosted by Iraq, France, and Oman. However, both Tehran and Riyadh decided to give full diplomatic credit to Beijing, where they flew to sign the deal, creating significant unease in the United States.

Competitive multi-polarity can be highly destabilising in geopolitical terms too. Allowing multi-polar bloc politics to undo the fragile strategic pause embraced in 2021 by Gulf and Middle Eastern actors would not ultimately serve the interests of any player. Confrontation by proxy between global players in regional Middle Eastern conflicts, such as Libya, Syria, or Yemen – as was the case, to a certain extent, in the early years following the Arab Spring – would lead to a fruitless draining of resources. With no global actor retaining a position of absolute hegemony in the region – a natural feature of multi-polarity – these players risk being sucked into those conflicts, which could easily spiral out of control and turn into quagmires. In a scenario where the JCPOA is not renewed and a Republican administration enters the White House in 2025, individual GCC capitals will adjust to the new US posture on Iran, but on the basis of their own perceptions of Tehran, as dissected in this volume. This is because GCC countries – like other regional actors – have interpreted the retrenchment of US hegemony in the region as an opportunity to act with autonomy more often, even when that entails misalignment with the USA, as in the case of the Russian invasion of Ukraine.

In fact, the absence of a single external hegemon in the region has substantial implications for global actors' engagement with it. Regional actors – chiefly the GCC monarchies – have started to oppose more vigorously the interference of non-regional actors in their backyard. They have leveraged the interests and concerns of their non-regional partners for their own gain. Therefore, global actors may swap transformative agendas with transactional programmes, privileging authoritarian stability and short-term objectives over longer-term sustainability. A more coherent approach would necessitate a better balance between these two extremes. Feeding a democracies-vs-autocracies paradigm is unsustainable, given that regional power brokers, such as the GCC monarchies, do not have a democratic system. Non-regional players should rather engage by emphasising opportunities for sustainable development. From food security to the climate crisis, from the energy transition to inflation and economic stagnation, the GCC countries seek to partner with global actors who can deploy resources and capabilities in triangulation in the wider region.[23]

Most importantly, the GCC countries will continue to seek partnerships with non-regional actors to balance the most relevant perceived threats. As this volume has shown, these are often intermestic threats triggered in no small part by socioeconomic and sociopolitical vulnerabilities. Global actors seeking to preserve or augment their influence in the GCC would be more successful in their quest when focusing on understanding and addressing these vulnerabilities and threat perceptions. This means first and foremost targeting policies on the specificities of each GCC country individually. A country such as the sultanate of Oman is likely to prioritise partnerships that can contribute to alleviating socioeconomic vulnerabilities, whereas Kuwait is likely to prefer partnerships that can bolster its institutional resilience. Both countries, as well as Qatar, seek non-regional partners that actively oppose new escalations of tensions within the Gulf. The UAE, Saudi Arabia, and Bahrain instead look for reliable partners that can bolster their own ability to project deterrence against intermestic threats, both by beefing up defence and security capabilities and by forging stronger security architectures.

This diverse set of expectations speaks of how different threat perceptions in the GCC remain dynamic and adapt to the new regional and global context. As the post-Arab Spring era comes to a close, ten years after a Tunisian street vendor set himself on fire in 2011, the GCC monarchies have transited from hyper-securitisation to a hedging strategy, built on diplomatic manoeuvre and consolidation of influence. Key questions remain as to the limits of this approach in the context of competitive multi-polarity and the tolerance for related risks. With their regimes having survived the post-2011 decade relatively unscathed, it remains to be seen how the GCC systems will adapt to a context where risk levels remain consistently at a high pressure point, but below the threshold of full-fledged threats.

Notes

1 Silvia Colombo, 'The GCC and the Arab Spring: A Tale of Double Standards', *International Spectator* 47:4 (2012), 110–126.
2 The securitisation of the 'Other' is analysed in Darwich, 'The Ontological (In) security of Similarity'.
3 See for instance Bianco and Stansfield, 'The Intra-GCC Crises'.
4 Philipp Amour (ed.), *The Regional Order in the Gulf Region and the Middle East* (Cham: Palgrave Macmillan, 2020).

5 *Ibid.*
6 Wæver, *Securitization and Desecuritization.*
7 Gengler, 'The Political Economy of Sectarianism in the Gulf'.
8 The main inspiration has been Buzan, *People, States and Fear.*
9 Regional interconnections are highlighted well in Gause, *The International Relations.*
10 The 'coup-proofing' policy is examined in Steffen Hertog, 'Rentier Militaries in the Gulf States: The Price of Coup-Proofing', *International Journal of Middle East Studies* 43:3 (2011), 400–402.
11 These have been underlined in several studies on security perceptions, including Jervis, *Perception and Misperception*; and Hermann and Hagan, 'International Decision Making'.
12 Eriksson and Noreen, 'Setting the Agenda of Threats'.
13 Hogarth and Goldstein, *Judgment and Decision Making.*
14 Gause, 'Understanding the Gulf States'; Davidson, 'The UAE, Qatar, and the Question of Political Islam'.
15 Darwich, 'The Ontological (In)security of Similarity'.
16 Interview by the author of a senior EU official, Brussels, 14 September 2022.
17 Interview by the author of a senior Emirati professor of political science, Dubai, 31 May 2022.
18 'Energy Imports Dependency', *Eurostat* (2021).
19 Jonathan Fulton, 'Systemic Change and Regional Orders: Asian Responses to a Gulf in Transition', *International Spectator* 56:2 (2022): 1–19.
20 'China–EU – International Trade in Goods Statistics', *Eurostat* (2021), https://ec.europa.eu/eurostat/statistics-explained/index.php?title=China-EU_-_international_trade_in_goods_statistics#:~:text=Between%20January%202021%20and%20December,EU%20countries%20increased%20by%2028.8%20%25 (accessed 5 August 2023).
21 'Association of Southeast Asian Nations (ASEAN)', yearly statistics, Office of the United States Trade Representative (2021), https://ustr.gov/countries-regions/southeast-asia-pacific/association-southeast-asian-nations-asean (accessed 5 August 2023).
22 Interview by the author of a former official from the United States National Security Council, Rome, 6 October 2021.
23 This point was reiterated by several GCC interlocutors: a senior Emirati expert from a UAE-based think tank during a private workshop in Brussels on 14 September 2022, an Omani economist in an interview with the author in Berlin on 15 September 2022, a member of the Saudi Shura Council interviewed by the author in Riyadh on 9 March 2022, and an official from Qatar's Ministry of Foreign Affairs interviewed in Doha on 28 March 2022.

Select bibliography

Aarts, Paul and Gerd Nonneman (eds). *Saudi Arabia in the Balance: Political Economy, Society, Foreign Affairs* (New York: New York University Press, 2005).

Abdullah, Abdulkhaleq. 'Ar-rabi'a al arabi: Wijhat nazar min al khalij al arabi' ('The Arab Spring: A Point of View from the Arabian Gulf'). *Al Mustaqbal Al Arabi* 391 (2011), 117–128.

Abdullah, Jamal. 'Motives and Consequences of Ambassador Withdrawals from Doha'. *Al Jazeera Centre for Studies* 24 (2014), https://studies.aljazeera.net/en/reports/2014/04/201441061248251708.html (accessed 24 July 2023).

Adler, Emanuel and Michael Barnett (eds). *Security Communities* (Cambridge: Cambridge University Press, 1998).

Ahmadian, Hassan. 'Iran and Saudi Arabia in the Age of Trump'. *Survival* 60:2 (2018), 133–150.

Alajmi, Abdulhadi. 'The Gulf Crisis: An Insight into Kuwait's Mediation Efforts'. *International Relations* 6:10 (2018), 537–548.

Al-Azri, Khalid. *Social and Gender Inequality in Oman: The Power of Religious and Political Tradition* (London: Routledge, 2012).

Albloshi, Hamad. 'Sectarianism and the Arab Spring: The Case of the Kuwaiti Shi'a'. *The Muslim World* 106:1 (2016), 109–126.

Albloshi, Hamad and Michael Herb. 'Karamet Watan: An Unsuccessful Nonviolent Movement'. *Middle East Journal*, 72:3 (2018), 408–430.

Al-Ghannam, Hesham and Mohammed Yaghi, 'Biden's Trip to Saudi Arabia: Successes and Failures'. Carnegie Endowment for International Peace (2022), https://carnegieendowment.org/sada/87662 (accessed 17 September 2022).

Alhasan, Hasan Tariq. 'The Role of Iran in the Failed Coup of 1981: The IFLB in Bahrain'. *Middle East Journal* 65:4 (2011), 603–617.

Al-Hashimi, Said. *Al-Rabi al-Umani: Qaraa fi al-Siyaqat wa-l-Dalalat (The Omani Spring: A Reading of Its Context and Implications)* (Beirut: Dar al-Farabi, 2013).

Al-Hashimi, Said Sultan. 'The Omani Spring: Towards the Break of a New Dawn'. Brief 52, Arab Reform Initiative, 27 November 2011, www.arab-reform.net/publication/the-omani-spring-towards-the-break-of-a-new-dawn/ (accessed 17 September 2022).

Al-Kuwari, Ali Khalifa. *Al Sha'hab Yurid Islah fi Qatar... Aidan (The People Want Reform in Qatar ... Too)* (Beirut: Al Maaref Forum, 2012).

Al-Kuwari, Maryam. 'State–Tribe Relations and Political Legitimacy in Qatar and Kuwait: A Comparative Study'. Ph.D. dissertation (University of Exeter, 2021).

Allen, Calvin and W. Lynn Rigsbee. *Oman under Qaboos: From Coup to Constitution, 1970–1996* (London and Portland: Frank Cass, 2000).

Almezaini, Khalid and Jean-Marc Rickli (eds). *The Small Gulf States: Foreign and Security Policies before and after the Arab Spring* (London: Routledge, 2016).

Al-Raqum, Badea A. 'A New Approach for Kuwait's National Defense Strategy', Strategy Research Project (Carlisle, PA: US Army War College, 2001), https://apps.dtic.mil/sti/pdfs/ADA391170.pdf (accessed 19 July 2023).

Al-Rashedi, Musallam. 'The UAE National Security Strategy in the 21st Century', thesis (United States Marine Corps, School of Advance Warfighting, Marine Corps University, 2005).

Al-Rasheed, Madawi. 'Sectarianism as Counter-Revolution: Saudi Responses to the Arab Spring'. *Studies in Ethnicity and Nationalism* 11:3 (2011), 513–526.

Al-Rasheed, Madawi (ed.). *Salman's Legacy: The Dilemmas of a New Era in Saudi Arabia* (Oxford: Oxford University Press, 2018).

Al-Rasheed, Madawi. *The Son King: Reform and Repression in Saudi Arabia* (Oxford: Oxford University Press, 2021).

Al-Rawi, Ahmed. 'Sectarianism and the Arab Spring: Framing the Popular Protests in Bahrain'. *Global Media and Communication* 11:1 (2015), 25–42.

Alsalloum, Khaled Abdulaziz and Mohamed Salman Tayie. 'The Present and Future of Kuwaiti–Iranian Relations and Their Influence on the Security of the Arabian Gulf'. *Asian Social Science* 14:1 (2017), 102–111.

Al-Saud, Naef bin Ahmed. 'Underpinning Saudi National Security Strategy', *Joint Force Quarterly* (2002), 124–130.

Al-Sayegh, Fatma. 'The UAE and Oman: Opportunities and Challenges in the Twenty-First Century', *Middle East Policy* 9:3 (2002), 124–137.

Alsharekh, Alnoud. 'Youth, Protest and the New Elite'. In Kristian Ulrichsen (ed.), *The Changing Security Dynamics of the Persian Gulf* (Oxford: Oxford University Press, 2018).

Al-Shehabi, Omar Hesham. 'Contested Modernity: Divided Rule and the Birth of Sectarianism, Nationalism, and Absolutism in Bahrain'. *British Journal of Middle Eastern Studies* 44:3 (2017), 333–355.

Al-Suweidi, Jamal (ed.). *Arabian Gulf Security: Internal and External Challenges* (Abu Dhabi: ECSSR, 2008).

Alwuhaib, Mohammad. 'Kuwait: The Crisis and Its Future'. Brief 63, Arab Reform Initiative, 12 November 2012, www.arab-reform.net/publication/kuwait-the-crisis-and-its-future/ (accessed 17 September 2022).

Al-Zo'by, Mazhar and Birol Başkan. 'Discourse and Oppositionality in the Arab Spring: The Case of the Muslim Brotherhood in the UAE'. *International Sociology* (2014), 401–417.

Amour, Philipp (ed.). *The Regional Order in the Gulf Region and the Middle East.* (Cham: Palgrave Macmillan, 2020).

Aras, Bülent and Pınar Akpınar. 'Turkish Foreign Policy and the Qatar Crisis'. IPC Policy Brief (Istanbul: Istanbul Policy Center, 2017).

Ardemagni, Eleonora. 'Strategic Borderlands: The UAE–Oman Rivalry Benefits Tehran'. Istituto studi di politica internazionale, 21 June 2019, www.ispionline.it/it/pubblicazione/strategic-borderlands-uae-oman-rivalry-benefits-tehran-23347 (accessed 17 September 2022).

Ayoob, Mohammed. *The Third World Security Predicament: State-Making, Regional Conflict and the International System* (Boulder, CO: Lynne Rienner, 1995.)

Azar, Edward and Chung-in Moon. 'Third World National Security: Toward a New Conceptual Framework'. *International Interactions* 11:2 (1984), 103–135.

Azoulay, Rivka. 'The Politics of Shi'i Merchants in Kuwait'. In Steffen Hertog, Giacomo Luciani, and Marc Valeri (eds), *Business Politics in the Middle East* (London: Hurst, 2013).

Azoulay, Rivka and Claire Beaugrand. 'Limits of Political Clientelism: Elites in Kuwait Fragmenting Politics', *Arabian Humanities* 4 (2015), 1–20.

Baabood, Abdullah. 'Dynamics and Determinants of the GCC States' Foreign Policy, with Special Reference to the EU'. In Gerd Nonneman (ed.), *Analysing Middle East Foreign Policies and the Relationship with Europe* (London: Routledge, 2005).

Baabood, Abdullah. 'Islamism in the Gulf Region'. In Khaled Hroub (ed.), *Political Islam: Context versus Ideology* (London: Saqi, 2010).

Baabood, Abdullah and Ahmed Baabood. 'Omani and Qatari Roles in the Yemen Crisis'. In Stephen W. Day and Noel Brehony (eds), *Global, Regional, and Local Dynamics in the Yemen Crisis* (Cham: Palgrave Macmillan, 2020).

Baharoon, Mohammed. 'The Keys to Reading the UAE's Strategic Map'. Middle East Institute, 5 April 2022, www.mei.edu/publications/keys-reading-uaes-strategic-map (accessed 11 August 2022).

Bahgat, Gawdat, Anoushiravan Ehteshami and Neil Quilliam (eds), *Security and Bilateral Issues between Iran and Its Arab Neighbours* (London: Palgrave Macmillan, 2017).

Baldwin-Edwards, Martin. 'Labour Immigration and Labour Markets in the GCC Countries: National Patterns and Trends'. Kuwait Programme on Development, Governance and Globalisation in the Gulf States, London School of Economics and Political Science, Research Paper 15 (2011), http://eprints.lse.ac.uk/55239/1/Baldwin-Edwards_2011.pdf (accessed 23 July 2023).

Barnett, Michael. 'Institutions, Roles and Disorder: The Case of the Arab States System'. *International Studies Quarterly* 37:3 (1993), 271–296.

Barnett, Michael and Gregory Gause. 'Caravans in Opposite Directions: Society, State and the Development of a Community in the Gulf Cooperation Council'. *Cambridge Studies in International Relations* 62:1 (1998), 161–197.

Barzegar, Kayhan. 'The Hard Chess Puzzle: Trump's "Maximum Pressure" versus Iran's "Maximum resistance"'. Al Jazeera Centre for Studies, 15 June 2020, https://tinyurl.com/54wa2y35 (accessed 17 September 2022).

Bassiouni, Mahmoud Cherif, Migel Rodley, Bardia Al-Awadhi, Philippe Kirsch, and Mahnoush H. Arsanjani. 'Report of the Bahrain Independent Commission of Inquiry, Presented in Manama, Bahrain, on 23 November 2011', www.bici.org.bh/BICIreportEN.pdf (accessed 17 September 2022).

Battaloglu, Nesibe. 'Saudi and Emirati Pivot to Russia and China: Shift of Axis or Extreme Hedging?'. *Politics Today*, 5 July 2022, https://politicstoday.org/saudi-and-emirati-pivot-to-russia-and-china/ (accessed 17 September 2022).

Beaugrand, Claire. 'Biduns in the Face of Radicalization in Kuwait', Arab Gulf States Institute in Washington, 18 August 2015, https://agsiw.org/biduns-in-the-face-of-radicalization-in-kuwait/ (accessed 17 September 2022).

Beaugrand, Claire. *Stateless in the Gulf: Migration, Nationality and Society in Kuwait* (London: IB Tauris, 2017).

Beblawi, Hazem. 'The Rentier State in the Arab World'. In Hazem Beblawi and Giacomo Luciani (eds), *The Rentier State: Nation, State and the Integration of the Arab World* (London: Croom Helm, 1987).

Bianco, Cinzia. 'Gulf Security after 2011: A Threat Analysis'. *Middle East Policy* 25:2 (2018), 27–41.

Bianco, Cinzia and Gareth Stansfield. 'The Intra-GCC Crises: Mapping GCC Fragmentation after 2011'. *International Affairs* 94:3 (2018), 613–635.

Brown, Nathan. 'Kuwait's 2008 Parliamentary Elections: A Setback for Democratic Islamism?' (Washington, DC: Carnegie Endowment for International Peace, 2008), Universitäts-und Landesbibliothek Sachsen-Anhalt, https://menadoc.bib liothek.uni-halle.de/menalib/content/pageview/1605846 (accessed 19 July 2023).

Bunzel, Cole. 'The Kingdom and the Caliphate: Duel of the Islamic States', Carnegie Endowment for International Peace (2016), https://carnegieendowment.org/files/Brief-Bunzel-Duel_of_The_Islamic_States.pdf (accessed 19 July 2023).

Buzan, Barry. 'New Patterns of Global Security in the Twenty-First Century'. *International Affairs* 67:3 (1991), 431–451.

Buzan, Barry. *People, States and Fear* (Boulder, CO: Lynne Rienner, 1991).

Cafiero, Giorgio and Joshua Hodge. 'The Saudi–Iranian Rivalry and the Gulf Littoral States', *LobeLog*, 22 June 2016, https://lobelog.com/the-saudi-iranian-rivalry-and-the-gulf-littoral-states/ (accessed 23 August 2022).

Cafiero, Giorgio and Theodore Karasik, 'Kuwait, Oman, and the Qatar Crisis'. Middle East Institute, 22 June 2017, www.mei.edu/publications/kuwait-oman-and-qatar-crisis (accessed 17 September 2022).

Caldwell, Dan. 'Flashpoints in the Gulf: Abu Musa and the Tunb Islands'. *Middle East Policy* 4:3 (1996), 50–57.

Casey, Michael. *The History of Kuwait* (London: Greenwood, 2007).

Colombo, Silvia. 'The GCC and the Arab Spring: A Tale of Double Standards'. *International Spectator* 47:4 (2012), 110–126.

Cooper, Scott. 'State-Centric Balance-of-Threat Theory'. *Security Studies* 13:2 (2003), 306–349.

Cordesman, Anthony. *The Gulf and the Search for Strategic Stability* (Boulder, CO: Westview, 1984).

Cordesman, Anthony. *Kuwait: Recovery and Security after the Gulf War* (New York: Routledge, 1997).

Cordesman, Anthony and Khalid R. Al-Rodhan. *Gulf Military Forces in an Era of Asymmetric Wars* (London: Greenwood, 2007).

Cronin, Stephanie and Nur Masalha. 'The Islamic Republic of Iran and the GCC States: Revolution to Realpolitik?'. Kuwait Programme on Development, Governance and Globalisation in the Gulf States, London School of Economics and Political Science, Research Paper 17 (2011).

Crystal, Jill. *Oil and Politics in the Gulf: Rulers and Merchants in Kuwait and Qatar* (Cambridge: Cambridge University Press, 1990).

Dannreuther, Roland. 'Russia and the Gulf States: Between West and East'. In Nikolay Kozhanov (ed.), *Russia's Relations with the GCC and Iran* (Singapore: Palgrave Macmillan, 2021), 109–131.

Darwich, May. 'The Ontological (In)security of Similarity: Wahhabism versus Islamism in Saudi Foreign Policy'. *Foreign Policy Analysis* 12 (2016), 469–488.

Davidson, Christopher. *Power and Politics in the Persian Gulf Monarchies* (London: Hurst, 2011).

Davidson, Christopher. *The United Arab Emirates: A Study in Survival* (Boulder, CO: Lynne Rienner, 2006).

Dazi-Héni, Fatiha. 'The Arab Spring Impact on Kuwaiti "Exceptionalism"'. *Arabian Humanities* 4 (2015) , https://doi.org/10.4000/cy.2868 (accessed 4 August 2023).

Dazi-Héni, Fatiha. 'The Gulf States and Israel after the Abraham Accords'. Arab Reform Initiative (2020), www.arab-reform.net/publication/the-gulf-states-and-israel-after-the-abraham-accords/ (accessed 19 July 2023).

Dekmejian, Hrair. 'The Rise of Political Islamism in Saudi Arabia'. *Middle East Journal* 48:4 (1994), 627–643.

DesRoches, David (ed.). 'GCC Security amid Regional Crises'. *Gulf Affairs*, Oxford Gulf & Arabian Peninsula Studies (OXGAPS) (2016).

Doran, Michael. 'The Trump Doctrine in the Middle East'. In Stanley A. Renshon and Peter Suedfeld (eds), *The Trump Doctrine and the Emerging International System* (Cham: Palgrave Macmillan, 2021).

Echagüe, Ana (ed.). *The Gulf States and the Arab Uprisings* (Madrid: Fundación para las Relaciones Internacionales y el Diálogo Exterior, 2013).

Echagüe, Ana. 'Oman: The Outlier', Fundación para las Relaciones Internacionales y el Diálogo Exterior, 27 November 2015, http://fride.org/publication/1279/oman:-the-outlier (accessed 17 September 2022).

Ehteshami, Anoushiravan. *Dynamics of Change in the Persian Gulf: Political Economy, War and Revolution* (London: Routledge, 2013).

Ehteshami, Anoushiravan and Steven M. Wright (eds). *Reform in the Middle East Oil Monarchies* (New York: Ithaca Press, 2008).

Eickelman, Dale. 'From Theocracy to Monarchy: Authority and Legitimacy in Inner Oman, 1935–1957'. *International Journal of Middle East Studies* 17:1 (1985), 3–24.

Eriksson, Johan and Erik Noreen. 'Setting the Agenda of Threats: An Explanatory Model'. Uppsala Peace Research Papers 6 (2002).

Fakhro, Elham. 'COVID and Gulf Foreign Policy'. International Crisis Group, 20 April 2020, www.crisisgroup.org/middle-east-north-africa/gulf-and-arabian-peninsula/covid-and-gulf-foreign-policy (accessed 12 September 2022).

Fakhro, Elham and Tareq Baconi. 'A Shared Vision: Security Convergence between the Gulf and Israel'. *Journal of Palestine Studies* (2022), 50–55.

Fakhro, Munira, 'The Uprising in Bahrain: An Assessment'. In Gary Sick and Lawrence Potter (eds), *The Persian Gulf at the Millennium: Essays in Politics, Economy, Security, and Religion* (London: St Martin's Press, 1997).

Fawcett, Louise (ed.). *International Relations of the Middle East* (Oxford: Oxford University Press, 2013).

Foley, Sean. 'The UAE: Political Issues and Security Dilemmas'. *Middle East Review of International Affairs* 3:1 (1999), 25–45.

Forstenlechner, Ingo and Emilie Jane Rutledge, 'The GCC's "Demographic Imbalance": Perceptions, Realities and Policy Options', *Middle East Policy Journal* 18:4 (2011), 25–43.

Forstenlechner, Ingo, Emilie Rutledge, and Rashed Salem Alnuaimi. 'The UAE, the "Arab Spring" and Different Types of Dissent'. *Middle East Policy* 19:4 (2012), 54–67.

Freer, Courtney. 'Rentier Islamism in the Absence of Elections: The Political Role of Muslim Brotherhood Affiliates in Qatar and the United Arab Emirates'. *International Journal of Middle East Studies* 49:3 (2017), 479–500.

Freer, Courtney. *Rentier Islamism: The Influence of the Muslim Brotherhood in Gulf Monarchies* (Oxford: Oxford University Press, 2018).

Fulton, Jonathan. 'China between Iran and the Gulf Monarchies'. *Middle East Policy* 28:3 (2021), 203–216.

Fulton, Jonathan and Li-Chen Sim (eds). *External Powers and the Gulf Monarchies* (London: Routledge, 2018).

Gause, Gregory. 'Balancing What? Threat Perception and Alliance Choice in the Gulf'. *Security Studies* 13:2 (2003), 273–305.

Gause, Gregory. 'Beyond Sectarianism: The New Middle East Cold War', Brookings Institution, 22 July 2014, www.brookings.edu/research/beyond-sectarianism-the-new-middle-east-cold-war/ (accessed 9 May 2022).

Gause, Gregory. *The International Relations of the Persian Gulf* (Cambridge: Cambridge University Press, 2009).

Gause, Gregory. 'Understanding the Gulf States'. *Democracy* 36 (2015), https://democracyjournal.org/magazine/36/understanding-the-gulf-states/ (accessed 29 July 2023).

Gengler, Justin. *Group Conflict and Political Mobilization in Bahrain and the Arab Gulf: Rethinking the Rentier State* (Bloomington: Indiana University Press, 2015).

Gengler, Justin. 'The Political Economy of Sectarianism in the Gulf'. Carnegie Endowment for International Peace (2016), https://carnegieendowment.org/files/Gengler_Sectarianism_Final.pdf (accessed 19 July 2023).

Gengler, Justin. 'Qatar's Ambivalent Democratization', *Foreign Policy*, 1 November 2011, https://foreignpolicy.com/2011/11/01/qatars-ambivalent-democratization/ (accessed 17 September 2022).

Gengler, Justin. 'Royal Factionalism, the Khawalid, and the Securitization of "the Shiʿa Problem" in Bahrain'. *Journal of Arabian Studies* 3:1 (2013), 53–79.

Gengler, Justin. 'Segregation and Sectarianism: Geography, Economic Distribution, and Sectarian Resilience in Bahrain'. In *Countering Sectarianism in the Middle East* (Washington, DC: RAND Corporation, 2019).

Gerges, Fawaz (ed.). *The New Middle East: Protest and Revolution in the Arab World* (Cambridge: Cambridge University Press, 2013).

Gerges, Fawaz. 'The Obama Approach to the Middle East: The End of America's Moment?'. *International Affairs* 89:2 (2013), 299–323.

Gervais, Victor. 'Du pétrole a l'armée: Les stratégies de construction de l'état aux Emirats Arabes Unis', Ph.D. dissertation (Institut de recherche stratégique de l'Ecole militaire, Paris, 2011).

Gresh, Geoffrey. *Gulf Security and the US Military: Regime Survival and the Politics of Basing* (Stanford: Stanford University Press, 2015).

Guzansky, Yoel. 'Defence Cooperation in the Arabian Gulf: The Peninsula Shield Force Put to the Test'. *Middle Eastern Studies* 50:4 (2014), 540–654.

Halliday, Fred. *Arabia without Sultans* (London: Saqi, 2013).

Hanieh, Adam. 'Bahrain'. In Paul Amar and Vijay Prashod (eds), *Dispatches from the Arab Spring: Understanding the New Middle East* (Minneapolis: University of Minnesota Press, 2013).

Harders, Cilja and Matteo Legrenzi (eds). *Beyond Regionalism? Regional Cooperation, Regionalism and Regionalization in the Middle East* (London: Ashgate, 2013).

Haykel, Bernard. 'Saudi Arabia vs the Arab Spring', *Project Syndicate*, 16 August 2011, www.project-syndicate.org/commentary/—udi-arabia-vs--the-arab-spring (accessed 23 August 2022).

Hedges, Matthew. *Reinventing the Sheikhdom: Clan, Power and Patronage in Mohammed bin Zayed's UAE* (Oxford: Oxford University Press, 2022).

Hedges, Matthew and Giorgio Cafiero. 'The GCC and the Muslim Brotherhood: What Does the Future Hold?'. *Middle East Policy* 24:1 (2017), 129–153, available at https://mepc.org/journal/gcc-and-muslim-brotherhood-what-does-future-hold (accessed 7 August 2023).

Hegghammer, Thomas. *Jihad in Saudi Arabia: Violence and Pan-Islamism since 1979* (Cambridge: Cambridge University Press, 2010).

Helfont, Samuel. 'The Muslim Brotherhood and the Emerging "Shia Crescent"', *Orbis* 53:2 (2009), 284–299.

Hermann, Margaret and Joe D. Hagan. 'International Decision Making: Leadership Matters'. *Foreign Policy* 110, special edn, *Frontiers of Knowledge* (Spring 1998), 124–137.

Hertog, Steffen. 'Rentier Militaries in the Gulf States: The Price of Coup-Proofing'. *International Journal of Middle East Studies* 43:3 (2011), 400–402.

Hertog, Steffen. 'The Sociology of the Gulf Rentier Systems: Societies of Intermediaries'. *Comparative Studies in Society and History* 52:2 (2010), 282–318.

Hill, Ginny and Gerd Nonneman. 'Yemen, Saudi Arabia and the Gulf States: Elite Politics, Street Protests and Regional Diplomacy'. Briefing paper, Chatham House (2011), www.chathamhouse.org/sites/default/files/public/Meetings/Meeting%20 Transcripts/120511yemen.pdf (accessed 20 July 2023).

Hinnebusch, Raymond and Anoushiravan Ehteshami (eds). *The Foreign Policies of Middle East States*, 2nd edn (Boulder, CO: Lynne Rienner, 2014).

Hitman, Gadi. 'Saudi Arabia's Wahhabism and Nationalism: The Evolution of Wataniyya into Qawmiyya'. *Digest of Middle East Studies* 27:1 (2018), 79–96.

Hogarth, Robin and William Goldstein. *Judgment and Decision Making: An Interdisciplinary Reader* (Cambridge: Cambridge University Press, 1996).

Hubbard, Ben. *MBS: The Rise to Power of Mohammed bin Salman* (New York: Tim Duggan Books, 2020).

Ibish, Hussein. 'The UAE's Evolving National Security Strategy'. Arab Gulf States Institute in Washington, 6 April 2017, www.agsiw.org/wp-content/uploads/2017/ 04/UAE-Security_ONLINE.pdf (accessed 23 August 2022).

Jervis, Robert. *Perception and Misperception in International Politics* (Princeton: Princeton University Press, 2017).

Jones, Clive. 'Saudi Arabia after the Gulf War: The Internal–External Security Dilemma', *International Relations* 12:6 (1995), 31–51.

Jones, Jeremy and Nicholas Ridout. *A History of Modern Oman* (Cambridge: Cambridge University Press, 2015).

Jones, Marc Owen. 'Hacking, Bots and Information Wars in the Qatar Spat'. In Marc Lynch (ed.), *The Qatar Crisis*, POMEPS Briefing 31 (October 2017), 8–10, https://pomeps.org/wp-content/uploads/2017/10/POMEPS_GCC_Qatar-Crisis. pdf (accessed 20 July 2023).

Jones, Toby. 'Rebellion on the Saudi Periphery: Modernity, Marginalization, and the Shia Uprising of 1979'. *International Journal of Middle East Studies* 38:2 (2006), 213–233.

Kabalan, Marwan. 'The Al-Ula GCC Summit'. *Insight Turkey* 23:1 (2021), 51–59.

Kamrava, Mehran (ed.). *International Politics of the Persian Gulf* (New York: Syracuse University Press, 2011).

Kamrava, Mehran. *Qatar: Small State, Big Politics* (New York: Cornell University Press, 2015).

Kamrava, Mehran. *Troubled Waters: Insecurity in the Persian Gulf* (New York: Cornell University Press, 2018).

Kausch, Kristina. 'Competitive Multipolarity in the Middle East'. *International Spectator* 50:3 (2015), 1–15.

Kaye, Dalia Dassa, Frederic Wehrey, and Michael Scott Doran. 'Arab Spring, Persian Winter: Will Iran Emerge the Winner from the Arab Revolt?'. *Foreign Affairs*, 1 July 2011, 183–188, www.foreignaffairs.com/articles/middle-east/2011-07-01/arab-spring-persian-winter (accessed 23 July 2023).

Kechichian, Joseph. *Oman and the World* (Washington, DC: RAND, 1995).

Kemp, Geoffrey and Janice Gross Stein (eds). *Powder Keg in the Middle East: The Struggle for Gulf Security* (Washington, DC: Rowman and Littlefield, 1995).

Khadduri, Majid. 'Iran's Claim to the Sovereignty of Bahrayn'. *American Journal of International Law* 45:4 (1951), 631–647.

Khoury, Philip Shukry and Joseph Kostiner (eds). *Tribes and State Formation in the Middle East* (Oakland: University of California Press, 1991).

Koch, Christian. 'The GCC as a Regional Security Organization'. *KAS [Konrad-Adenauer-Stiftung] International Reports* (2010), 23–35.

Korany, Bahgat. 'Strategic Studies and the Third World: A Critical Evaluation'. *International Social Science Journal* 38:4 (1986), 547–562.

Kosebalaban, Hasan and Mohammed Ayoob (eds). *Religion and Politics in Saudi Arabia: Wahhabism and the State* (Boulder, CO: Lynne Rienner, 2009).

Kostiner, Joseph. 'The Search for Gulf Security: The Politics of Collective Defense'. *Middle East Contemporary Survey* 16 (1992), 237–244.

Krane, Jim. *City of Gold: Dubai and the Dream of Capitalism* (London: Macmillan, 2009).

Krieg, Andreas (ed.). *Divided Gulf* (Singapore: Palgrave Macmillan, 2019).

Lacey, Robert. *Inside the Kingdom: Kings, Clerics, Modernists, Terrorists, and the Struggle for Saudi Arabia* (London: Penguin, 2009).

Lacroix, Stéphane. *Awakening Islam: The Politics of Religious Dissent in Contemporary Saudi Arabia* (Cambridge, MA: Harvard University Press, 2011).

Lacroix, Stéphane. 'Is Saudi Arabia Immune?'. *Journal of Democracy* 22:4 (2011), 48–59.

Lawson, Fred. 'Neglected Aspects of the Security Dilemma'. In Rex Brynen, Bahgat Korany, and Paul Noble (eds), *The Many Faces of National Security in the Arab World* (London: Palgrave Macmillan, 1993).

Lefebvre, Jeffrey. 'Oman's Foreign Policy in the Twenty-First Century', *Middle East Policy Council* 12:1 (2010), 99–114.

Legrenzi, Matteo. *The GCC and the International Relations of the Gulf: Diplomacy, Security and Economic Coordination in a Changing Middle East* (London: Bloomsbury, 2015).

Legrenzi, Matteo (ed.). *Security in the Gulf: Historical Legacies and Future Prospects* (London: Routledge, 2013).

Long, David and Christian Koch (eds). *Gulf Security in the Twenty-First Century* (London: IB Tauris, 1997).

Longva, Anh Nga. 'Nationalism in Pre-Modern Guise: The Discourse on Hadhar and Badu in Kuwait'. *International Journal of Middle East Studies* 38:2 (2006), 171–187.

Louër, Laurence. 'The Politics of Labor Policy Reform in Bahrain'. *Gulf Affairs* (2015), 9–12, https://sciencespo.hal.science/hal-03459681/document (accessed 30 July 2023).

Louër, Laurence. 'Sectarianism and Coup-Proofing Strategies in Bahrain'. *Journal of Strategic Studies* 36:2 (2013), 245–260.

Lynch, Marc. 'Obama and the Middle East: Rightsizing the US Role'. *Foreign Affairs*, September/October 2015, www.foreignaffairs.com/articles/middle-east/obama-and-middle-east (accessed 20 July 2023).

Lynch, Marc (ed.). *The Qatar Crisis*, POMEPS Briefing 31 (October 2017), https://pomeps.org/wp-content/uploads/2017/10/POMEPS_GCC_Qatar-Crisis.pdf (accessed 20 July 2023).

Mabon, Simon. 'The Battle for Bahrain: Iranian–Saudi Rivalry', *Middle East Policy Council* 19:2 (2012), 84–97.

Mabon, Simon. 'The End of the Battle for Bahrain and the Securitization of Bahraini Shi'a'. *Middle East Journal* 73:1 (2019), 29–50.

Mabon, Simon. *Houses Built on Sand: Violence, Sectarianism and Revolution in the Middle East* (Manchester: Manchester University Press, 2021).

Mabon, Simon and Robert Mason. *Gulf States and the Horn of Africa: Interests, Influences and Instability* (Manchester: Manchester University Press, 2022).

Mabon, Simon, Samira Nasirzadeh, and Eyad Alrefai. 'De-Securitisation and Pragmatism in the Persian Gulf: The Future of Saudi–Iranian Relations'. *International Spectator* 56:4 (2021), 66–83.

Maisel, Sebastian. 'The New Rise of Tribalism in Saudi Arabia'. *Nomadic Peoples* 18:2 (2014), 100–122.

Majidyar, Ahmad Khalid. 'Is Sectarian Balance in the United Arab Emirates, Oman, and Qatar at Risk?'. American Enterprise Institute, 21 October 2013, www.aei.org/research-products/report/is-sectarian-balance-in-the-united-arab-emirates-oman-and-qatar-at-risk/ (accessed 17 September 2022).

Malmvig, Helle. 'Power, Identity and Securitization in Middle East: Regional Order after the Arab Uprisings'. *Mediterranean Politics* 19:1 (2014), 145–148.

Matthiesen, Toby. 'Hizbullah al-Hijaz: A History of the Most Radical Saudi Shi'a Opposition Group', *Middle East Journal* 64:2 (2010), 179–197.

Matthiesen, Toby. 'A "Saudi Spring"? The Shi'a Protest Movement in the Eastern Province 2011–2012'. *Middle East Journal* 66:4 (2012), 628–659.

Matthiesen, Toby. *Sectarian Gulf: Bahrain, Saudi Arabia, and the Arab Spring that Wasn't* (Stanford: Stanford University Press, 2013).

Matthiesen, Toby. 'The World's Most Misunderstood Martyr'. *Foreign Policy*, 8 January 2018, https://foreignpolicy.com/2016/01/08/the-worlds-most-misunderstood-martyr/ (accessed 20 July 2023).

Menshawy, Mustafa and Simon Mabon. 'The Muslim Brotherhood Faultline in Saudi–Qatari Relations: Domestic Divisions and Regional Rivalry'. *Insight Turkey* 23:4 (2021), 51–62.

Miller, Rory. *Desert Kingdoms to Global Powers: The Rise of the Arab Gulf* (New Haven: Yale University Press, 2016).

Mitchell, Jocelyn Sage. 'Beyond Allocation: The Politics of Legitimacy in Qatar'. Ph.D. dissertation (Georgetown University, 2013).

Mogielnicki, Robert. 'Oman's Economic Reforms Struggle to Keep Pace with Mounting Challenges', Arab Gulf States Institute in Washington, 22 October 2020, https://agsiw.org/omans-economic-reforms-struggle-to-keep-pace-with-mounting-challenges/ (accessed 18 September 2022).

Nathan, Fabien. 'Natural Disasters, Vulnerability and Human Security'. In Hans Günter Brauch, Úrsula Oswald Spring, John Grin *et al.* (eds), *Facing Global*

Environmental Change: Environmental, Human, Energy, Food, Health and Water Security Concepts. Hexagon Series on Human and Environmental Security and Peace 4 (Berlin: Springer-Verlag, 2009).

Niblock, Tim. *Saudi Arabia: Power, Legitimacy and Survival* (London: Routledge, 2006).

Niblock, Tim and Steve Hook (eds). *The United States and the Gulf: Shifting Pressures, Strategies and Alignments* (Berlin: Gerlach Press, 2015).

Obaid, Nawaf. 'A Saudi Arabian Defense Doctrine'. Defense and Intelligence Projects, Belfer Center for Science and International Affairs (Cambridge, MA: President and Fellows of Harvard College, 2014), https://ciaotest.cc.columbia.edu/wps/isp/0031181/f_0031181_25247.pdf (accessed 20 July 2023).

Olver-Ellis, Sophie. 'Building the New Kuwait: Vision 2035 and the Challenges of Diversification'. Kuwait Programme, London School of Economics and Political Science (2020), http://eprints.lse.ac.uk/103198/1/Olver_Ellis_building_the_new_Kuwait_published.pdf (accessed 20 July 2023).

Partrick, Neil. 'The GCC: Gulf State Integration or Leadership Cooperation?'. Kuwait Programme on Development, Governance and Globalisation in the Gulf States, London School of Economics (2011), Research Paper 19, http://eprints.lse.ac.uk/55660/1/__lse.ac.uk_storage_LIBRARY_Secondary_libfile_shared_repository_Content_Kuwait%20Programme_Partrick%202011%20paper.pdf (accessed 20 July 2023).

Partrick, Neil. 'Kuwait: The Permanent Struggle for Security', 14 August 2018, www.neilpartrick.com/blog/kuwait-the-permanent-struggle-for-security (accessed 17 September 2022).

Partrick, Neil. 'Nationalism in the Gulf States'. Research Paper 5, Centre for the Study of Global Governance: Kuwait Programme on Development, Governance, and Globalisation in the Gulf States (2009), Research Paper 5, https://eprints.lse.ac.uk/55257/1/Patrick_2009.pdf (accessed 20 July 2023).

Partrick, Neil and Francis Toase (eds). 'Gulf Security: Opportunities and Challenges for the New Generation', RUSI Whitehall Papers 51 (London: RUSI, 2000).

Peck, Malcolm. *The United Arab Emirates: A Venture in Unity* (Boulder, CO: Westview Press, 1986).

Peterson, J. E. *Defending Arabia* (London: Croom Helm, 1986).

Phillips, Christopher. *The Battle for Syria: International Rivalry in the New Middle East* (New Haven: Yale University Press, 2016).

Potter, Lawrence and Gary Sick. *Security in the Persian Gulf: Origins, Obstacles, and the Search for Consensus* (New York: Macmillan, 2002).

Priess, David. 'Balance-of-Threat Theory and the Genesis of the Gulf Cooperation Council'. *Security Studies* 5:4 (1996), 143–171.

Quamar, Muddassir. 'Saudi Arabia's Strategic Partnership with the United States: Fraying at the Margins?'. *Strategic Analysis* (2022), 1–14.

Ramazani, Rouhullah. 'Iran's Islamic Revolution and the Persian Gulf'. *Current History* 84:498 (1985), 5–8.

Razzak, Weshah. 'Examining the Performance of Oman's Economy'. Research Paper 103379, University of Munich, 2020.

Rickli, Jean-Marc. 'New Alliances Dynamics in the Gulf and Their Impact on the Small GCC States'. *Third World Thematics* 1:1 (2016), 132–150.

Rizvi, Sajjad. 'Political MobilizatiIn and the Shi'i Religious Establishment (Marja'iyya)'. *International Affairs* 86:6 (2010), 1299–1313.

Roberts, David. 'Qatar and the Brotherhood'. *Survival*, 56:4 (2014), 23–32.

Roberts, David. 'Qatar and the Muslim Brotherhood: Pragmatism or Preference?'. *Middle East Policy* 21:3 (2014), 84–94.

Roberts, David. 'Qatar and the UAE: Exploring Divergent Responses to the Arab Spring'. *Middle East Journal* 71:4 (2017), 544–562.

Roberts, David. *Qatar: Securing the Global Ambitions of a City State* (London: Hurst, 2017).

Roberts, David. 'Qatar's Domestic Stability and the Gulf Crisis'. Policy Watch 2847, Washington Institute for Near East Policy, 18 August 2017, www.washingtonin stitute.org/policy-analysis/qatars-domestic-stability-and-gulf-crisis (accessed 17 September 2022).

Romano, J. and Lee Seeger. 'Rentierism and Reform: Youth Unemployment and Economic Policy in Oman'. Institute for Middle East Studies, IMES Paper Capstone Series (May 2014), https://cpb-us-e1.wpmucdn.com/blogs.gwu.edu/dist/6/1613/files/2018/11/Romano-Seeger-Capstone-Final-xlu6ps.pdf (accessed 20 July 2023).

Russell, James. 'Environmental Security and Regional Stability in the Persian Gulf'. *Middle East Policy* 16:4 (2009), 90–101.

Sabab, Bilal. 'Can the House of Saud Survive ISIS?'. *Foreign Affairs*, 11 June 2015, www.foreignaffairs.com/articles/2015–06–11/can-house-saud-survive-isis (accessed 23 August 2022).

Sadjadpour, Karim. 'The Battle of Dubai: The United Arab Emirates and the US–Iran Cold War'. Carnegie Endowment for International Peace (2011), https://carnegieendowment.org/files/dubai_iran.pdf (accessed 23 July 2023).

Said, Basma Mubarak. 'The Future of Reform in Oman', *Contemporary Arab Affairs* 9:1 (2016), 46–67.

Said, Basma Mubarak. 'Oman, Iranian Rapprochement and a GCC Union'. Al Jazeera Centre for Studies, 21 January 2014, https://studies.aljazeera.net/en/reports/2014/01/20141218365065800.html (accessed 17 September 2022).

Saidy, Brahim. 'Qatari–US Military Relations: Context, Evolution and Prospects'. *Contemporary Arab Affairs* 10:2 (2017), 286–299.

Saikal, Amin. 'The United States and Persian Gulf Security'. *World Policy Journal* 9:3 (1992), 515–531.

Schenker, David. 'The Shift in Saudi Foreign Policy'. Policy Analysis, Washington Institute for Near East Policy, 10 February 2016, www.washingtoninstitute.org/policy-analysis/view/the-shift-in-saudi-foreign-policy (accessed 23 August 2022).

Shehabi, Ala'a. 'Why Is Bahrain Outsourcing Extremism?'. *Foreign Policy*, 29 October 2014, https://foreignpolicy.com/2014/10/29/why-is-bahrain-outsourc ing-extremism/ (accessed 30 August 2022).

Shehabi, Manal. 'Quantifying Long-Term Impacts of COVID-19 and Oil Price Shocks in a Gulf Oil Economy'. Oxford Institute for Energy Studies (2021), www.oxfordenergy.org/wpcms/wp-content/uploads/2021/06/Quantifying-Long-Term-Impacts-of-COVID-19-and-Oil-price-Shocks-in-a-Gulf-Oil-Economy-MEP25.pdf (accessed 23 July 2023).

Shifrinson, Joshua and Stephen Wertheim. 'Biden the Realist'. *Foreign Affairs*, 9 September 2021, https://www.foreignaffairs.com/articles/united-states/2021-09-09/biden-realist (accessed 23 July 2023).

Shihabi, Ali. 'The Iranian Threat: The Saudi Perspective'. London School of Economics and Political Science blog, 15 June 2018, https://blogs.lse.ac.uk/mec/2018/06/15/the-iranian-threat-the-saudi-perspective/ (accessed 23 August 2022).

Sick, Gary and Lawrence Potter (eds). *The Persian Gulf at the Millennium* (New York: St Martin's, 1997).

Steinberg, Guido. 'The Gulf States and the Muslim Brotherhood'. Project on Middle East Political Science, 9 March 2014, https://pomeps.org/the-gulf-states-and-the-muslim-brotherhood (accessed 17 September 2022).

Takriti, Abdel Razzaq. *Monsoon Revolution: Republicans, Sultans, and Empires in Oman, 1965–1976* (Oxford: Oxford University Press, 2013).

Tavana, Daniel and Abdullah al-Khonaini. 'Kuwait Voted This Weekend. Who Won?', *Washington Post*, 8 December 2020, www.washingtonpost.com/politics/2020/12/08/kuwait-voted-this-weekend-who-won/ (accessed 17 September 2022).

Tétreault, Mary Ann. *Stories of Democracy: Politics and Society in Contemporary Kuwait* (New York: Columbia University Press, 2000).

Tétreault, Mary Ann, Gwenn Okruhlik, and Andrzej Kapiszewski (eds). *Political Change in the Arab Gulf States: Stuck in Transition* (Boulder, CO: Lynne Rienner, 2011).

Ulrichsen, Kristian (ed.). *The Changing Security Dynamics of the Persian Gulf* (London: Hurst, 2017).

Ulrichsen, Kristian. *Insecure Gulf: The End of Certainty and the Transition to the Post-Oil Era* (New York: Columbia University Press, 2011).

Ulrichsen, Kristian. 'Internal and External Security in the Arab Gulf States'. *Middle East Policy* 16:2 (2009), 39–58.

Ulrichsen, Kristian. *Qatar and the Arab Spring* (Oxford: Oxford University Press, 2014).

Ulrichsen, Kristian. *Qatar and the Gulf Crisis: A Study of Resilience* (Oxford: Oxford University Press, 2020).

Ulrichsen, Kristian. 'Rebalancing Regional Security in the Persian Gulf'. Center for the Middle East, Rice University's Baker Institute for Public Policy (2020), www.bakerinstitute.org/research/rebalancing-regional-security-persian-gulf (accessed 23 July 2023).

Ulrichsen, Kristian. *The United Arab Emirates: Power, Politics and Policy-Making* (London: Routledge, 2016).

Ulrichsen, Kristian. 'Walking the Tightrope: Kuwaiti–Iranian Relations in the Aftermath of the Abdali Affair'. *IndraStra Global* 8 (2017), www.ssoar.info/ssoar/handle/document/53497 (accessed 23 July 2023).

Valeri, Marc. 'High Visibility, Low Profile: The Shi'a in Oman under Sultan Qaboos', *International Journal of Middle East Studies* 42:2 (2010), 251–268.

Valeri, Marc. 'Islamist Political Societies in Bahrain: Collateral Victims of the 2011 Popular Uprising'. In Hendrik Kraetzschmar and Paola Rivetti (eds), *Islamists and the Politics of the Arab Uprisings: Governance, Pluralisation and Contention* (Edinburgh: Edinburgh University Press, 2018).

Valeri, Marc. 'Simmering Unrest and Succession Challenges in Oman'. Carnegie Endowment for International Peace (2015), https://carnegieendowment.org/2015/01/28/simmering-unrest-and-succession-challenges-in-oman-pub-58843 (accessed 17 September 2022).

Valeri, Marc. 'The Ṣuḥār Paradox: Social and Political Mobilisations in the Sultanate of Oman since 2011', *Arabian Humanities* 4 (2015), https://doi.org/10.4000/cy.2828 (accessed 23 July 2023).

Vasiliev, Alexei. *The History of Saudi Arabia* (London: Saqi, 2000).

Vohar, Anchal. 'Erdoğan's War with Arab Monarchies Is Over'. *Foreign Policy*, 22 March 2022, https://foreignpolicy.com/2022/03/22/erdogan-turkey-uae-saudi-arabia-monarchy-islamism/ (accessed 17 September 2022).

Wæver, Ole. *Securitization and Desecuritization* (Copenhagen: Centre for Peace and Conflict Research, 1993).

Wæver, Ole and Barry Buzan. *Regions and Powers* (Cambridge: Cambridge University Press, 2003).

Wehrey, Frederic. 'The Forgotten Uprising in Eastern Saudi Arabia', Carnegie Endowment for International Peace (2013), https://carnegieendowment.org/files/eastern_saudi_uprising.pdf (accessed 23 July 2023).

Wehrey, Frederic. *Sectarian Politics in the Gulf* (New York: Columbia University Press, 2013).

Wehrey, Frederic, David E. Thaler, Nora Bensahel, *et al.* 'Arab Perceptions of the Iranian Threat'. In *Dangerous but Not Omnipotent: Exploring the Reach and Limitations of Iranian Power in the Middle East* (Washington, DC: RAND, 2009), 129–152.

Wiegand, Krista. 'Bahrain, Qatar, and the Hawar Islands: Resolution of a Gulf Territorial Dispute'. *Middle East Journal* 66:1 (2012), 79–96.

Wilkinson, John Craven. *The Imamate Tradition of Oman* (Cambridge: Cambridge University Press, 1987).

Williamson, Scott and Nathan J. Brown. 'Kuwait's Muslim Brotherhood under Pressure'. *Foreign Policy*, 20 November 2013, http://foreignpolicy.com/2013/11/20/kuwaits-muslim-brotherhood-under-pressure/ (accessed 17 September 2022).

Yom, Sean and Gregory Gause. 'Resilient Royals: How Arab Monarchies Hang On'. *Journal of Democracy* 23:4 (2012), 74–88.

Zahlan, Rosemarie Said. *The Creation of Qatar* (London: Croom Helm, 1979).

Zahlan, Rosemarie Said. *The Making of the Modern Gulf States: Kuwait, Bahrain, Qatar, the United Arab Emirates and Oman* (London: Routledge, 2016).

Zunes, Stephen. 'Bahrain's Arrested Revolution'. *Arab Studies Quarterly* 35:2 (2013), 149–164.

Index

EU authorised representative for GPSR:
Easy Access System Europe, Mustamäe tee 50,
10621 Tallinn, Estonia
gpsr.requests@easproject.com